Fifth Edition

D0207156

FOCUS ON PSYCHOLOGY

A Guide to Mastering
PETER GRAY'S PSYCHOLOGY

Mary Trahan

WORTH PUBLISHERS

Focus on Psychology

A Guide to Mastering Peter Gray's **Psychology**, Fifth Edition
by Mary Trahan

Printed in the United States of America

ISBN 10: 0-7167-4585-2
ISBN 13: 978-0-7167-4585-3

First Printing 2006

Worth Publishers
41 Madison Avenue
New York, NY 10010
www.worthpublishers.com

Contents

To the Student

Why This Guide Is Written As It Is

I have written this guide to help you master Peter Gray's *Psychology*, fifth edition. The guide is interactive—like a tutorial or like my own style of classroom teaching. I write something, and you write something back; often our back-and-forth writing amounts to a brief conversation about the ideas presented in Peter Gray's textbook. The guide is intended to do more than develop a knowledge base in your mind. It is my hope that you will not only only come to understand psychology better but will gain a deeper understanding of what it *means* to understand, and will see better how to achieve understanding in your other studies. Additionally, I hope you will develop an increased confidence in your own ability to think and to learn.

This study guide puts into practice some of the principles psychologists have discovered through investigations of learning and memory, namely, the importance of organization and elaboration. Organization repeatedly has been shown to facilitate the learning, retention, and use of information. It is not only the organization of the information on the page, but the organization of the information in the mind that matters. The former merely facilitates the latter. I have tried to produce a study guide that helps you to organize what you are putting into your memory. Elaboration involves *doing* something active and meaningful with the material you read, not just transferring it passively from the textbook page to your mind to the study guide page. We are engaging in elaboration when we draw parallels, summarize, produce examples, criticize, compare, ponder analogies, and apply general concepts to specific cases. Elaboration, in short, involves thinking. And thinking is not only the most effective way to learn, it is also the most interesting!

How to Use This Guide

This guide is not intended to be a supplement to your study of the textbook; nor is it simply a means of checking your understanding after you have finished studying. It is designed to be your guide in studying the text. Each chapter of the study guide has the following features:

1. An **introductory summary** gives you an overview or "map" of the chapter in the textbook and an initial acquaintance with some of its major ideas before you begin to read the chapter.

2. **Italicized instructions** advise you on how to proceed at each step in the study process—letting you know, for example, when to read the chapter thoroughly and when to skim it, when to go on to the next section and when to review first.

3. The **Integrated Study Workout** is the heart of the study guide. Divided into sections according to the major topics of the text chapter, the Workout contains a variety of questions as well as brief passages that help to put the questions in context. Often hints are provided that direct you to examine a relevant table or graph. The questions help you to identify what is most important in the text-book, to break sections down into manageable parts, and to probe the material for critical ideas.

   Preceding the Workout is a table that shows which study guide questions are related to each of the Focus Questions in the text. The Focus Questions are designed to help you concentrate on the purpose of each segment of the text. If your instructor has recommended that your exam preparation include or center on specified Focus Questions, the corresponding study guide material would make a particularly effective review.

4. Two **Self-Tests** will help you to assess your understanding. Each Self-Test contains fifteen multiple-choice questions and two essay questions.

5. **Answers** are provided for selected items from The Integrated Study Workout, generally those items that are objective or have very short answers. Answers for all multiple-choice questions, many accompanied by explanatory eom-ments, and model answers to essay questions are also included, along with textbook page references.

Because of the organization of each study guide chapter and the instructions that guide you through them, I need say little more about how to use this study guide. However, I do wish to make two suggestions: One is that you read and im-plement the study recommendations that Peter Gray has provided in the first chap-ter of his text. The second is that you avoid an all-or-none attitude in your study-ing. I hope you will make the time to complete each chapter of this guide, because doing so will maximize your learning. But please do not feel that you must answer every single question to make its use worthwhile. Doing three-fourths of the ques-tions is better than doing none. Further, do not feel that you must write out all of your answers in complete sentences. The correct few words will usually help you most. Make sure your answers are clear, organized, and complete enough to be valuable to *you*. After all, this is your guide—only you will read it.

I wish you success in your studies and encourage you to write to me if you have any comments or suggestions.

Mary Trahan

Acknowledgments

Many thanks to Peter Gray for writing such a wonderful text and for somehow managing to improve it to a remarkable extent on each successive revision. It is a textbook that is truly worth studying, an exceptional accomplishment. I find this fifth edition of his book—and the vision and work it took to produce it—especially impressive. I feel fortunate indeed that my chance to "teach on paper" came with Peter Gray's book. I also owe a debt of gratitude to all the staff at Worth Publishers, who have helped me to shape this study guide from its inception. Worth is a remarkable publisher, with an uncommon commitment to excellence and innovation. On this fifth edition, I particularly wish to thank Sharon Merritt, Eve Conte, Stacey Alexander, and Tracey Kuehn for their fine work and support.

To my colleagues and students over the years, who have taught me about psychology and about teaching, thanks. I am indebted to my teachers at Loyola University in New Orleans, where I began my study of psychology; to faculty and students at the University of Michigan, where, as a graduate student, I developed a love for psychology and a devotion to teaching; and especially to many students and colleagues at Randolph-Macon College for the rich variety of teaching experiences afforded me.

As always thanks to my friends. I know how blessed I am to have them.

Foundations for the Study of Psychology

READ the introduction below before you read the chapter in the text.

Psychology is defined as the science of behavior and the mind. Like all sciences, psychology attempts to answer questions through the systematic collection and logical analysis of objectively observable data.

Psychology became a formal, recognized scientific discipline in 1879 when Wilhelm Wundt founded the first university psychology laboratory. Even before the official beginnings of psychology, developments in philosophy and science prepared the way for it. For example, Descartes' dualism, Hobbes's materialism, British empiricism in philosophy, as well as the work of Darwin and pioneering physiologists in the sciences helped to lay the groundwork for a science of psychology. Progress in these disciplines established the ideas that behavior is physically caused and that behavior and the mind are shaped by experience and by natural selection.

Psychologists study their complex subject matter by investigating different types of causal processes; that is, by investigating at different levels of analysis. They may explore neural, genetic, cognitive, developmental, or other bases for mental experience and behavior. Some specialties within psychology are defined by their level of analysis but others are defined more in terms of their topic, such as perceptual psychology and clinical psychology.

Psychology is an academic discipline related to the natural sciences, social sciences, and humanities. It is also a profession. Professional psychologists may work to add to our knowledge of mind and behavior or to apply that knowledge for practical ends. They are employed in settings that include colleges and universities, elementary and secondary schools, various clinical settings, business, and government.

Chapter 1 closes with a discussion of special features of the textbook that can really assist your learning—if you use them. These include the focus questions and section reviews along with headings designed to guide your reading.

LOOK over the table of contents for this chapter in your textbook before you continue with your study.

Notice that there are focus questions in the margins of the text for your use in studying the material. The following chart lists which Study Guide questions relate to which focus questions.

Focus Questions	Study Guide Questions
Introduction and Three Foundation Ideas for Psychology: A Historical Overview	
1	1–3
2–3	4–6
4	7
5	8–9
6	10
7–8	11–13
9	14–15
10	16–18
The Scope of Psychology	
12–15	1
16	2
17	3–5
Thoughts About Using This Book and Its Special Features	
18	1–2
19	3
20	4

The Integrated Study Workout

COMPLETE one section at a time.

Introduction AND *Three Foundation Ideas for Psychology: A Historical Overview*   (pages 1–9)

CONSIDER these questions before you go on. They are designed to help you start thinking about this subject, not to test your knowledge.

Where and when did psychology get its start?

Is it really possible for us to study behavior and the mind scientifically?

Is psychology's development related to other academic areas, such as philosophy or biology, or is it an isolated field of study?

How are the mind and the body related?

READ this section of your text lightly. Then go back and read thoroughly, completing the Workout as you proceed.

Psychology, the science of behavior and the mind, emerged in the second half of the nineteenth century.

1. Psychology is the science of _____—
   the observable actions, of a person or animal—
   and _____—an individual's
   sensations, perceptions, memories, motives,
   emotions, thoughts, and other subjective
   experiences, as well as unconscious knowledge
   and operating rules.

2. What does it mean to say that psychology is a science?

Psychology, the science of behavior and the mind, emerged in the second half of the nineteenth century. Ideas that arose and were discussed in other disciplines beforehand laid the foundation for a science of psychology.

3. Briefly, what are the three foundational ideas identified in the text?
   a.

   b.

   c.

The very idea of psychology would have been unimaginable without earlier developments in philosophy. René Descartes, a French philosopher, was a key figure in these developments.

4. Explain the doctrine of dualism accepted by the church in the seventeenth century.

5. How did Descartes' version of dualism make way for a science of behavior?

6. How would a strict adherence to Descartes' theory limit psychology?

Thomas Hobbes, a British contemporary of Descartes, departed much further from the church's accepted position on dualism.

7. What ideas were central to Thomas Hobbes's materialism?

Seeing the body as a machine open to scientific study helped physiology to advance. Progress in physiology during the nineteenth century then further helped to create an intellectual climate in which psychology could develop.

8. How did physiology's new understanding of reflexes help to lay the foundation for a scientific psychology?

9. Describe the view known as reflexology.

10. What influences came from an increased understanding of localization of function in the brain?

The thinking of the British empiricists was also critical to the emergence of psychology.

11. According to the British empiricists such as Locke, Hartley, and the Mills, what is the original basis of all knowledge and thought?

12. What was the role of association by contiguity according to the empiricists?

13. How has empiricist philosophy influenced psychology?

Nativist philosophers such as Kant and Leibniz in Germany espoused a view opposite to empiricism.

14. What is the basic idea of nativism? Why must it at some level be correct?

15. Distinguish between *a priori* and *a posteriori* knowledge.

The ideas that Darwin presented in *On the Origin of Species* were revolutionary, affecting not only biology, but also philosophy, and laying yet more foundation for psychology.

16. What was Darwin's fundamental idea?

17. How did Darwin's evolutionary viewpoint highlight the *function* of behavior?

    b. genetic

    c. evolutionary

18. What are some major influences of Darwin's work on the field of psychology?

    d. learning

The Scope of Psychology (pages 9–18)

CONSIDER these questions before you go on. They are designed to help you start thinking about this subject, not to test your knowledge.

---

    e. cognitive

How can something as complicated as the mind or behavior be studied scientifically?

Is psychology considered a natural science? a social science? or one of the humanities?

    f. social

What kind of work do psychologists do, and where do they do it?

READ this section of your text lightly. Then go back and read thoroughly, completing the Workout as you proceed.

---

    g. cultural

Psychologists endeavor ultimately to explain various aspects of the mind and behavior. To do this fully, they seek to understand causal processes at different levels of analysis.

1. For each level of analysis that follows, give a brief definition, identify the type of cause being explored, and name the type of psychologist who focuses on that level.

    a. neural

Like medicine, history, physics, or literature, psychology incorporates a number of specialties. Some, as you have seen, are defined primarily by a certain level of analysis. Others are defined more by topic than level of analysis.

2. List and be sure you can differentiate the topic-based specialties described in the text.

Colleges and universities are generally made up of departments representing specific academic disciplines. Often, we speak of disciplines as falling into one of three divisions—natural sciences, social sciences, and humanities.

3. How does psychology fit into this way of categorizing the disciplines? Explain your answer.

The many influences in psychology's past have helped to make psychology a very diverse field today. That diversity is evident not only in the content of academic psychology but also in the many professional endeavors of psychologists.

4. What kinds of educational credentials do professional psychologists generally have?

5. List four types of settings in which psychologists work, and indicate the kind of activity they might carry out in each.

a.

b.

c.

d.

Thoughts About Using This Book and Its Special Features   (pages 19–23)

CONSIDER these questions before you go on. They are designed to help you start thinking about this subject, not to test your knowledge.

What can you do to get the most out of this text and by extension out of this course?

READ this section of your text lightly. Then go back and read thoroughly, completing the Workout as you proceed.

1. What is the challenge presented by reading a textbook as opposed to a nonfiction book you have chosen outside of coursework?

2. What should your goals be in reading?

3. What are focus questions? How can they help you?

4. How can the headings and section reviews be of value to you? How can you make the best use of them?

Be sure to READ the Concluding Thoughts at the end of the chapter. Note important points in your Workout. Then consolidate your learning by answering the focus questions in the margins of the text.

After you have studied the chapter thoroughly, CHECK your understanding with the Self-Test that follows.

Self-Test 1

Multiple-Choice Questions

1. Darwin felt that natural selection:
   a. could not help us to explain evolution.
   b. could help us to understand anatomy but not behavior.
   c. could be applied to plants and nonhuman animals but not to humans.
   d. gradually formed the present anatomy and behavior of living things.

2. Descartes' theory of human action is a version of dualism because it includes both:
   a. mind and behavior.
   b. mind and spirit.
   c. body and soul.
   d. philosophy and science.

3. The British empiricists believed that thought ultimately derives from:
   a. logical analysis.
   b. the brain's innately determined physiology.
   c. free will.
   d. sensory experience.

4. Which important advance in nineteenth-century physiology helped to prepare the way for scientific psychology?

   a. new understanding of the neurological basis of reflexes
   b. rejection of the idea that specific parts of the brain have specific functions
   c. discovery of the basic arrangement of the nervous system
   d. discovery of an anatomical basis for the distinction between the conscious mind and the unconscious mind

5. As defined in the chapter, psychology is the science of:
   a. behavior.
   b. the brain.
   c. the mind.
   d. behavior and the mind.

6. The person usually credited with the founding of scientific psychology is:
   a. Sechenov.
   b. Darwin.
   c. Wundt.
   d. Kant.

7. Reflexology contributed most directly to the development of:
   a. evolutionary psychology.
   b. behavioral genetics.
   c. abnormal psychology.
   d. behaviorism.

8. Jalila wonders how she should structure rewards and punishments to reduce the time she spends playing computer games. She is most likely to find the information she needs in a textbook on
   a. personality psychology.
   b. abnormal psychology.
   c. learning psychology.
   d. cognitive psychology.

9. Hobbes's materialism most directly influenced the development of:
   a. nativism.
   b. physiology.
   c. dualism.
   d. evolutionary psychology.

10. Which of the following levels of analysis fits *least* well with the other three?
    a. neural
    b. cognitive
    c. genetic
    d. evolutionary

Essay Question

1. Contrast empiricist and nativist views on the origins of knowledge.

After you have assessed your understanding on the basis of Self-Test 1 and have tried to strengthen your preparation in any areas of weakness, GO ON to Self-Test 2.

Self-Test 2

Multiple-Choice Questions

1. The causes of behavior can be examined at different _____, such as neural, genetic, cognitive, or cultural.
   a. levels of analysis
   b. psychocentric levels
   c. functional levels
   d. localizations of function

2. An increased understanding of reflexes in the 19th century was key to the development of:
   a. nativism.
   b. dualism.
   c. psychology.
   d. empiricism.

3. Darwin's primary emphasis on the _____ of behavior was a major influence on evolutionary psychology.
   a. mechanisms
   b. learning
   c. complexity
   d. functions

4. For psychologists, 1879 has historical significance because it was the year that the:
   a. first psychologist was hired by a hospital.
   b. first laboratory of psychology was opened at a university.
   c. first book on empiricism was published.
   d. psychologist Wilhelm Wundt was born.

5. According to Descartes' version of dualism:
   a. even some complex behaviors can occur without any involvement of the soul.
   b. the body has exclusive control over behavior, while the soul has exclusive control over thought.
   c. all behavior involves interaction with the soul.
   d. the body fully controls both behavior and thought.

6. The law of association by contiguity was central to:
   a. the 17th century church's version of dualism.
   b. Descartes' version of dualism.
   c. British empiricism.
   d. the theory of natural selection.

7. The person sitting next to you on the plane tells you that her work involves stimulating a small area of a cat's brain to learn if there are any effects on its hunting behaviors. You could correctly say, "Oh, you're a _____."
   a. behavioral neuroscientist
   b. behavioral geneticist
   c. developmental psychologist
   d. cognitive psychologist

8. Cognitive psychology, unlike the psychology of learning, focuses on:
   a. experience.
   b. the mind.
   c. personality.
   d. behavior.

9. Suppose your roommate is writing a senior thesis about the following topic: Effects of Spousal Pressure on Adherence to an Exercise Program. Your roommate's thesis mostly falls within _____ psychology.
   a. cognitive
   b. cultural
   c. social
   d. developmental

10. According to Kant, one cannot obtain _____ without _____.
    a. *a priori* knowledge; *a posteriori* knowledge
    b. *a posteriori* knowledge; *a priori* knowledge
    c. *a priori* knowledge; natural selection
    d. natural selection; *a priori* knowledge

Essay Question

11. Discuss the ways that Descartes helped to prepare the way for a scientific psychology. Also point out any limits that his philosophy set on such a science.

Answers

Introduction and Three Foundation Ideas for Psychology

1. behavior; the mind

Self-Test 1

1. **d.** (p. 8)

2. **c.** (p. 3)

3. **d.** (p. 6)

4. **a.** (p. 4)

5. **d.** (p. 1)

6. **c.** Wundt's laboratory at the University of Leipzig represented an official acceptance of psychology by the academic establishment and provided a firm basis for the growth of the field. (p. 2)

7. **d.** (p. 5)

8. **c.** (p. 12)

9. **b.** Hobbes's views portrayed the body as a machine open to scientific study, and physiology as seeking to understand the mechanisms of the body through science. (p. 4)

10. **b.** (p. 10)

11. According to the empiricists, all knowledge comes from sensory experience of the world around us. They believed that even complex thoughts and ideas came ultimately from this source. Such ideas and thoughts were considered to be based on linking more elementary ideas together. The most basic principle proffered to explain such links was the concept of association by contiguity originally suggested by Aristotle. The nativists, in contrast, claimed that some knowledge and rules of operation are native, that is, innate, to the human mind. As Kant explained it, such knowledge is *a priori*. This inborn *a priori* knowledge is necessary to be able to acquire further knowledge from experience. This second type of knowledge he labeled *a posteriori*. (p. 7)

Self-Test 2

1. **a.** (p. 10)

2. **c.** (p. 4)

3. **d.** (p. 8)

4. **b.** (p. 2)

5. **a.** (p. 3)

6. **c.** (p. 6)

7. **a.** (p. 10)

8. **b.** (p. 13)

9. **c.** (p. 14)

10. **b.** (p. 7)

11. Descartes' dualism suggested the existence of a body and a soul, both of which affect behavior. According to the theory, the body can control even some complex behavior directly, without any involvement of the soul. Descartes argued that any human activity that is essentially like an activity an animal can perform does not require the soul, since animals were assumed to have no souls. Descartes thus offered a new view of the body as a mechanism that follows natural laws and can therefore be understood through science. How-

ever, the nonmaterial soul was believed by Descartes to be responsible for all thought. Unlike the body itself, the soul was not subject to natural law. Rather, it was thought to have free will. Because it was not operating under natural law, the soul, and the behaviors it willed the body to per-

form, could not be studied by science. This would clearly set profound limits on the aims of scientific psychology. Thought and any behavior governed by thought would be essentially outside its scope. (p. 3)

Methods of Psychology

chapter 2

READ *the introduction below before you read
the chapter in the text.*

Psychology employs scientific methods to answer questions about behavior and the mind. Scientific methods involve the systematic collection and analysis of objective, publicly observable data. The classic story of Clever Hans, a horse purported to have extensive knowledge of many subjects, such as history and arithmetic, illustrates the value of a scientific approach.

The scientific process involves the use of facts to develop theories. From theories, scientists derive hypotheses about what will happen under specific conditions. Then they test their hypotheses—producing more facts.

To produce and evaluate facts, hypotheses, and theories, psychological researchers employ various strategies. These strategies can be categorized along three dimensions. One dimension is research design: Some studies involve controlled experimentation; others search for correlations between variables; and others simply describe behavior systematically. Another dimension is the setting: Some research is conducted in laboratories, but other studies are carried out in natural environments—in classrooms, public parks, city streets, or sports arenas, for example. The third dimension is the data-collection method: In some cases, the data may consist of information reported by the individuals being studied. Alternatively, the data may come from direct observations and measurements made by the researchers.

Statistical analysis is used to help psychologists understand the meaning of the data collected through research. Descriptive statistics summarize the data in useful ways. Inferential statistics indicate whether patterns in the data are reliable or repeatable, given that data are always somewhat affected by random variation.

Research must be designed with various precautions in place. For example, care must be taken in selecting research subjects and assigning them to groups. Even the way a variable is measured requires careful consideration. Some safeguards must be used to keep the researchers' expectations from affecting the data. Other safeguards must be used because the expectations of research subjects can produce misleading data. Finally, a number of research guidelines exist for ethical purposes, to protect the rights and welfare of research subjects.

LOOK *over the table of contents for this chapter in your
textbook before you continue with your study.*

Notice that there are focus questions in the margins of the text for your use in studying the material. The following chart lists which Study Guide questions relate to which focus questions.

Focus Questions	Study Guide Questions
Lessons from Clever Hans	
1–3	1–5
Types of Research Strategies	
9	1, 4–9
10	2, 10–11
11	3, 12–15
Statistical Methods in Psychology	
12	1–4
13	5–8
14	9
15	10
16	11
Minimizing Bias in Psychological Research	
17	1
18	2
19	3

The Integrated Study Workout

COMPLETE one section at a time.

Introduction AND *Lessons from Clever Hans* (pages 25–28)

CONSIDER these questions before you go on. They are designed to help you start thinking about this subject, not to test your knowledge.

What concepts and attitudes are essential for a scientific approach to knowledge?

Is skepticism important only for combatting deliberate attempts to deceive?

Is there a difference between a theory and a hypothesis?

READ this section of your text lightly. Then go back and read thoroughly, completing the Workout as you proceed.

As scientists, psychologists attempt to answer their research questions through the systematic collection and analysis of objective, publicly observable data. The story of Clever Hans helps to teach us some important lessons about the scientific approach.

1. What was claimed for Clever Hans? Who made the claim?

2. Was the case of Clever Hans a deliberate hoax? Explain.

3. How did the psychologist Oskar Pfungst uncover the truth about Clever Hans? What was his final conclusion about the basis for Hans's amazing performance?

4. Define these terms: *fact, theory,* and *hypothesis.* Make sure your answer explains how they are related.

5. What are the major lessons to be learned from the case of Clever Hans?

   a.

   b.

   c.

Types of Research Strategies   (pages 29–34)

CONSIDER these questions before you go on. They are designed to help you start thinking about this subject, not to test your knowledge.

If optimism were found to be correlated with career success, would it mean that optimism causes greater career success?

What makes an experiment an experiment?

What other methods besides experiments do psychologists use to study behavior and the mind?

Can psychologists study behavior in a natural setting? in a laboratory?

READ this section of your text lightly. Then go back and read thoroughly, completing the Workout as you proceed.

You will understand psychological research better if you appreciate the variety of research strategies used. Below are listed three dimensions of research strategies—the research design, the research setting, and the method of data collection. Identify the different categories of each dimension below. (See text p. 34)

1. The research design:

   a. _____ A procedure in which a researcher systematically varies one or more independent variables and notes any change in one or more dependent variables, while holding other variables constant.

   b. _____ A study in which a researcher observes or measures two or more variables to find relationships among them but does not manipulate any variables.

   c. _____ A study in which the goal is not the systematic investigation of relationships between variables but rather the description of behavior.

2. Research settings:

   a. _____ Subjects are studied in a specially designated area that allows better control of environmental conditions or facilitates data collection.

   b. _____ Subjects are studied in an environment not specially set up for purposes of research, such as a park, a restaurant, a kindergarten, or a living room.

3. Data-collection methods:

   a. _____ The people being studied rate or describe their own behavior or mental state in some way.

   b. _____ The researcher observes and records the behavior of interest.

4. Categorize each of the following situations along the three dimensions of research strategy.

   a. A developmental psychologist has randomly divided elderly residents of a nursing home into three groups, each of which receives a different type of treatment intended to enhance life satisfaction. At the end of the study, the psychologist asks the residents to rate their life satisfaction using a series of questions.

   Type of design? _____

   Type of setting? _____

   Type of data collection? _____

   b. A psychologist is interested in spatial skills as they relate to aviation safety. Subjects who are licensed pilots are brought in and tested on a special apparatus that simulates various emergencies. The apparatus records how quickly and appropriately the subjects maneuver the "aircraft" to avoid imminent danger. The psychologist wants to see whether performance on this apparatus is related to scores on a paper and pencil test of spatial ability.

   Type of design? _____

   Type of setting? _____

   Type of data collection? _____

   c. A clinical psychologist wants to better understand the means by which social support systems help terminally ill patients in a hospice. The psychologist sits in on group support sessions and family visits of selected patients, carefully recording what happens.

   Type of design? _____

   Type of setting? _____

   Type of data collection? _____

Experiments allow researchers the greatest degree of control and permit strong conclusions about cause and effect.

5. How do the terms *independent variable* and *dependent variable* relate to the terms *cause* and *effect*?

6. In the following examples, indicate which are variables by writing *V* in the blank provided.

   ____ a. intelligence test score

   ____ b. height of adult males

   ____ c. number of days in a week

   ____ d. major in college

7. In the following situations, indicate independent variables with *IV* and dependent variables with *DV*.

   a. A researcher randomly assigns subjects to groups that differ in size (_____). All subjects are then asked to perform the same task. The researcher measures the average amount of work each person does (_____).

   b. Subjects report childhood memories that come to mind (_____) after being exposed to verbal, visual, or smell cues (_____) associated with common childhood experiences.

   c. Researchers observe how long subjects work on a word puzzle (_____) after being told that they are good or poor puzzle solvers (_____).

   d. Subjects are prescribed varying dosages of a drug (_____) designed to reduce symptoms of depression. After a month, they are rated by themselves, by family members, and by counselors on various dimensions related to depression (_____).

   e. Researchers calculate the average academic grades of children (_____) at 3 months, 6 months, 1 year, and 2 years after the death of a parent (_____).

8. What is the difference between a within-subject and a between-groups experiment?

Correlational studies can provide useful and interesting information when it is not possible to manipulate a variable directly. A psychologist cannot, for example, assign subjects to different genders or occupations.

9. Correlational studies do not permit us to draw cause-effect conclusions the way experiments do.

   a. Why is this so?

   b. Consider Diana Baumrind's work on parental discipline styles. Why would cause-effect conclusions based on this study be inappropriate?

Research can be conducted in a laboratory setting or in a field setting. Each has certain advantages and drawbacks.

10. What are the special advantages and limitations of laboratory studies? of field studies?

11. What is a field experiment?

Psychologists can collect data in a number of different ways within two broad categories.

12. Two major ways of collecting self-report data are _____ and _____.

13. Two major ways of collecting observational data are _____ and _____.

14. Provide two concrete examples of each data-collection method mentioned above. (Use examples from the text, or, better yet, make up your own examples.)

   a. self-report

   b. observational

15. Compare the advantages and disadvantages of self-report methods, naturalistic observation, and tests.

Statistical Methods in Psychology (pages 35–39)

CONSIDER these questions before you go on. They are designed to help you start thinking about this subject, not to test your knowledge.

What does it mean when someone says two things are correlated?

Science has the reputation of being quantitative. How does psychology make use of math?

READ this section of your text lightly. Then go back and read thoroughly, completing the Workout as you proceed.

Data are useful only to the extent that they can be summarized and interpreted. Statistical procedures are critical to that step in the research process.

1. Descriptive statistics help us to

   _____ a set of data.

The mean and median are measures of central tendency. They help to summarize the data by giving us one "typical" number that serves to represent the whole data set. (*Hint:* Look at Table 2.1, text p. 35.)

2. The mean of the numbers 4, 6, 9, 8, 3 is

   _____.

3. The median of the numbers 8, 6, 5, 10, 12 is

   _____.

Variability is the extent to which the scores in a set of data differ from one another. The standard deviation is a common measure of variability. (In a sense, the measure of variability tells us how well the measure of central tendency represents the data set. For example, if all the scores in the set are fairly similar, the mean might represent them well. If there are widely differing scores, the mean would represent them less well.)

4. Which set below has the higher variability? (Circle a or b)

   a. 3 6 7 6 8 5

   b. 1 5 2 9 4 11

A correlation coefficient is a descriptive statistic that expresses the strength and direction of the relationship between two variables. (*Hint:* Look at Figure 2.3, text p. 36, for the items below.)

5. A correlation coefficient can vary between

   _____ and _____.

6. The sign + or − indicates whether the relationship is positive or negative—in other words, the _____ of the relationship.

7. The absolute value of the coefficient indicates the _____ of the relationship. Lower numbers indicate_____ relationships, while higher numbers indicate _____ relationships. Numbers at or near zero indicate _____ correlation.

8. In the following scatter plot, what kind of correlation is indicated—negative or positive? weak, moderate, or strong?

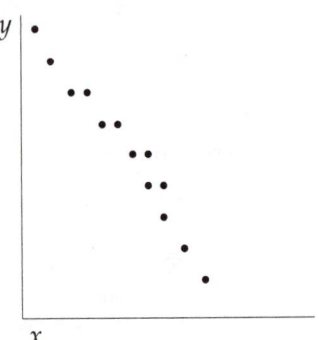

Data are always subject to a certain amount of random or chance variation. These random influences can keep us from seeing real, systematic patterns in the data, somewhat the way noise on a phone call prevents us from hearing the speaker's voice clearly. They can also make it appear as if certain patterns exist when in reality they do not. Inferential statistics help us to decide when the patterns we see are real and repeatable, not just a product of chance.

9. Explain what it means to say that a given set of results is significant at the 5 percent level.

10. What elements are taken into account in determining statistical significance?

    a.

    b.

    c.

11. Statistical significance is not the same as practical significance. Explain, then make up an example of a research result that has statistical but no real practical significance.

Minimizing Error and Bias in Psychological Research   (pages 39–44)

CONSIDER these questions before you go on. They are designed to help you start thinking about this subject, not to test your knowledge.

What are some issues you should consider in deciding how much you should trust the results of a psychological study?

Are scientists as objective as they ideally would like to be, or are they sometimes swayed by their own biases, like nonscientists?

READ this section of your text lightly. Then go back and read thoroughly, completing the Workout as you proceed.

Considerable care is involved in designing sound research studies. There are several known sources of bias and error in research, and researchers must constantly guard against them.

1. Explain the difference between error and bias. Why is bias a much more serious problem?

2. How can a biased sample come about in an experiment? in a descriptive study?

The measurement procedure used by the researcher is an important factor in minimizing error and bias.

3. What does it mean to say a measure is reliable? What problem results from low reliability?

9. An experimental that guards against both observer- and subject-expectancy effects is called a(n) _____ experiment.

10. Which kind of expectancy effect produced the apparent phenomenon of facilitated communication?

4. Define *validity*. What problem results from low validity?

5. Can a measurement be reliable and yet not be valid? Give an example to support your answer.

Ethical Issues in Psychological Research
(pages 44–46)

CONSIDER these questions before you go on. They are designed to help you start thinking about this subject, not to test your knowledge.

What are the most serious ethical challenges encountered in psychological research?

Do psychologists give serious attention to ethical issues involved in using animals as research subjects?

What kinds of ethical principles do psychologists observe?

6. A measurement procedure has _____ validity if it seems to make sense on the surface. A measurement procedure has _____ validity to the extent that it correlates well with another, more direct index of the same characteristic.

READ this section of your text lightly. Then go back and read thoroughly, completing the Workout as you proceed.

Bias can also result from the wishes and expectations brought into the research situation by either observers or subjects.

Those who conduct psychological research are obliged to observe ethical as well as scientific principles.

7. How can an observer's expectations bias results? How can we avoid such observer-expectancy effects in experiments?

1. List the three major issues in research with human subjects.

   a. _____

   b. _____

   c. _____

2. How do researchers deal with these issues?

   a.

8. Explain the concept of a subject-expectancy effect. What is the best way to avoid this problem?

   b.

   c.

3. What are the ethical obligations of researchers who use animal subjects?

4. What are some steps the profession as a whole has taken to oversee ethical practices in psychological research?

Be sure to READ the Concluding Thoughts at the end of the chapter. Note important points in your Workout. Then consolidate your learning by answering the focus questions in the margins of the text.

After you have studied the chapter thoroughly, CHECK your understanding with the Self-Test that follows.

Self-Test 1

Multiple-Choice Questions

1. Which of the following is a lesson that should be learned from the case of Clever Hans?
   a. We must not be misled by science's claims of objectivity.
   b. Unless we take a skeptical approach to any situation, we may be led to believe what is simply not true.
   c. When an unusual and interesting claim is made, we should suspend our skepticism and look first for evidence that supports the claim.
   d. The intelligence of nonhuman species should not be underestimated out of human arrogance.

2. Which of the following is the mean of the numbers 2, 4, 4, 6, 9?
   a. 2   c. 5
   b. 4   d. 25

3. A procedure in which the researcher systematically varies one variable, holding all others constant, to see if another variable is affected, is called a(n):
   a. correlational study.
   b. observational study.
   c. experiment.
   d. double-blind study.

4. An experimenter wants to see whether caffeine has any effect on the ability to concentrate on a visual task. In this study, the caffeine would be the:
   a. independent variable.
   b. between-groups variable.
   c. dependent variable.
   d. within-subject variable.

5. Cause is to effect as _____ is to _____.
   a. constant; variable
   b. dependent variable; independent variable
   c. independent variable; dependent variable
   d. experiment; correlational study

6. A psychologist tries to find out whether there is any relationship between the number of older siblings a child has and the size of the child's vocabulary at age 3. This is an example of a(n):
   a. experiment.
   b. correlational study.
   c. descriptive study.
   d. laboratory study.

7. A psychologist explores the behavior of children in their first competitive sports experience, recording the variety and frequency of various social behaviors. What type of research strategy is involved here?
   a. experimental
   b. correlational
   c. descriptive
   d. within-subject

8. The purpose of descriptive statistics is to:
   a. help us decide whether research conclusions based on the data are warranted.
   b. help us collect data more efficiently.
   c. help us summarize data in a meaningful way
   d. do all of the above.

9. The chapter categorizes research strategies in terms of:
   a. research design, description, and data analysis
   b. data collection, type of experiment, and statistical analysis.
   c. research design, setting, and data-collection method.
   d. observation, correlation, and setting.

10. Which of the following is the median of the numbers 25, 5, 15, 20, 30?
   a. 5
   b. 15
   c. 19
   d. 20

11. A psychologist uses test X to measure a person's creativity. The test is administered several times with widely varying results. Test X apparently lacks:
    a. observer expectancy.
    b. face validity.
    c. a double blind.
    d. reliability.

12. A result is termed "statistically significant" if it:
    a. is probably due to chance.
    b. cannot possibly be due to chance.
    c. has less than a 5 percent probability of being due to chance.
    d. is large enough to be of practical importance.

13. The host of a radio call-in show asks listeners to phone in their views on affirmative action—for, against, or not sure. The results are suspect because of:
    a. a sample that is probably biased.
    b. high criterion validity.
    c. the fact that the study is merely descriptive.
    d. the between-groups nature of the experiment.

14. The value of a correlation coefficient can vary between:
    a. 1.00 and 100.00.
    b. −10.00 and +10.00.
    c. 0.00 and 1.00.
    d. −1.00 and +1.00.

15. Clever Hans's abilities were apparently due to:
    a. placebo effects.
    b. low reliability.
    c. observer expectancy.
    d. a double-blind procedure.

Essay Questions

16. How do facts, theories, and hypotheses fit into psychology?

17. What are the three major ethical issues that must be considered in psychological research with human subjects? How do psychologists deal with these issues?

After you have assessed your understanding on the basis of Self-Test 1 and have tried to strengthen your preparation in any areas of weakness, GO ON to Self-Test 2.

Self-Test 2

Multiple-Choice Questions

1. Which of the following describes an independent variable?
   a. a variable that is studied on its own without relationship to any other variables
   b. the variable the researcher observes and measures in an experiment
   c. the variable the researcher deliberately manipulates in an experiment
   d. a variable that is held constant in an experiment

2. Which type(s) of research design permit(s) direct cause-and-effect conclusions?
   a. experiments
   b. correlational studies
   c. descriptive studies
   d. both experiments and correlational studies

3. A within-subject experiment is one in which:
   a. there is only a single subject.
   b. a given subject experiences all the different conditions of the experiment.
   c. the data are collected by self-report.
   d. the experimenter is interested only in the subjective experiences of the subject.

4. A psychologist varies the amount of practice time provided for different sets of subjects in a target-shooting task. The question is whether accuracy will be affected. The psychologist is conducting a:
   a. correlational study.
   b. between-groups experiment.
   c. within-subject experiment.
   d. descriptive study.

5. A psychologist asks people to complete a confidential questionnaire to determine whether physical fitness is related to self-esteem. The psychologist is conducting a(n) ____ study.
   a. experimental   c. double-blind
   b. correlational   d. descriptive

6. A psychologist visits a chemical plant to interview people engaged in a labor strike there. This would be:
   a. an experiment in which data collection is by self-report.
   b. a correlational study in which data collection is observational.
   c. a descriptive study in which data collection is observational.
   d. a field study in which data collection is by self-report.

7. A study examines the effect of different incentives ($5 versus $50) on people's willingness to perform a mildly embarrassing task. In this study, _____ would be the independent variable and _____ would be the dependent variable.
   a. incentive; willingness to perform the task
   b. willingness to perform the task; incentive
   c. incentive; whether subjects receive $5 or $50
   d. willingness to perform the task; the number of people tested

8. We often use _____ as an indicator of the variability in a data set.
   a. the standard deviation
   b. central tendency
   c. a correlation coefficient
   d. the mean

9. A procedure that succeeds in measuring what it is intended to measure is said to be:
   a. unbiased.   c. valid.
   b. reliable.   d. correlated.

10. Which of the following correlation coefficients would indicate the strongest correlation between two variables?
   a. −0.80   c. +0.50
   b. 0.00   d. +0.75

11. Suppose a research result shows a difference between the two groups studied. Suppose further that inferential statistics show that the likelihood of the difference being due to chance is 30 percent. Is the result statistically significant by the usual standards?
   a. Yes.
   b. No.
   c. Well, yes and no—it's 70 percent significant.
   d. It's impossible to say based on the information provided.

12. In an experiment, which of the following factors is *not* taken into account in a test of statistical significance?
   a. the size of the observed difference between means
   b. the number of times the study has been repeated
   c. the number of subjects
   d. the variability of the data in each group

13. The more consistent the result of a measurement procedure when used on the same subject under the same conditions, the more _____ the measure is.
   a. reliable   c. independent
   b. unbiased   d. valid

14. Which of the following is the mean of the numbers 10, 20, 30, 40, 100?
   a. 10   c. 40
   b. 30   d. 55

15. If the results of an experiment are actually due to the beliefs of the subjects and not to a real effect of the independent variable, we say:
   a. the subjects are blind.
   b. the study involves a double blind.
   c. there is bias.
   d. there is a within-subject effect.

Essay Questions

16. Briefly describe the case of Clever Hans, and explain the lessons we should learn from it.

17. Explain the phenomena of observer-expectancy and subject-expectancy effects in research. What measures can be taken to guard against them?

Answers

Types of Research Strategies

1. a. experiment
   b. correlational study
   c. descriptive study

2. a. laboratory
   b. field

3. a. self-report
   b. observational

4. a. experiment; field; self-report
   b. correlational; laboratory; observational
   c. descriptive; field; observational

6. Items **a**, **b**, and **d** are variables, whereas **c** is a constant.

7. a. IV, DV
   b. DV, IV
   c. DV, IV
   d. IV, DV
   e. DV, IV

2. questionnaire; interview

3. naturalistic observation; test

Statistical Methods in Psychology

1. summarize

2. 6

3. 8

4. Set b has higher variability

5. −1.00 and +1.00

6. direction

7. strength; weaker; stronger; no

8. a strong negative correlation

Minimizing Error and Bias in Psychological Research

5. Yes. For example, eye color would be a reliable but not valid measure of honesty.

6. face; criterion

9. double-blind

Ethical Issues in Psychological Research

1. a. right to privacy
   b. possible discomfort or harm
   c. use of deception

Self-Test 1

1. b. (pp. 27–28)

2. c. (p. 35)

3. c. Only the experiment involves this much control. It is the control that allows conclusions about cause-and-effect relationships from experimental data. (p. 29)

4. a. (p. 29)

5. c. (pp. 29–30)

6. b. (p. 31)

7. c. (p. 32)

8. c. (p. 35)

9. c. (p. 29)

10. d. Remember, the median is the middle number when numbers are ranked from lowest to highest. The mean, on the other hand, is the arithmetic average. (p. 35)

11. d. (pp. 40)

12. c. Scientists have established 5 percent as an arbitrary cutoff point. The rationale is that a 5 percent chance that a result could be due to random factors is a small enough chance to take a gamble on because we would be wrong only 5 percent of the time. (p. 37)

13. a. (pp. 39–40)

14. d. (p. 35)

15. c. (p. 41)

16. Psychology, like all scientific endeavors, seeks to explain its subject matter—in this case behavior and the mind—objectively. In other words, it relies on fact rather than pure opinion or speculation. A psychologist carrying out research in some area of inquiry would attempt to make sense of known facts (or observations), perhaps producing a theory that explains them. That theory would then be used to produce hypotheses, that is, predictions about what would be observed in particular circumstances. Then those predictions are systematically tested, and the facts or observations produced by the test may well lead to further theorizing, predicting, and testing. (p. 27)

17. The three major ethical issues involved in psychological research are the right to privacy, the possibility of discomfort or harm to subjects, and deception. The first issue demands that information obtained from or about subjects be dealt with in a way that safeguards the individual's anonymity. Both the issues of privacy and harm or discomfort can be handled largely by obtaining informed consent from subjects and by letting them know they can quit the study at any point. Psychologists must also compare the potential risks to subjects with the potential scientific benefits for humankind before entering into the research. If risks can be avoided or minimized, there is an obligation to do that. Deception is probably the most controversial issue. Opponents say deception is never acceptable, but others counter that it is comparatively rare, generally benign, and often scientifically necessary. (pp. 44–45)

Self-Test 2

1. c. (p. 29)

2. a. (p. 29)

3. b. (p. 29)

4. b. (p. 30)

5. b. (p. 31)

6. d. (p. 32)

7. a. (p. 29)

8. a. (p. 35)

9. c. (p. 40)

10. a. To assess the strength of the relationship, look only at the absolute value of the coefficient, not the sign. The second strongest correlation coefficient among the alternatives would be d. Alternative b indicates the absence of any relationship between the two variables. (p. 36)

11. b. The arbitrary cutoff point to establish statistical significance is often 5 percent. Below the cutoff, the results are considered significant; above the cutoff, the results are considered not significant. In other words, if the results had only a 5 percent or lower probability of occurring by chance, then we are essentially "betting" that they aren't due only to chance. There is no such thing as a partially significant result. Further, if there really were a 30 percent chance that our results were due to random factors, it would be a very risky bet to proclaim that they really weren't. (p. 37)

12. b. (pp. 37–38)

13. a. (p. 40)

14. c. (p. 35)

15. c. (p. 39)

16. Clever Hans was a horse owned by a retired German schoolteacher named von Osten. Von Osten tried to prove his hypothesis that horses were as smart as people and simply needed to be educated to show that they were. After several years of training, Hans could apparently answer questions about math, geography, history, and other subjects by moving his head or tapping his hoof. Von Osten's claims were widely accepted, even by many scientists. However, a psychologist by the name of Oskar Pfungst discredited Hans in a series of careful experiments. When Hans was prevented from receiving subtle unintentional cues from his "teacher" or others in his admiring audiences, he was unable to answer the questions put to him. This case is a classic lesson in the value of skepti cism in science. We must not accept something as true just because we would like it to be true or because on casual observation it appears to be true. We must test a claim and see whether it can be explained in some other fashion than the one we favor. It is also a lesson about the importance of making observations under carefully controlled and systematically varied conditions. Further, the case of Clever Hans can serve as an illustration of observer-expectancy effects, a problem that results when a researcher inadvertently cues a subject as to what is expected from him or her. (pp. 26–28)

17. One difficulty that psychological researchers often face comes from the very fact that they and their subjects are intelligent, thinking creatures. The researcher on the one hand and the subject on the other may both be affected by expectations. The researcher may unwittingly pass on expectations to the subject, who may just as unwittingly (or deliberately) comply with those expectations. If that happens, the results of the study are not a reflection of nature as the researcher hoped they would be. Instead, they are just a reflection of the researcher's own beliefs. Likewise, the researcher's observations and judgments may be influenced by his or her own expectations. For example, if the researcher expects the subject to behave nonaggressively in a particular situation, behavior that is ambiguous or even slightly aggressive may be perceived as nonaggressive. These kinds of effects, which stem from what the observer believes or expects, are referred to as observer-expectancy effects. Subjects, too, may develop their own expectations. For example, a subject who knows she is receiving a drug intended to suppress appetite may experience appetite suppression for reasons due to the expectation, not the drug. In other words, the observed appetite suppression could be due to a placebo effect. Blind and double-blind studies can be very useful in preventing expectancy effects. In blind studies, the observers are not given access to information that could fuel observer-expectancy effects. In other words, they are unaware of a given subject's treatment condition and thus have no basis to apply their expectations. In double-blind studies, both the observer *and* the subject are unaware of what treatment the subject is receiving. Thus double-blind studies protect against both observer- and subject-expectancy effects. (pp. 41–44)

Genetic and Evolutionary Foundations of Behavior

READ the introduction below before you read the chapter in the text.

Chapter 3 focuses on the impact of genetics and evolutionary adaptation on behavior. Adaptation is a means of accommodating to changed circumstances. (Evolution is just one level on which adaptation occurs; another is learning, which will be considered in Chapter 4.)

Genes, the biological units of heredity, affect our anatomy and physiology and, through these, behavioral characteristics. They exert their influences by one, and only one, means—by governing the manufacture of the body's many different protein molecules. Genes always work in interaction with environmental influences. This chapter explains how genetic information is passed down from one generation to the next through sexual reproduction. Such concepts as genetic diversity, genotypes and phenotypes, and dominant and recessive genes are explained.

In some cases, a single gene can affect a particular aspect of behavior or cause genetic disorders that have behavioral consequences. But most differences among individuals stem from the combined effects of many genes in interaction with the environment. We call these polygenic characteristics. Polygenic characteristics vary in degree from one individual to another—that is, each individual will have more or less of the characteristic. In contrast, in the case of single-gene differences, individuals differ in type rather than degree.

The mechanism by which evolutionary adaptation takes place is natural selection, a concept originated by Charles Darwin. Darwin argued that inheritable changes that enhance the chances of survival and reproduction tend to be passed on to the next generation while inheritable changes that hinder survival or reproductive chances are lost. In current evolutionary thinking, Darwin's critical insights are combined with a modern understanding of genes.

People have long engaged in selective breeding—reproducing plants and animals in such a way that desirable traits are developed, enhanced, or continued. Evolution depends on natural selection, defined above, in which the demands of life in a particular environment determine what is a "desirable trait." Genetic diversity provides the raw material for natural selection, but environmental change propels the process. It is important to recognize that evolution does not involve foresight, since common misconceptions about evolution stem from this erroneous assumption.

Functionalism, which emphasizes the purposes of behavior, is well suited to an evolutionary viewpoint. However, not all characteristics that emerge through evolution should be assumed to be useful.

The chapter next explores instinctual or species-typical behaviors, such as speaking in humans or dam-building in beavers. Although biological preparedness is the foundation for such behaviors, learning can be involved in—even critical to—their development. Cross-species comparisons of species-typical behaviors are enlightening. Two types of comparisons—homology and analogy—are used in trying to understand the evolutionary development and functions of behaviors.

One major focus of the evolutionary perspective has been sexual behavior. Robert Trivers, for example, has suggested that the relative parental investments required of males and females of a given species will strongly affect the mating patterns seen in that species. Thinking in evolutionary terms has also helped us understand the greater aggressiveness of male primates as compared with females of their species. Helping behavior in humans and other species can be explained as consistent with natural selection, as well. The chapter also describes fallacies in evolutionary thinking that we should avoid.

Notice that there are focus questions in the margins of the text for your use in studying the material. The following chart lists which Study Guide questions relate to which focus questions.

Focus Questions	Study Guide Questions
Review of Basic Genetic Mechanisms	
1–2	1–4
3	5
4–5	6–14
6–7	15–21
Inheritance of Behavioral Traits	
8	1–3
9	4
10	5–7
11	8
12	9
13–14	10–12
Evolution by Natural Selection	
15	1
16	2–4
17	5–7
18	8
Natural Selection as a Foundation for Functionalism	
19	1–2
20	3–5
21	6
Natural Selection as a Foundation for Understanding Species-Typical Behaviors	
22–23	1–3
24	4
25	5
26	6
27–28	7–9
29	10–12
30	13
Evolutionary Analyses of Mating Patterns	
31	2–3
32	4
33	5–6
34	7–9
35	10
36	11–12
37	13
38	14–16
Evolutionary Analyses of Hunting and Helping	
41	1–6
42–43	7–8

The Integrated Study Workout

COMPLETE one section at a time.

Introduction AND *Review of Basic Genetic Mechanisms*   (pages 49–55)

CONSIDER these questions before you go on. They are designed to help you start thinking about this subject, not to test your knowledge.

How can a microscopic physical thing like a gene affect something psychological such as verbal ability?

How are genes passed down from parents to children?

READ this section of your text lightly. Then go back and read thoroughly, completing the Workout as you proceed.

Genes are the basic building blocks of heredity. If we want to understand the genetic contribution and evolutionary forces that shape behavior, we must understand how genes exert their effects and how they are transmitted from one generation to the next.

1. Do genes affect behavior directly? Explain.

2. Genes affect physical development by directing the synthesis of _____ molecules. The structure of every cell in the body is made up of _____ proteins, and proteins called _____ control the rate of chemical reactions in the cells. Specifically, each gene provides the code that determines the sequence of _____ in a single type of protein. Physically, genes are segments of long molecules of _____

It is very important to understand that the effects of genes are always interwoven with the effects of the environment. Neither one alone can affect the biology or the behavior of an individual.

3. In the context of this chapter, what does *environment* mean?

9. What is the purpose of mitosis? How is the genetic material in one resulting cell related to the genetic material in the other resulting cell?

4. How are genes thought to play a part in long-term behavioral changes resulting from experience?

10. Since the cells in all parts of your body (excluding egg and sperm cells) have the same gene content, how can the cells end up being so different from one another—cells in your stomach lining versus cells in your brain, for example?

5. The same genotype can produce different phenotypes.

_____ The set of genes that the individual inherits

_____ The observable properties of the body and behavioral traits.

It is useful to understand how genetic material is passed down from parents to offspring in sexual reproduction.

6. Strands of DNA are arranged in cells in structures called _____.

7. How many pairs of chromosomes are in a normal human cell (except an egg or sperm cell)?

8. One pair of chromosomes are sex chromosomes. How do the sex chromosomes of males and females differ?

11. Meiosis is the type of cell division that produces

_____ or _____ cells. Through the _____ exchange of genetic material and subsequent _____, several genetically different egg or sperm cells are formed. The number of chromosomes in each egg or sperm cell produced is _____.

In human sexual reproduction, the egg and sperm cells unite, combining their genetic information.

12. The union of an egg and a sperm produces a single new cell called a(n) _____, which contains 23 _____ of chromosomes. The zygote then grows through the process of _____. Each zygote is genetically _____.

13. Explain the evolutionary advantage of reproducing sexually as opposed to asexually.

Cells can divide in two ways. One type of cell division is mitosis, the other, meiosis. An understanding of meiosis is important for understanding the hereditary transmission of genetic information and the way that genetic diversity comes about.

14. Identify the two types of twins, giving two names for each type. How are the twins genetically related in each type?

We often talk about chromosomes in terms of pairs. In the case of humans, we usually say there are 23 pairs of chromosomes, not 46 chromosomes, although both are true. The pairing is emphasized because it has important consequences. It is not only the chromosomes that are paired but also the genes they carry. (*Hint:* Look at Figure 3.4 on text page 54.)

15. Different genes that could potentially occupy the same locus on a pair of chromosomes are called

_____.

16. If the two genes paired at a given locus are identical, the individual is _____ at that locus and if the genes are different, the individual is _____ at that locus.

17. What does it mean to say an allele is dominant? to say an allele is recessive? Are all gene pairs either dominant or recessive? Explain.

18. In each of the following cases, assume that there is an allele *M* which is dominant and an allele *m* which is recessive. Indicate which allele (*M* or *m*) will be expressed in the phenotype for each case.

_____ **a.** The individual is heterozygous.

_____ **b.** The individual is homozygous for *M*.

_____ **c.** The individual is homozygous for *m*.

Gregor Mendel is famous for his elegant studies of genetics in peas. Mendel's work, done in the nineteenth century, still offers a clear picture of certain hereditary patterns.

19. In one experiment, Mendel studied wrinkled-seed peas and round-seed peas. Explain Mendel's breeding procedure.

20. Why did all of the F_1 generation have round seeds?

21. Why did three-fourths of the F_2 generation have round seeds and the other one-fourth wrinkled seeds? (*Hint:* Look at Figure 3.5 on text page 54.)

Inheritance of Behavioral Traits   (pages 55–61)

CONSIDER these questions before you go on. They are designed to help you start thinking about this subject, not to test your knowledge.

What clues lead scientists to believe that differences among individuals on some specific trait are due to a single gene or to many genes?

Can a single gene affect more than one aspect of development or functioning?

READ this section of your text lightly. Then go back and read thoroughly, completing the Workout as you proceed.

In some cases, a behavioral trait is controlled by a single gene locus and inherited in a Mendelian pattern. Scott and Fuller revealed just such a pattern in the behavior of two dog breeds—cocker spaniels and basenjis. In other words, they showed that a particular behavioral trait was controlled by a single gene locus with one allele dominant over another. (*Hint:* See Figures 3.6 and 3.7 on text page 56.)

1. How did purebred cocker and basenji puppies react when approached by a human who was a stranger to them?

2. When dogs of the two breeds were crossbred, how did the resulting (F_1) offspring behave in the same fear test?

3. When dogs of the F_1 generation were mated, what did the researchers observe with respect to the offspring's fearfulness? What conclusion was supported regarding the genetic basis of this type of behavior in cockers and basenjis.

4. Do these results indicate that fear in dogs is controlled by a single gene locus? that environment is irrelevant to the matter of fear in cockers and basenjis? Support your answer.

A Mendelian pattern of inheritance is also found to underlie a specific language disorder in the KE family.

5. Describe the specific language disorder found primarily in the KE family.

6. What does the pattern of inheritance for this disorder suggest about its genetic basis? Specifically, is the abnormal gene dominant or recessive?

7. What does the normal gene do that the abnormal gene fails to do?

Some people have more friends than others. Some people sleep longer on average than others. Some people learn musical skills more easily than others. Most of the differences among individuals reflect the combined influences of many genes (in interaction with the environment, of course), not the effects of single genes.

8. Characteristics affected by many different genes are called _____ traits. When we measure differences among individuals in such traits, they will differ from one another in _____ rather than in type. In other words, individuals will not fall into distinct _____ or groups as they do in the case of single-gene traits. Most often, the set of scores obtained for polygenic traits approximates a(n) _____ distribution. (*Hint:* Look at Figure 3.9 on text page 58.)

Selective breeding has been practiced for thousands of years to produce more desirable strains of plants and animals. Scientists have used selective breeding to produce strains of animals with specialized behavioral tendencies.

9. What is the basic approach followed in selective breeding?

Robert Tryon's work with "maze bright" and "maze dull" rats clearly pointed out that even complex behaviors, such as a rat's ability to learn a maze, can be powerfully influenced by genetic variation.

10. How did Tryon produce the two strains of rats? How did he control for the possibility that the rats' "maze brightness" or "maze dullness" was due to what they learned from their mothers rather than to their genes?

11. Why is it important to note that Tryon tested his subjects only on their ability to learn one particular task?

Psychologists often would like to assess the relative contributions of genetic and environmental variation for polygenic behavioral traits in humans.

12. How can such questions be studied in humans?

Evolution by Natural Selection   (pages 61–64)

CONSIDER these questions before you go on. They are designed to help you start thinking about this subject, not to test your knowledge.

Did Darwin know about genes when he developed his theory of evolution?

Since evolution is supposed to involve adaptation, how does nature "know" which traits will be adaptive in future generations?

Can individuals inherit traits that their parents have acquired through experience?

How fast does evolution take place?

READ this section of your text lightly. Then go back and read thoroughly, completing the Workout as you proceed.

The publication of Charles Darwin's *The Origin Species* in 1859 was a landmark event. It has ha tremendous impact on the way we understand bot biological and psychological issues. Darwin used th familiar concept of selective breeding—which h termed *artificial selection*—as a point of reference. Hi major point was that nature, too, involves a kind of se lective breeding. He called this *natural selection*.

1. Explain the concept of natural selection.

Darwin developed his theory without knowing any thing about genes. Mendel's work, a first step towar understanding genes, was not known in the scien tific world. Darwin knew only that *something* existe that was passed on from one generation to the nex and something that could change, forming the basi for evolutionary changes in a species.

2. List two sources of the genetic variability that i the foundation of evolution. Which is the ultimat source of genetic variation?

3. What is a mutation? Is it likely to be helpful o harmful? How does this fit in with natural selec tion?

4. Explain Lamarck's notion of the inheritance of ac quired characteristics. Is this idea accepted today?

:volutionary change is propelled by environmental :hange.

5. Specify some aspects of the environment that might change and thereby lead to evolutionary change?

6. Is evolutionary change always slow and steady? Support your answer with an example.

7. Can complex genetic changes occur as rapidly as simpler changes? Why or why not?

People sometimes fall into intellectual traps in thinking about evolution. Several related misconceptions stem from the mistaken assumption that evolution involves foresight.

8. State three specific forms this fundamental misunderstanding can take.

a.

b.

c.

Why do newborn infants tightly grasp objects placed in their hands?

How can we even attempt to discover the reasons for behaviors that evolved in the very distant past?

Did every characteristic of a species evolve for a particular purpose?

READ this section of your text lightly. Then go back and read thoroughly, completing the Workout as you proceed.

Psychologists are of course interested in the effects of evolution on behavior.

1. Briefly explain how the process of natural selection can affect behavior.

2. How compatible is the functionalist approach in psychology with an evolutionary perspective on behavior?

Psychologists and biologists who take an evolutionary perspective distinguish between two kinds of explanations of behavior.

3. Define the terms below.
   a. ultimate explanation

   b. proximate explanation

Natural Selection as a Foundation for Functionalism (pages 64–68)

CONSIDER these questions before you go on. They are designed to help you start thinking about this subject, not to test your knowledge.

---

4. Are ultimate and proximate explanations of be- havior necessarily incompatible? Support your an- swer.

An ultimate explanation may be plausible, even ele- gant, and yet be incorrect. We must be careful to in- sist on scientific evidence in evaluating an explanation.

5. What kinds of evidence can be used to evaluate a particular ultimate explanation?

We must also realize that a characteristic doesn't nec- essarily exist because it is in itself useful.

6. Briefly present four reasons why a given trait or behavior may not be functional.

    a.

    b.

    c.

    d.

Natural Selection as a Foundation for Understanding Species-Typical Behaviors (pages 68–76)

CONSIDER these questions before you go on. They are designed to help you start thinking about this subject, not to test your knowledge.

Are there certain behaviors that seem to mark a dog as "doggy" or a fish as "fishy" or a person as "hu- man"?

Do facial expressions mean the same thing across dif- ferent cultures, or does each culture develop its own code?

READ this section of your text lightly. Then go back and read thoroughly, completing the Workout as you proceed.

Behavior patterns so characteristic of a species that they help to identify the species, such as dam build- ing in beavers or speaking in humans, are called in- stinctive or species-typical behaviors. Human emo- tional expressions can be regarded as examples of species-typical behaviors. This idea was advanced by Darwin and has been supported by recent scientific re- search.

1. What kind of atlas did Paul Ekman and Wallace Friesen produce and how did they do it? (*Hint:* See Figure 3.13 on text page 69.)

2. Summarize Eibl-Eibesfeldt's evidence for the uni- versality of the eyebrow flash.

3. Does it necessarily follow that a universal non- verbal signal like the eyebrow flash is free of cul- tural influence?

4. Comment on the role of learning in the development of species-typical behaviors. Give two examples.

t is the degree of biological preparedness involved in a behavior that determines whether we call it species-typical.

5. What is biological preparedness? Illustrate the concept with either human walking or human talking.

6. Why is it better to treat species-typical behavior as a relative concept rather than an absolute one?

An important means of better understanding human traits (or the traits of any given species) is to compare species. The similarities found can be enlightening.

7. It is important to distinguish two different classes of cross-species similarities. (*Hint:* See Figures 3.18 and 3.19 on text pages 74 and 75.)

   a. A(n) _____ is any similarity between species that exists because of convergent evolution.

   b. A(n) _____ is any similarity between species that exists because of their common ancestry.

   c. _____ has taken place when different species independently evolve a common characteristic because they have similar habitats or lifestyles.

8. In practice, how can we distinguish between similarities based on homology and those based on analogy?

9. What is the particular value of studying homologies?

Homologies have been useful in understanding the evolution of smiling, laughing, and other behaviors.

10. Two kinds of human smiles can be differentiated: Describe them briefly.

11. What is the silent bared-teeth display seen in monkeys and apes? What kind of human smile is it thought to be related to? What can we learn from comparing the way this display functions in macaques and chimpanzees?

12. What is the relaxed open-mouth display seen in monkeys and apes? What is its apparent meaning? How is it related to laughing and the happy smile in humans?

Analogies can also provide clues about species-typical traits.

13. How are analogies useful? What can they *not* tell us?

Evolutionary Analyses of Mating Patterns
(pages 76–82)

CONSIDER these questions before you go on. They are designed to help you start thinking about this subject, not to test your knowledge.

Is sexual jealousy adaptive?

Why do some species have long-term male-female sexual relationships while others do not?

Can human mating behavior be reasonably explained in evolutionary terms?

Why are males bigger and stronger than females in some species and not in others?

READ this section of your text lightly. Then go back and read thoroughly, completing the Workout as you proceed.

Patterns of mating are an especially interesting area of study because mating is critical to the survival of any sexual species and because mating is a fundamental social behavior.

1. In _____, one male mates with more than one female. In _____, one female mates with more than one male. In _____, one male and one female bond only with one another. In _____, members of a group containing more than one male and more than one female mate with one another.

Robert Trivers has related various patterns of courtship and mating behavior to a concept he calls parental investment.

2. Define *parental investment*.

3. What general principle relates parental investment to courtship and mating patterns in Trivers's theory?

Polygyny is the most common mating pattern among mammalian species.

4. According to Trivers, why does high female parental investment and low male parental investment lead to each of the following?
   a. polygyny

   b. large size of males

   c. high selectivity in the female's choice of a mate

The primary mating pattern for some species of fish and birds is polyandry.

5. Why does polyandry make more sense for egg-laying species than for mammals?

6. How do sex differences in the polyandrous species known as spotted sandpipers support Trivers's theory?

By far the most common mating pattern for birds is monogamy.

7. What conditions should lead to equal parental investment and thus monogamy?

8. How is equal parental investment related to sex differences in size and strength?

9. In what kinds of species is monogamy common? Give specific examples.

10. What evolutionary reasons might underlie the fact that social monogamy is not always matched by sexual monogamy?

Chimpanzees and bonobos are among the clearest examples of species that have a polygynandrous mating pattern.

11. What evolutionary advantages might be conferred by polygynandry in chimpanzees and bonobos?

12. Contrast mating behavior in bonobos with that in chimpanzees.

Human mating patterns lie somewhere between monogamy and polygyny. Long-term mating bonds are the norm everywhere. Where it is legal, polygyny exists, with some men having two or more wives, but even in such cultures, most marriages are monogamous.

13. How does the mix of monogamy and polygyny in humans fit with Trivers's theory?

In humans, the emotions of romantic love and sexual jealousy serve important functions.

14. How widespread are these emotions in humans? What evolutionary purposes do they serve?

15. How do humans compare with other species in terms of love and jealousy?

Lust and unfaithfulness also appear to have an evolutionary foundation.

16. In evolutionary terms, why might unfaithfulness occur?

Evolutionary Analyses of Hurting and Helping
(pages 82–88)

CONSIDER these questions before you go on. They are designed to help you start thinking about this subject, not to test your knowledge.

Do animals help each other or is that an exclusively human phenomenon?

Why are men generally more violent than women?

READ this section of your text lightly. Then go back and read thoroughly, completing the Workout as you proceed.

Though members of a given species may fight with one another even to the point of injury or death, they may also help one another. Help sometimes takes the form of cooperation, and at other times appears to be altruistic.

1. Correctly identify each of the following.

a. _____ occurs when an individual helps another at the expense of its own survival or reproductive capacity.

b. _____ is any behavior that increases the survival or reproductive capacity of another individual.

c. _____ involves an individual's helping another while at the same time helping itself.

2. How does kin selection theory explain the occurrence of altruistic behavior?

3. What evidence supports kin selection theory as it applies to animals? to humans?

4. How does reciprocity theory explain the occurrence of altruistic behavior?

5. Has behavior consistent with reciprocity theory been observed in the animal world? among humans?

6. In what sense are both theories attempting to redefine altruistic behavior as not really altruistic?

In considering human behavior from an evolutionary perspective we must be aware of certain fallacies that can lead to distorted conclusions.

7. What is the naturalistic fallacy? Illustrate your answer with an example of such distorted thinking.

8. What is the deterministic fallacy? Illustrate your answer with an example of such distorted thinking.

Be sure to READ the Concluding Thoughts at the end of the chapter. Note important points in your Workout. Then consolidate your learning by answering the focus questions in the margins of the text.

After you have studied the chapter thoroughly, CHECK your understanding with the Self-Test that follows.

Self-Test 1

Multiple-Choice Questions

1. Genes that can occupy the same locus—and can thus pair with one another—are called:
   a. homozygous.
   b. dizygotic.
   c. alleles.
   d. dominant genes.

2. Suppose a person well-informed in the area of genetics refers to "genes for spatial ability." A correct interpretation of this phrase would be:
   a. "genes that directly control a person's ability to process spatial information and have no other function."
   b. "genes that produce a particular anatomy and physiology, which in turn affect a person's spatial ability."
   c. "genes that directly control cognitive ability in general and spatial ability in particular."
   d. that it's a joke since genes have no effect (direct or indirect) on psychological functioning.

3. Meiosis results in egg and sperm cells containing _____ number of chromosomes contained in each of the body's other cells.
   a. exactly the same
   b. half the
   c. twice the
   d. four times the

4. The value of sexual—as opposed to asexual—reproduction is the production of offspring that are:
   a. genetically diverse.
   b. genetically uniform.
   c. genetically similar to their parents.
   d. numerous.

5. Genes affect both physical development and behavior by directing the synthesis of:
   a. DNA.
   b. chromosomes.
   c. alleles.
   d. structural proteins and enzymes.

6. The majority of violence carried out by male primates is related somehow to:
   a. protection of offspring.
   b. competition for food and water.
   c. competition for territory.
   d. sex.

7. Any characteristic that varies in a continuous fashion in a population should be presumed:
   a. to be polygenic.
   b. to be based on a single gene.
   c. to involve whole chromosomes rather than individual genes.
   d. not to be genetically influenced.

8. Tryon's attempt to selectively breed "maze bright" and "maze dull" rats:
   a. resulted in failure.
   b. showed that only very small differences could be produced, even over 20 generations.
   c. showed that large differences could be produced over several generations.
   d. proved that genes are more important than environment in determining intelligence.

9. In the process called *natural selection*:
   a. the breeding of certain domestic animals is controlled to produce desirable traits in future generations.
   b. inherited traits helpful in overcoming barriers to survival and reproduction are more likely to be passed down to offspring.
   c. genes that will be helpful in suiting offspring to future environments are selected for.
   d. nature "selects" the traits of the next generation by way of a random shuffle of genes.

10. If chance factors alone cause the gene pools in two populations of a species to differ, we refer to the situation as:
    a. genetic drift.
    b. mutation.
    c. artificial selection.
    d. a homology.

11. The rate of evolutionary change:
    a. is slow and steady.
    b. depends primarily on population size.

c. depends on environmental change.

d. was initially rapid but has slowed progressively over the years.

12. John W. believes that male aggression toward women is controlled by genes and is an unchangeable fact of human nature. His thinking illustrates:

a. reciprocity theory.
b. kin-selection theory.
c. the naturalistic fallacy.
d. the deterministic fallacy.

13. Similarities between species that are due to convergent evolution are called:

a. analogies.
b. homologies.
c. analogies in mammals and homologies in non-mammalian species.
d. homologies in mammals and analogies in non-mammalian species.

14. The ability of premature human infants to support their weight with the gasp reflex is probably an example of:

a. the inheritance of acquired characteristics.
b. a vestigial characteristic.
c. a genetic side effect.
d. reciprocity.

15. According to Robert Trivers, polygyny is related to _____ parental investment.

a. high female/low male
b. low female/high male
c. equal male and female
d. no particular pattern of

Essay Questions

16. Discuss nepotism in the context of the kin-selection theory of altruism.

17. Does evolution involve foresight? Explain.

After you have assessed your understanding on the basis of Self-Test 1 and have tried to strengthen your preparation in any areas of weakness, GO ON to Self-Test 2.

Self-Test 2

Multiple-Choice Questions

1. Which of the following is true of polygenic effects?

a. Most measurable differences between people can be explained in terms of single genes; that is, they are not polygenic.
b. Without examining the genetic material itself, there is no way to determine whether a characteristic is polygenic in origin.
c. Polygenic effects are generally brain disorders, while single-gene effects are positive, useful traits.
d. The distribution of scores for a polygenic trait often approximates a normal distribution.

2. The normal human cell (other than egg or sperm cells) contains _____ pairs of chromosomes.

a. 12   c. 23
b. 22   d. 46

3. The process by which cells divide for the purpose of normal body growth is:

a. mitosis.
b. meiosis.
c. transcription.
d. protein synthesis.

4. We can assume that _____ are genetically identical.

   a. identical twins
   b. fraternal twins
   c. both identical and fraternal twins
   d. no two people

5. A friend of yours has brown eyes and her mother has blue eyes. Assuming that blue is recessive and brown is dominant, you can conclude that your friend:

   a. is heterozygous for eye color.
   b. is homozygous for eye color.
   c. is monozygotic for eye color.
   d. is brown-eyed as far as phenotype is concerned, but you can infer nothing about her genotype.

6. When Mendel crossed purebred wrinkled-seed peas with purebred round-seed peas, he found that all of the F_1 generation had round seeds. When he bred the F_1 peas with one another, he found that:

   a. the F_2 peas all had round seeds.
   b. the F_2 peas all had wrinkled seeds.
   c. half the F_2 peas had round seeds and the other half had wrinkled seeds.
   d. three-fourths of the F_2 peas had round seeds and the other one-fourth had wrinkled seeds.

7. The primary job of genes is to direct the sequence of _____ that make up each type of protein molecule.

   a. DNA
   b. amino acids
   c. RNA
   d. enzymes

8. Which of the following is true of mutations?

   a. Mutations have little effect on the course of evolution because they are so rare.
   b. Mutations are errors in the replication process; as such, they inevitably lead to harmful changes in the structure of DNA.
   c. Although mutations usually have harmful consequences, they are sometimes helpful.
   d. Mutations are the new collections of genes that result from the random rearrangement of genes in sexual reproduction.

9. Which of the following represents a question posed from a functionalist perspective?

   a. At what rate does evolution take place?
   b. Which species are most closely related to one another?
   c. What are the possible uses of the human voice?
   d. Why do dogs have such a keen sense of smell?

10. The human taste for sugar, which may have several negative health consequences, can be understood as a:

    a. vestigial characteristic.
    b. genetic side effect.
    c. species-typical behavior.
    d. result of nutritional deprivation.

11. Birds, some insects, and some mammals can fly. Similarities among these groups are not due to common ancestry and would thus represent:

    a. homologies.
    b. analogies.
    c. vestigial characteristics.
    d. learning.

12. An *ultimate explanation* of behavior is an explanation of:

    a. the mechanism that actually produces the behavior.
    b. the immediate environment conditions that bring on the behavior.
    c. the form a behavior will ultimately take upon further evolution.
    d. why a particular evolutionary development offered an adaptive advantage.

13. A species in which an individual female generally mates with several males would be classified as:

    a. polygynandrous.   c. polygynous.
    b. polyandrous.   d. monogamous.

14. Female bonobos dominate males by virtue of their:

    a. greater size and strength.
    b. greater intelligence.
    c. greater speed and agility.
    d. strong alliances.

15. When we assume that human genetic biases toward certain behaviors cannot be countered by learning or culture, we are falling prey to the _____ fallacy.

    a. deterministic   c. naturalistic
    b. species-typical   d. genetic dominance

Essay Questions

16. Give evidence of the fact that male primates are generally more violent than female primates and discuss it from an evolutionary perspective.

17. How can we explain behavior that appears to be altruistic? Isn't such behavior entirely inconsistent with natural selection?

Answers

Introduction and Review of Basic Genetic Mechanisms

2. protein; structural; enzymes; amino acids; DNA

5. genotype; phenotype

6. chromosomes

7. 23

11. egg; sperm; random; cell divisions; 23

12. zygote; pairs; mitosis; unique

15. alleles

16. homozygous; heterozygous

18. a. *M*, **b.** *M*, **c.** *m*

Inheritance of Behavioral Traits

8. polygenic; degree; categories; normal

Natural Selection as a Foundation for Understanding Species-Typical Behaviors

7. a. analogy **b.** homology **c.** convergent evolution

Evolutionary Analyses of Mating Patterns

1. polygyny; polyandry; monogamy; polygynandry

Evolutionary Analyses of Hurting and Helping

1. a. Altruism **b.** Helping **c.** Cooperation

Self-Test 1

1. c. (p. 53)

2. b. Genes have their effect only by controlling the manufacture of proteins. In that way, they affect an individual's anatomy and physiology. Their effects on behavior are due to the particular anatomy and physiology they create and are thus indirect (p. 50)

3. b. There are 23 pairs of chromosomes in most of the body's cells, but only 23 chromosomes in an egg or sperm cell. When the egg and sperm combine to form the zygote, the full complement of 23 pairs of chromosomes is restored. (p. 52)

4. a. Sexual reproduction essentially "shuffles the genetic deck" to produce great diversity in offspring. Diversity offers an evolutionary advantage in that some of the many different types of individuals created may be capable of adapting more successfully to changing environmental conditions and may thus survive and reproduce. (p. 53)

5. d. (p. 50)

6. d. (p. 83)

7. **a.** A polygenic characteristic can often be described in terms of a normal distribution. A single-gene kind of pattern is indicated by step-wise variation. It involves a categorical rather than a graded difference. (p. 58)

8. **c.** (pp. 59–60)

9. **b.** Remember that natural selection acts to produce offspring better suited to the current environment, not some future environment. Natural selection is driven by success or failure in that current environment. It cannot be affected by an unforeseen future. (p. 61)

10. **a.** (p. 67)

11. **c.** (p. 63)

12. **d.** (p. 87)

13. **a.** Convergent evolution refers to a situation in which similarities of environment or lifestyle lead to similar but independent evolutionary developments. The root of the similarity is not genetic relatedness. In this case, we have an analogy, not a homology. (p. 72)

14. **b.** It may help to remember that a vestige is a leftover trace of something from the past. (p. 66)

15. **a.** (p. 76)

16. Nepotism is the tendency for people to help kin more than nonkin. In a number of societies, related individuals are more likely to share goods and land with one another than with nonkin and to collaborate more—for example, in hunting. Kin tend to come to one another's aid more than nonkin—for example, in taking orphaned children within the family. Also, violence may be lower among related individuals than among unrelated individuals in similar living arrangements. The evolutionary explanation for this would be that individuals helping kin or sharing with kin are helping to perpetuate genes they share with those individuals. (p. 85)

17. One of the most common errors people make in thinking about evolutionary adaptation is to assume it involves foresight. It does not. Natural selection operates on the basis of the current environment, not on the basis of some future environment. This should be obvious given the way natural selection operates. Selection comes about only because individuals with genes helpful in overcoming obstacles to reproduction pass those genes on, whereas individuals with unhelpful or harmful genes will tend not to pass them on since they will have fewer or no offspring. Future environments can't sort individuals into those two categories—those who successfully reproduce and those who don't. Only the present environment can. (p. 63)

Self-Test 2

1. **d.** (p. 58)

2. **c.** (p. 52)

3. **a.** (p. 52)

4. **a.** (p. 53)

5. **a.** Since your friend's mother has blue eyes and blue is recessive, you know her genotype; she has two blue-eye alleles. Since your friend received one of her genes for eye color from her mother, she must have one blue-eye allele. Since she's brown-eyed, the other allele must be a dominant brown-eye allele from her father. (p. 54)

6. **d.** The original purebred round-seed peas had only round-seed alleles to contribute to offspring, whereas purebred wrinkled-seed peas had only wrinkled-seed alleles. In the F_1 generation, all peas have one round-seed allele and one wrinkled-seed allele. Because the F_1 generation all had round seeds, we know that round-seed alleles are dominant. When F_1 peas are bred with one another, one-fourth of the peas will have two wrinkled-seed alleles, one-fourth will have two round-seed alleles, and the remaining peas will have one of each type of allele. But because round-seed alleles are dominant, all but the one-fourth with two wrinkled-seed alleles will be round-seeded. (p. 54)

7. **b.** (p. 50–51)

8. **c.** As the text states, mutation is ultimately the basis of all genetic variation, because it alone introduces truly new genetic information. (p. 62)

9. **d.** The functionalist seeks to understand actual behaviors, not potential behaviors, and the ways they promoted survival and reproduction in the species. (p. 64)

10. **a.** (p. 66)

11. **b.** The case described is one resulting from convergent evolution. (p. 72)

12. d. (p. 65)

13. b. (p. 76)

14. d. (p. 84)

15. a. (p. 87)

16. Male primates are more aggressive than female primates as a general rule. Female aggression occurs, but is more limited in scope, severity, and frequency. Male aggression often has to do with sex. Male monkeys and apes may kill infants fathered by others to stop their mothers from lactating so they will again be available sexually. They may fight with other males to improve their status and attractiveness and may violently force females to submit to sex. The pattern holds for humans, with men being much more violent than women; sexual jealousy is a primary motive. Such male aggression increases the chances of the male passing on his genes. There is not such an advantage for females given their higher parental investment. (p. 83)

17. Both kin-selection and reciprocity theories try to reframe behavior that is apparently selfless as behavior that is in some sense selfish. Kin-selection theory suggests that the gene promoting the "altruistic" act in an individual may be destroyed, but other copies of the same gene in the individual's kin will be saved as a result; in this case, it is the gene that is "selfish." In reciprocity theory, there is an expectation of the favor being returned at some future time. This theory can help to explain behavior that seems altruistic being directed toward non-kin. Female coalitions among bonobos are an example from animal behavior. Humans are the greatest practitioners of reciprocal helping, though. They have effective ways to keep track of help given, and emotions—such as a sense of fairness—that promote reciprocity. (pp. 85–86)

Basic Processes of Learning

chapter 4

READ the introduction below before you read the chapter in the text.

Learning involves adaptation to the environment that occurs within an individual's lifetime. It is a set of processes through which experience can have an effect on an individual's future behavior. As a central topic in psychology, with relevance to many different subfields, learning has been much studied and much debated over the course of psychology's history.

One category of learning that has been intensively studied is classical conditioning, which involves the learning of reflexes. Ivan Pavlov discovered classical conditioning as a by-product of his research on digestive processes. He then switched his focus to this type of learning, analyzing the process through which it occurs and studying various phenomena of classical conditioning, such as extinction, spontaneous recovery, generalization, and discrimination. This chapter discusses conditioned emotional reactions and drug reactions in illustrating the practical significance of classical conditioning.

Unlike classical conditioning, which focuses on reflexive behavior, operant conditioning involves learning to perform certain actions to produce certain consequences: We study to get good grades, we buy food to alleviate hunger, we work for money, and so on. The most fundamental idea in operant conditioning is Edward Thorndike's law of effect. According to the law of effect, the probability of performing a given behavior in a given situation depends on the effects it has had in past experience in that situation. B. F. Skinner was the best-known investigator in this area and in fact coined the term *operant conditioning*. Some basic concepts related to operant conditioning are reinforcers, shaping, extinction, schedules of partial reinforcement, discriminative stimuli, and punishment.

The chapter addresses major theoretical issues; the nature of what is learned in classical and operant conditioning, for example. It compares the S-R (stimulus-response) perspective associated with some early behaviorists with the cognitive perspective.

The S-R perspective characterizes learning solely in terms of observable stimuli and responses. Early behaviorists such as John B. Watson and B. F. Skinner insisted that what takes place inside the learner is irrelevant to scientific psychology because it cannot be observed and thus cannot be investigated scientifically.

Advocates of the cognitive perspective contend that the very things S-R theorists would leave out— those mysterious unseen processes inside the learner— are the things one must study to really understand learning. The essential point of the cognitive theorist is that learning involves information that is meaningful to the learner. It causes the learner to expect or predict certain things to happen under certain circumstances. The chapter explains how classical and operant conditioning can be understood from this perspective and presents evidence to support the cognitive view. The cognitive perspective is also applied to other topics in the chapter.

Natural selection has produced some types of activities that are specially designed to promote learning. These include play, exploration, and observation. Play is valuable as a means of learning survival skills, while exploration provides information about the environment. Observational learning occurs in nonhuman animals, but its most complex form (imitation) is found only in humans and some other primates.

In addition to the general learning abilities covered in most of the chapter, natural selection has resulted in some specialized learning abilities useful to particular species. This helps to explain special cases of learning involving food aversion and food preference. It also helps us to understand why some stimuli work better than others in experiments that attempt to condition fear, what happens when baby birds become imprinted, and specialized place-learning abilities.

LOOK over the table of contents for this chapter in your textbook before you continue with your study.

Notice that there are focus questions in the margins of the text for your use in studying the material. The following chart lists which Study Guide questions relate to which focus questions.

Focus Questions	Study Guide Questions
Classical Conditioning I: Fundamentals	
1	3–7
2	8
3	9–13
4	15
5	16–18
6	19
Classical Conditioning II: Beyond the Fundamentals	
7	1–2
8	3–4
9–10	5–9
11	10
12	11
13	12
14–15	13–15
16	16
Operant Conditioning I: Fundamentals	
17	3–4
18	5–7
19	8
20	9
21	10
22	11
23	12–14
24	15–17
25	18–20
Operant Conditioning II: What Is Learned?	
26	1–3
27	4–5
28	6
29	7–8
30	9
31	10
Activities Designed for Learning: Play, Exploration, and Observation	
32	1–2
33	3–4
34	5
35	6–7
36	8–14
37	5–16
Specialized Learning Abilities: Filling in the Blanks in Species-Typical Behavior Patterns	
38	2–4
39	5
40	6
41	7
42	8
43	9
44	10
45	11

The Integrated Study Workout

COMPLETE one section at a time.

Introduction* AND *Classical Conditioning I: Fundamentals   (pages 91–96)

What kinds of responses can be classically conditioned?

Why do we often start to salivate at the very sight of an advertisement for a tasty food?

READ the chapter introduction and this section of your text lightly. Then go back and read thoroughly, completing the Workout as you proceed.

Learning lies at the heart of psychology. There is hardly an area of psychology that does not need to consider learning. The social psychologist, the personality theorist, and the clinical psychologist are all dealing with individuals who bring a history of learning to current situations. Cognitive psychologists and, of course, learning psychologists deal with it even more directly. Learning depends on mechanisms provided by natural selection. These mechanisms allow individual members of a species to adapt to the constant environmental change they will face in their lives.

1. Define *learning*, making sure to clarify all essential terms.

2. Indicate, by circling *yes* or *no*, whether the individual's behavior in each case is due to learning.

   Yes No **a.** A new employee in the customer service department watches videotapes of employees handling difficult customers effectively; then she handles her first grouch with aplomb by using the same techniques.

   Yes No **b.** A toddler touches a hot stove and then immediately withdraws his hand and starts crying.

   Yes No **c.** A student passes a bakery on the way to class one morning and finds that the sight of the fresh bread literally makes her mouth water.

   Yes No **d.** A child receives warm applause and praise after singing for dinner guests; then he volunteers to sing again on a similar occasion.

Psychologists have spent decades studying classical conditioning—with considerable success. They have discovered basic principles that underlie this type of learning and have developed some interesting and useful applications of those principles. To understand classical conditioning, you will need to learn some essential terminology—beginning with words such as *reflex*. Classical conditioning concerns the learning of reflexes.

3. Define *reflex*.

4. **a.** A(n) _____ is a particular, well-defined event in the environment.

   b. A particular, well-defined bit of behavior is a(n) _____.

5. Give three examples of a stimulus and three examples of a response.

6. Why is it important to note that reflexes are mediated by the nervous system?

7. A decline in the magnitude of a reflexive response when the stimulus is repeated several times in succession is called _____, which qualifies as a simple form of

   _____.

Ivan Pavlov, a Russian physiologist, is a key figure in the study of classical conditioning. Even before he discovered classical conditioning, he was well-known for his staunch devotion to scientific research and for his work on digestive reflexes.

8. How did Pavlov come to discover classical conditioning?

A phenomenon that was at first only a nuisance soon attracted Pavlov's scientific eye. Once he realized he could study it as a reflex he began to analyze classical conditioning through a number of carefully controlled experiments. In his early experiments, he broke classical conditioning down into its elementary parts and gave them descriptive names. (See Figure 4.2 on text page 93 for help in answering the following questions.)

9. Explain the concept of a conditioned reflex. Why is the term *conditioned* used?

10. What is a conditioned stimulus? a conditioned response?

11. What is an unconditioned stimulus? an unconditioned response?

12. Identify the following aspects of Pavlov's classic experiment, in which a dog learned to salivate in response to a bell.

a. The *conditioned reflex* involved was

_____.

b. The *unconditioned stimulus* was

_____.

c. The *unconditioned response* was

_____.

d. The *conditioned stimulus* was the

_____.

e. The *conditioned response* was

_____.

13. Trace the course of classical conditioning by answering the following questions about the same experiment you described in item 12 above.

a. How did the dog respond to the food prior to its pairing with the bell?

b. How did the dog respond to the bell prior to its pairing with the food?

c. How did the dog respond to the bell after it was paired with the food?

Classical conditioning is not just a phenomenon that psychologists study in laboratories. It is something you encounter in everyday life.

14. Produce two simple examples of classically conditioned responses that a person or animal might make under appropriate circumstances. (See the examples on text page 94 and try to think of analogous situations.)

a.

b.

Pavlov and his colleagues did hundreds of experiments on classical conditioning. In the course of that work, they uncovered a number of phenomena that are still considered of major importance. One issue—the permanence of conditioned reflexes (or the lack of permanence)—was of particular interest to Pavlov.

15. Answer the following questions concerning extinction. (*Note:* Students often make a leap from the term *extinction* to saying that a response has become "extinct." However, the proper terminology is to say a response has been *extinguished*.)

a. What is extinction and under what conditions does it occur?

b. Does extinction mean that the learning that took place has been totally erased? Explain.

c. Are the neurons involved in extinction the same as those involved in conditioning?

Pavlov's team also studied the complementary phenomena of generalization and discrimination.

16. What is generalization? How does an organism's response change as the test stimulus becomes less and less similar to the actual conditioned stimulus?

READ this section of your text lightly. Then go back and read thoroughly, completing the Workout as you proceed.

Behaviorism is an approach within psychology that has been important in several ways. It has helped to establish psychology as an objective, scientific endeavor as well as teach us a great deal about learning.

1. Describe the major characteristics and goals of behaviorism.

17. Describe the procedure of discrimination training. How does it affect an organism's tendency to generalize?

John B. Watson was a pioneer in the area of behaviorism and in the application of classical conditioning to human behavior.

2. What did behaviorists like Watson see as essential ideas in Pavlov's work?

18. How can classical conditioning and discrimination training be used to study an animal's sensory capabilities?

A major question in learning theory concerns the nature of the connection that is forged through classical conditioning. One camp has proposed an S-R interpretation, the other an S-S interpretation. (See Figure 4.13 on text page 114.)

19. Can the meaning of a stimulus serve as a basis for generalization or is it only physical characteristics that matter? Support your answer.

3. According to the S-R view of classical conditioning, the animal learns a new

_____. This view was favored by

_____. According to the S-S view

of classical conditioning, however, the animal

learns a(n) _____ between the

_____ and the _____.

_____ espoused this view, but

_____ rejected it because it

involved _____.

Classical Conditioning II: Beyond the Fundamentals (pages 96–104)

CONSIDER these questions before you go on. They are designed to help you start thinking about this subject, not to test your knowledge.

Can an emotional response like fear be learned? Can it be unlearned?

Does classical conditioning have any practical applications?

Considerable research has been done to settle the S-R versus S-S dispute. Robert Rescorla's work is illustrative.

4. Describe Rescorla's research procedure. Which position did his data support? What did the *other* theory predict?

c.

9. Why have some cognitive psychologists programmed computers to simulate expectation and prediction?

The S-S view of classical conditioning is inherently more cognitive than the S-R view, because it assumes that the learner has a mental representation of the unconditioned stimulus.

5. Cognitive theorists describe this mental

   representation as a(n) _____ of the

   _____.

From an evolutionary perspective, classical conditioning serves to prepare the body for biologically significant things like danger, food, or a sex partner.

6. How does expectancy theory help to explain why the conditioned response is often different from the unconditioned response?

10. How did Watson and Rayner condition fear in a baby named Albert?

7. How does Rescorla describe the learning organism in classical conditioning?

11. What is the appetizer effect and how can classical conditioning explain it?

8. List three types of evidence supporting the notion that the learner uses the conditioned stimulus to predict the arrival of the unconditioned stimulus.
   a.

12. How has sexual arousal been conditional in experiments? Does it actually appear to aid reproduction?

b.

Some of the most fascinating and practical work in classical conditioning has involved conditioned drug reactions.

13. Describe the results of Pavlov's experiment on conditioned drug reactions.

How can we develop desirable habits in ourselves and eradicate bad ones?

READ this section of your text lightly. Then go back and read thoroughly, completing the Workout as you proceed.

---

14. What is a conditioned counteractive drug effect? (Be sure to describe the underlying mechanism.)

Throughout each day, we engage in behaviors that have consequences (environmental changes or stimuli). We turn a key in a lock and are thus able to open a door. We give money to a clerk and leave a store happily bearing some new treasure. We smile at someone and receive a smile in return. We try to carry too many books at once and watch them tumble into a heap at our feet.

1. Why are the terms *operant* and *instrumental* used to describe certain responses?

15. How can conditioned counteractive drug effects help to explain drug tolerance and some drug overdose cases?

16. Discuss classical conditioning as it relates to drug relapse after withdrawal.

2. Define operant (or instrumental) conditioning.

Edward Thorndike was studying learning at about the same time as Pavlov but was approaching it from a very different angle. And the term "operant" was not yet in use.

3. Describe Thorndike's basic experimental procedure.

Operant Conditioning I: Fundamentals (pages 104–112)

CONSIDER these questions before you go on. They are designed to help you start thinking about this subject, not to test your knowledge.

How do the consequences of a behavior affect the chances of that behavior occurring again?

How would a learning psychologist explain the fact that some people study hard and others never open a book? that some people are compulsively neat and others are hopelessly messy? that some people save their money and others spend as if there were no tomorrow?

Pavlov's training procedure allowed him to elicit the response he wanted, and he focused on stimuli that preceded that response. Thorndike, in contrast, had to wait until an animal produced the response that led to the consequence of an open door and thus to food.

4. State Thorndike's law of effect.

Though B. F. Skinner did not originate the law of effect, he spent many years studying and extending this simple but powerful idea. In fact, he gave us some of the tools we use to study this type of learning and much of the language we use to talk about it.

5. Either describe or draw and label a Skinner box. Why is it a more efficient research tool than a puzzle box? (*Hint:* Look at Figure 4.10 on text page 107.)

Operant conditioning is a term coined by Skinner. You have already defined operant conditioning above, but it would be a good idea to look back at that definition now.

6. Define *reinforcer*.

7. In what way are money and food different types of reinforcers?

Skinner argued that operant conditioning determines virtually all of our behavior. It may not seem to us that we are being controlled by relationships between our responses and their consequences, but that doesn't mean it isn't so.

8. Can people be operantly conditioned without even realizing it? Briefly describe an experiment that supports your answer and relate it to the learning of motor skills.

9. Describe the technique of shaping. Why is it sometimes necessary? Give an example to illustrate how shaping might be carried out.

10. The absence of reinforcement for a response and the resulting decline in response rate are both called _____.

11. Every occurrence of a particular response is reinforced in _____ reinforcement. In contrast, a response is reinforced only sometimes in _____ reinforcement.

Partial reinforcement is more precisely described in terms of four types of schedules, which are related to specific rates and patterns of responding in the individual being reinforced. The behavior produced by two of these schedules of reinforcement is especially resistant to extinction. Schedules are either fixed or variable and either ratio-based or interval-based.

12. Write the name of the schedule that applies in each of the following cases. The response alternatives are fixed-ratio (FR), variable-ratio (VR), fixed interval (FI), and variable-interval (VI).

_____ **a.** A response must be emitted a certain average number of times before a reinforcer is given.

_____ **b.** A specific unchanging period of time following a reinforced response must elapse before another response is reinforced.

_____ c. Reinforcement becomes available only after some average amount of time has elapsed, but the exact amount of time at any given point is unpredictable for the learner.

_____ d. This schedule underlies many gambling systems and helps to explain gambling behavior.

_____ e. A specific unchanging number of responses must be made before reinforcement will be given.

13. In general, _____ (ratio/interval) schedules produce faster responding.

14. Which schedules produce the greatest resistance to extinction? Why?

Reinforcement, which increases the chances that a particular response will occur, can be either positive or negative. It is important that you clearly understand what the terms *positive* and *negative* refer to (and what they don't refer to).

15. Define *positive reinforcement*. What is a positive reinforcer? Give two examples of positive reinforcement.

16. Define *negative reinforcement*. What is a negative reinforcer? Give two examples of negative reinforcement.

17. What do the terms *positive* and *negative* refer to in these cases? What do they not refer to?

Operant conditioning can involve punishment as well as reinforcement.

18. What is punishment? In what sense is it the opposite of reinforcement?

19. What is positive punishment? negative punishment? (*Hint:* Look at Figure 4.12 on text page 112.)

20. A stimulus that serves as a positive reinforcer, such as money, can become a(n) _____ punisher. A stimulus that acts as a negative reinforcer, such as a queasy feeling in the stomach, can become a(n) _____ punisher.

Operant Conditioning II: What Is Learned?
(pages 112–117)

CONSIDER these questions before you go on. They are designed to help you start thinking about this subject, not to test your knowledge.

What actually happens in the learner's mind when operant conditioning takes place?

What would happen to the rate of operant responding if the magnitude of the reinforcer were suddenly increased or decreased?

When is it—and when is it not—a good idea to deliberately reinforce someone's behavior? For example, is it a good idea to give a child money for reading or for practicing the piano?

READ this section of your text lightly. Then go back and read thoroughly, completing the Workout as you proceed.

As we have already noted, in operant conditioning, reinforcers are stimuli that follow the response. But operant behavior is also influenced by stimuli that precede it. The individual must learn when a given response will be rewarded.

1. What is a discriminative stimulus?

2. How does operant behavior come under the control of a discriminate stimulus?

3. After operant discrimination training, the learner will _____ to stimuli perceived as sufficiently similar to the discriminative stimulus.

4. How did Herrnstein use operant discrimination training to study concept understanding in pigeons?

5. What did Herrnstein's results show and what does this suggest?

As with classical conditioning, there have been theoretical disputes about the very nature of what is learned in operant conditioning. On one side of the debate were S-R theorists and on the other were more cognitive theorists.

6. Contrast the strict S-R view and the cognitive view.

7. What did Tolman mean when he characterized operant conditioning as the learning of a means-end relationship?

8. Briefly explain how Tolman supported his view with a study of maze-learning in rats.

9. What are reward contrast effects? How do they support the cognitive view of operant conditioning?

10. Explain the overjustification effect. What does it suggest about using rewards to influence children's behavior?

Activities Designed for Learning: Play, Exploration, and Observation (pages 118–124)

CONSIDER these questions before you go on. They are designed to help you start thinking about this subject, not to test your knowledge.

What is the point of exploration?

Why do people and animals play?

How is play fighting different from real fighting?

What can be learned through observation?

Through natural selection, drives for (or behavioral tendencies toward) play, exploration, and observation have developed because these activities promote learning.

1. How is the behavior involved in these activities different from operant behavior? Use play as a specific example.

2. Play behavior can be distinguished from serious (non-play) behavior in that it

    a. _____

    b. _____

    c. _____

    d. _____

    e. _____

3. According to Groos, play evolved as a way for young animals to _____ the _____ they would need to survive.

4. Briefly present two types of evidence for Groos's view.

Though Groos thought of exploration as a type of play, most theorists today consider exploration and play to be distinct categories.

5. How are play and exploration different in their evolutionary function?

6. Comment on the interplay of curiosity, novelty, and fear in exploration.

7. How do we know that animals actually acquire useful information through exploration?

8. Define *observational learning*. List some species that have been shown capable of observational learning.

9. It is generally believed to be _____ and _____ that make observation helpful even to nonprimates.

10. Explain and give examples for the terms used to answer item 9 above.

    a.

    b.

11. What is imitation?

12. Imitation is cognitively _____ (simpler/more complex) than stimulus enhancement and goal enhancement.

13. It is not certain which species of mammals are capable of imitation but at least some nonhuman _____ can.

14. Briefly discuss evidence that some behavior in wild chimpanzees depends on imitation.

Albert Bandura, the foremost investigator of human observational learning, states that this type of learning has two functions. One is to learn specific motor skills and the other is to learn general modes or styles of behaving.

15. Give an example of a person learning each of the following through observation.
    a. a specific motor skill

    b. a general mode or style of behavior

16. Summarize Bandura's experiment with the Bobo doll. Point out how it illustrates both functions of observational learning.

Specialized Learning Abilities: Filling the Blanks in Species-Typical Behavior Patterns (pages 124–130)

CONSIDER these questions before you go on. They are designed to help you start thinking about this subject, not to test your knowledge.

If nature were to build in certain kinds of specialized learning abilities, what types of activities do you think they might concern?

How do animals know which foods are safe to eat and which are not?

How do baby ducks know who to follow around?

READ this section of your text lightly. Then go back and read thoroughly, completing the Workout as you proceed.

Both the behavioral and cognitive perspectives have worked to develop general principles of learning that apply across situations.

1. What do we mean by specialized learning abilities?

Finding food that is safe to eat is a significant undertaking for many species, especially omnivorous creatures such as rats and humans.

2. How has food-aversion learning been demonstrated experimentally?

3. What are two characteristics that distinguish this type of learning from traditional examples of classical conditioning?

4. Why do the special characteristics of food-aversion learning make sense in the context of a natural environment?

Animals have to find foods that are not only safe but also nutritious. Apparently, learning is involved in food preference, as well as food aversion.

5. How did an experiment show that rats will choose the food containing a vitamin they need? How can the rats' behavior be explained?

6. Describe Clara Davis's findings when she allowed babies to choose their own diets. Why should we be cautious in interpreting her results?

7. What evidence suggests that social learning plays a part in food selection?

8. How has natural selection prepared young omnivores to learn what to eat?

Nature seems to have equipped animals with other special learning abilities in addition to those involved in food selection.

9. Present evidence showing that some stimuli, such as snakes, can become conditioned fear stimuli more easily than others. Why is this the case?

10. Describe imprinting. What is meant by a critical period? Are all stimuli equally likely choices for young birds to be imprinted on?

11. What are some examples of specialized place-learning abilities?

Be sure to READ the Concluding Thoughts at the end of the chapter. Note important points in your Workout. Then consolidate your learning by answering the focus questions in the margins of the text.

After you have studied the chapter thoroughly, CHECK your understanding with the Self-Test that follows.

Self-Test 1

Multiple-Choice Questions

1. What term is defined as "any process through which experience at one time can alter an individual's behavior at a future time?"
   a. behaviorism   c. reflex
   b. learning   d. habituation

2. As compared with serious (non-play) behavior, play behavior is more likely to:
   a. be unrelated to species-typical behaviors.
   b. occur when there is a strong, immediate need state.

c. involve a great deal of repetition.

d. all of the above.

3. A specific, well-defined event in the environment is called a(n):

a. reflex.
b. stimulus.
c. operant.
d. response.

4. In classical conditioning, a(n) _____ comes to elicit a response only as a result of training.

a. conditioned stimulus
b. unconditioned stimulus
c. unconditioned response
d. discriminative stimulus

5. Exploration is:

a. merely a form of play.
b. designed to promote skill learning.
c. a more primitive, widespread behavior than play.
d. not a product of natural selection.

6. Spontaneous recovery is defined as the:

a. equivalent of extinction.
b. partial restoration of an extinguished response after further pairing of the conditioned stimulus with the unconditioned stimulus.
c. partial restoration of an extinguished response after the passage of time.
d. full restoration of the individual to the state that existed prior to conditioning.

7. We could best explain why someone might feel sleepy on returning to a room where he or she had frequently taken sedatives in terms of:

a. a conditioned drug reaction.
b. observational learning.
c. spontaneous recovery.
d. imprinting.

8. The law of effect lies at the heart of the form of learning called:

a. classical conditioning.
b. habituation.
c. operant conditioning.
d. observational learning.

9. The overjustification effect involves a change in the:

a. amount of work that is required in order to be rewarded.
b. meaning of a behavior and thus the likelihood of engaging in it.
c. conditions under which a particular behavior will be rewarded.

d. schedule of partial reinforcement, which results in greater resistance to extinction.

10. The existence of reward contrast effects supports the _____ view of _____ conditioning.

a. S-R; classical
b. S-R; operant
c. cognitive; classical
d. cognitive; operant

11. If the arrival of a stimulus following a response increases the likelihood of that response recurring, we know by definition that the stimulus is a:

a. discriminative stimulus.
b. secondary reinforcer.
c. positive reinforcer.
d. negative reinforcer.

12. Classical conditioning generally _____ occur if the conditioned and unconditioned stimuli are presented simultaneously, a fact supporting _____ views.

a. does; S-S
b. does; S-R
c. does not; S-S
d. does not; S-R

13. If reinforcement depends on the average number of responses produced (e.g., 10), with a different number of responses required on each occasion (e.g., 7, 11, 12), the learner is on a:

a. fixed-interval schedule.
b. fixed-ratio schedule.
c. variable-interval schedule.
d. variable-ratio schedule.

14. Rats deprived of the vitamin thiamine will:

a. tend to eat all foods unselectively despite their nutritional deficiency.
b. lose their ability to differentiate foods on the basis of taste and will thus fail to avoid poison.
c. come to prefer foods containing thiamine after sampling various foods even though thiamine is tasteless.
d. consequently become incapable of learning operant responses.

15. Animals can more easily learn to:

a. fear certain types of stimuli as compared with other types.
b. avoid harmful foods if they become sick after eating them.
c. choose the right foods if they observe an adult model doing so.
d. All of the above are true.

Essay Questions

6. What is generalization in classical conditioning? How can a learner be taught not to generalize?

7. Explain the difference between reinforcement and punishment, between positive and negative reinforcement, and between positive and negative punishment.

After you have assessed your understanding on the basis of Self-Test 1 and have tried to strengthen your preparation in any areas of weakness, GO ON to Self-Test 2.

Self-Test 2

Multiple-Choice Questions

1. A puppy watches its mother swat her paw under the sofa to retrieve a tennis ball which she proceeds to chew. The puppy later shows more interest in the tennis ball than he had previously. This is an example of _____, a form of _____.
   a. imitation; observational learning
   b. stimulus enhancement; observational learning
   c. imitation; exploration
   d. stimulus enhancement; exploration

2. What kind of conditioning involves the learning of reflexes?
   a. habituation
   b. classical conditioning
   c. operant conditioning
   d. both classical and operant conditioning

3. A noise may startle you enough to make you jump. If it occurs several times, you will jump less and less each time. This is an instance of:
   a. a conditioned reflex.
   b. habituation.
   c. extinction.
   d. spontaneous recovery.

4. Stimuli similar to the conditioned stimulus are able to elicit the conditioned response in the phenomenon called:
   a. latent learning.
   b. habituation.
   c. generalization.
   d. discrimination.

5. You may find yourself salivating in response to a television commercial that shows a luscious dessert. This behavior would best be explained by:
   a. classical conditioning.
   b. operant conditioning.
   c. observational learning.
   d. discrimination training.

6. One group of rats receives tasty food pellets for each response, while another group receives not-so-tasty pellets for each response. When the first group is then treated like the second, they:
   a. stop responding altogether.
   b. continue to respond at a higher rate than the second group.
   c. drop to a response rate equal to that of the second group.
   d. drop to a response rate below that of the second group.

7. Which schedule of partial reinforcement underlies many gambling systems and may help to explain compulsive gambling?
   a. fixed interval
   b. fixed ratio
   c. variable interval
   d. variable ratio

8. Watson and Rayner did a classic study with a rat and a baby named Albert, which demonstrated that _____ be classically conditioned.
   a. fear can
   b. fear cannot

c. food preferences can
d. food preferences cannot

9. Sam has a habit of launching into long political tirades by saying, "Well, here's how I see it." As soon as she hears this, Betsy excuses herself and thereby escapes the rest of the speech. Betsy has learned to take advantage of a(n):

a. conditioned stimulus.
b. discriminative stimulus.
c. observational response.
d. positive punisher.

10. A stimulus that can serve as a positive reinforcer can:

a. also serve as a positive punisher.
b. also serve as a negative punisher.
c. also serve as a negative reinforcer.
d. only serve as a positive reinforcer.

11. Gregory Razran performed an experiment in which lemon juice was squirted into the mouths of college students just before a printed word was presented to them. He found that:

a. the students could not be conditioned to verbal stimuli.
b. the actual conditioned stimuli that elicited salivation were not the word meanings but the physical appearance of the words.
c. students later generalized, salivating to the words that meant the same thing as the original words more than to sound-alike words.
d. students could not learn to salivate in response to words, though they could learn other reflexive responses.

12. The technique in which successively closer approximations to the desired response are reinforced is:

a. backward conditioning.
b. discrimination training.
c. continuous reinforcement.
d. shaping.

13. Tolman and Honzik showed that rats acquired useful information from exploring a maze, but only showed evidence of that learning when rewarded. In other words, the experiment revealed:

a. reward contrast effects.
b. latent learning.
c. the overjustification effect.
d. goal enhancement.

14. A child who learns how to behave at a birthday party by seeing how other children behave is exhibiting:

a. observational learning.
b. classical conditioning.
c. instrumental conditioning.
d. exploration.

15. Imprinting:

a. is a type of observational learning found in all species studied so far.
b. occurs only during a critical period.
c. occurs equally well if the stimulus is a human as when the stimulus is a female of the species.
d. has not yet been reasonably explained in terms of adaptive value.

Essay Questions

16. Edward Tolman claimed that operant conditioning involves the learning of means-end relationships. Explain Tolman's view and present evidence for or against it.

17. Interpret and present an argument for the following statement: Learning mechanisms are products of natural selection and as such are suited to help a species deal with biologically important matters.

Answers

Introduction AND *Classical Conditioning I: Fundamentals*

2. a. yes, b. no, c. yes, d. yes

5. a. stimulus
   b. response

7. habituation; learning

2. a. salivating in response to a bell
   b. food placed in the mouth
   c. salivation
   d. bell
   e. salivation

Classical Conditioning II: Beyond the Fundamentals

3. S-R connection; Watson; connection; conditioned stimulus; unconditioned stimulus; Pavlov; Watson; mental entities (Watson was joined in his views by other behaviorists.)

5. expectation; unconditioned stimulus

Operant Conditioning I: Fundamentals

10. extinction

11. continuous; partial

12. a. VR, b. FI, c. VI, d. VR, e. FR

13. ratio

20. negative; positive

Operant Conditioning II: What Is Learned?

3. generalize

Activities Designed for Learning: Play, Exploration, and Observation

3. practice species-specific skills

9. stimulus enhancement; goal enhancement

12. more complex

13. primates

Self-Test 1

1. **b.** (p. 91)

2. **c.** (p. 118)

3. **b.** (p. 92)

4. **a.** (p. 93)

5. **c.** (p. 120)

6. **c.** The conditioned response will be fully restored if the conditioned stimulus is once again paired with the unconditioned stimulus, but spontaneous recovery refers specifically to the case in which the mere passage of time is sufficient to partially restore the extinguished response. (p. 94)

7. **a.** The physical surroundings in which the drug is taken may act as a conditioned stimulus. (p. 94)

8. **c.** (p. 106)

9. **b.** (p. 117)

10. **d.** (p. 116)

11. **c.** If the removal of the stimulus following the response had increased the likelihood of the response, we would have known the stimulus was a negative reinforcer. (p. 111)

12. **c.** A situation in which the conditioned and unconditioned stimuli occur together in time is not an effective means of producing classical conditioning. From the cognitive perspective—the S-S theory of classical conditioning—this makes sense. If the two are simultaneous, the conditioned stimulus cannot produce an expectancy that the unconditioned stimulus will occur. (pp. 97–99)

13. **d.** (p. 110)

14. **c.** (pp. 125–126)

15. **d.** (pp. 124–127)

16. Generalization in classical conditioning is demonstrated when the learner produces a conditioned response to a stimulus other than the original conditioned stimulus. The strength of the subject's response to a new stimulus depends on its similarity to the actual conditioned stimulus: the closer it is to the conditioned stimulus, the closer the response will be to the usual conditioned response.

A learner can be taught not to generalize through discrimination training. This procedure involves (1) pairing the conditioned stimulus with the unconditioned stimulus in further trials and (2) presenting the stimulus to which the learner generalized *without* the unconditioned stimulus. The learner eventually continues to respond to the conditioned stimulus and no longer generalizes to the other stimulus. (p. 95)

17. Reinforcement and punishment differ in terms of their effects on the likelihood of a behavior recurring. They not only differ in this regard; they are opposites. Reinforcement occurs when the consequences of a response increase the chances that the response will occur again, while punishment occurs when the consequences of a response decrease the chances that the response will occur again.

    Both positive and negative reinforcement involve increasing the likelihood of a response through the consequences of that response. But in positive reinforcement, the consequence involves the *arrival* of some stimulus, such as praise or money or food. In negative reinforcement, the consequence involves the *removal* of some stimulus, such as shock or a headache or forced confinement.

    Positive and negative punishment also both involve the same behavioral result—a decrease in the likelihood of the behavior. Positive punishment involves the *arrival* of some stimulus, such as shock or a headache or forced confinement, contingent on a behavior. Negative punishment involves the *removal* of a stimulus, such as praise or money or food. (pp. 111–112)

Self-Test 2

1. **b.** (p. 122)

2. **b.** (p. 92)

3. **b.** (p. 92)

4. **c.** (p. 95)

5. **a.** (pp. 92–93)

6. **d.** This reward contrast effect is evidence that they have learned to expect a certain level of reward for their response. (p. 116)

7. **d.** The gambler is being influenced by the unpredictability of the reinforcement schedule. In the past, reinforcement sometimes occurred after the gambler played just once or twice, other times on after extended playing. One never knows, thin the gambler, when the next win is due. (p. 110)

8. **a.** (pp. 100–101)

9. **b.** (p. 113)

10. **b.** A positive reinforcer is one for which th learner is willing to work. It is also presumably stimulus whose removal would be punishing hence, it is a negative punisher. Remember that th terms *positive* and *negative* refer to *presentation* an *removal*, respectively. *Reinforcer* and *punisher* refe to consequences that, respectively, *increase* and *d crease* the behaviors they follow. (pp. 111–112)

11. **c.** Razran's results support the cognitive view point because they show that what matters abou the stimulus is its meaning. (pp. 95–96)

12. **d.** (p. 109)

13. **b.** (pp. 121–122)

14. **a.** (p. 123)

15. **b.** (p. 128)

16. As a cognitively oriented theorist, Edward Tolma was comfortable interpreting behavioral phenom ena in terms of mental entities. He was suggestin that what takes place through operant condition ing is the acquisition of knowledge by the learne specifically knowledge about which action shoul lead to which result under which circumstance The learner can then use that knowledge to fit cu rent needs or desires and current conditions. I other words, the learner comes to know whic means will lead to particular ends.

    Tolman's view found substantial support. I one experiment, for example, hungry rats learne to lever-press for either sugar water or dry food Then they were deprived of water and thus mad thirsty. When tested with no reinforcement avail able, the thirsty rats that had learned to expec sugar water from lever presses performed this ac tion much more than rats that had learned to ex pect dry food from the same action. Reward con trast effects provide another example suggestin that Tolman was right. Animals that have receive a big reinforcer for an operant and are the switched to a small reinforcer don't respond a much as animals that received a small reinforce all along. This makes sense if we assume that th animal had a certain conception of what ought to happen, but it doesn't make sense in strict S-R terms. (p. 115)

7. Natural selection operates under the pressure of the survival and reproductive needs of a particular species in a particular environment. It produces in each species tools for dealing with those needs in that environment. Learning mechanisms are examples of such tools. They are an inborn means of modifying behavior to suit the demands an organism faces in its lifetime.

A number of different findings in research on learning make sense if we view them in this evolutionary perspective. For example, there are apparently innate tendencies in learning that affect which stimuli can become conditioned fear stimuli. In an attempt to repeat the Watson and Rayner experiment using Little Albert, an experimenter tried to condition fear to blocks and pieces of fabric rather than to a rat. It didn't work. One explanation is that we are biologically predisposed to fear some things (like rats) but not other things (like blocks).

Research on food aversion provides another line of support for the evolutionary view. Food-aversion learning seems to be special—different in important ways from classical or operant conditioning. For example, the events that need to be linked through learning—the food and the subsequent illness—can be separated in time by a whole day. In fact, if the food tasting and the illness occur within a few minutes of one another, the food aversion will not be learned. In typical classical conditioning, on the other hand, the two events must occur close together in time if learning is to take place. (pp. 124–127)

The Neural Control of Behavior

chapter 5

READ *the introduction below before you read
the chapter in the text.*

The nervous system is the basis of all that we refer to as psychological—thoughts, feelings, moods, behaviors. It coordinates and directs all of our actions. The most fundamental structure of the nervous system is a cell called a neuron. Although neurons play different roles and come in a variety of sizes and shapes, all can be described in terms of the same functional parts, including dendrites, axons, and axon terminals. A neuron's dendrites receive incoming information; its axon carries neural impulses; and its axon terminals release chemical messengers that influence other cells at junctions called synapses.

The neuron is different from other cells of the body in that it is capable of carrying signals. Those signals take the form of nerve impulses called action potentials, which involve the movement of electrically charged particles across the cell's membrane. The impulses travel down the axon to the axon terminals, where, through synaptic transmission, the neuron sends messages to other cells.

Researchers have at their disposal a number of methods for mapping the functions of the brain. Some, such as EEG, PET scans, and fMRI scans offer important ways to study the human brain noninvasively. Other more invasive techniques, such as producing localized brain damage (lesions), brain stimulation, or recording from single neurons can be used in nonhuman subjects.

The human nervous system consists of two main parts—the central nervous system (brain and spinal cord) and the peripheral nervous system (the nerves). The nerves connect the brain and spinal cord to sensory organs, muscles, and glands. Each nerve is a bundle of axons. (Do not confuse nerves with neurons.)

In the central nervous system, the spinal cord functions as a conduit between the brain and many of the nerves in the peripheral nervous system. It is also responsible for organizing certain rhythmic movements and for mediating spinal reflexes—behaviors that can be triggered and carried through to completion without the help of the brain.

The brain controls all other behaviors. Beginning just above the spinal cord are the subcortical structures of the brain, such as the brainstem, cerebellum, thalamus, hypothalamus, and limbic system, each with particular functions. The cerebral cortex, the outermost and most massive part of the brain, is divided into two symmetrical hemispheres—right and left. The cortex is critical to high-level processes, such as language and decision making, as well as to sensory and motor functions.

In many cases, the functions of the nervous system are organized hierarchically, with the most primitive, reflexive responses in the spinal cord at the lowest level and the most complex types of control in the cortex at the highest level. Movement control illustrates this hierarchical organization. Another characteristic of brain organization is that higher functions such as language are distributed asymmetrically across the left and right hemispheres.

Learning changes the brain. For example, rats exposed to an enriched environment with greater opportunity for learning experiences had thicker cortexes, larger cortical neurons, and more fully developed synapses than rats in an impoverished environment. More evidence has come from a variety of studies on animals and humans. Strengthening of synapses through long-term potentiation serves as a foundation for learning.

Besides the nervous system, the other major mode of communication within the body is the hormonal system. Hormones are chemical messengers that are released from endocrine glands and other organs and are delivered to various target tissues through the bloodstream. They produce a variety of effects, playing important roles in the development of anatomical differences between males and females and in the body's response to stressful situations, for example. The hormonal system and the nervous system are intimately related. In many ways, the hormonal system is under the control of the brain. Also, some hormones are chemically identical to neurotransmitters.

Drugs differ from hormones in that they are not produced inside the body but are introduced from outside. Like hormones, drugs are carried by the blood and taken up in target tissues of the body. Also like hormones, drugs can affect synaptic transmission, but the brain protects itself from some such substances by the blood-brain barrier.

LOOK over the table of contents for this chapter in your textbook before you continue with your study.

Notice that there are focus questions in the margins of the text for your use in studying the material. The following chart lists which Study Guide questions relate to which focus questions.

The Integrated Study Workout

COMPLETE one section at a time.

Introduction AND Neurons: Cells That Create the Mind   (pages 133–141)

CONSIDER these questions before you go on. They are designed to help you start thinking about the subject, not to test your knowledge.

What is a neuron? Is it the same as a nerve?

What actually happens when a neuron carries an electrical impulse?

How do neurons pass information among themselves?

READ these sections of your text lightly. Then go back and read thoroughly, completing the Workout as you proceed.

Despite the brain's rather unassuming appearance, even some ancients, such as the Greek physician Hippocrates, recognized it to be the organ of thought, feeling, and behavioral control. This represented a major difference of opinion, as other early thinkers credited the heart with these responsibilities. Students are often surprised to see that a psychology text includes a chapter on the brain (and the nervous system of which it is a part) because they expect that subject to be reserved for biologists. But if psychology is the science of mind and behavior, shouldn't we understand the organ that makes mind and behavior possible? Psychologists have answered "yes" to that question from the beginning, and the "yes" becomes increasingly insistent as new research uncovers more and more of the secrets of this amazing organ.

Let's begin with the basic units of the nervous system. To understand the way the nervous system works, you must have a solid understanding of individual cells.

1. The basic units, the "building blocks," of the nervous system are called _____. The human brain contains about ____ billion of them. A _____ is a bundle of _____ (well, of their axons) in the _____ nervous system, which extends from the _____ nervous system to the rest of the body. The central nervous system consists of the _____ and the _____. (See Figure 5.1 on text page 135.)

2. List and briefly describe three types of neurons by function. Indicate how many of each type are thought to exist in the human nervous system. (See Figure 5.2 on text page 135.)

   a.

   b.

   c.

3. Different neurons have many of the same basic parts in common though they vary in shape. Label the diagram of a typical motor neuron below. This type of neuron is generally used to illustrate the basic parts of a neuron in textbooks. (See Figure 5.3 on text page 135.)

4. Each part of a neuron is specialized for some function. Write the name of the part that performs each of the following functions.

_____ a. Thin, tube-shaped extensions that increase the surface area for receiving incoming signals from other neurons

_____ b. A small swelling that can release a chemical substance onto a receiving cell, such as another neuron or a muscle cell.

_____ c. The widest part of the cell, which contains the cell nucleus and other basic machinery common to all cells

_____ d. A thin, tubelike structure that carries electrical impulses (messages) from the cell body toward other cells

_____ e. A casing that wraps tightly around the axons of some neurons

5. A neuron sends a message to another cell first by carrying an impulse called a(n) _____ potential which travels down the _____. An action potential is _____ or _____; in other words, all action potentials in a given neuron have the same _____. A neuron conveys a weaker or stronger message with the _____ of its action potential.

6. What is the cell membrane? intracellular fluid? extracellular fluid?

7. Identify the electrically charged chemicals in the internal and external fluid environments of the inactive (resting) neuron. Also indicate their charge and location.

Name	Type of charge	Location

   a. _____

   b. _____

   c. _____

   d. _____

8. Now place chemical symbols (e.g., Na$^+$) representing the various chemicals named in question #7 on the following diagram. The diagram represents a section of axon in an inactive or resting neuron.

9. What is the resting potential? How big is it? How is it relevant to the action potential?

10. What is the action potential?

The action potential can be broken down into two major phases: depolarization and repolarization. Now let's trace the events of an action potential in detail. (See Figure 5.5 on text page 137 for questions 11–12 below.)

11. The cell membrane initiates the action potential by opening thousands of tiny _____.
This allows _____ ions to rush into the neuron. Two forces cause this movement to take place. They are a(n) _____ force and a(n) _____ force. As a result of this movement, the electrical charge across the cell membrane becomes momentarily _____ inside relative to outside. This shift in electrical balance constitutes the _____ phase.

12. Immediately after depolarization, _____ begins. As the sodium channels close up, channels that permit only _____ ions to pass through open. These _____ charged ions are repelled by the positive charge

_____ the cell and thus move _____. As a result of this movement, the electrical charge across the cell membrane returns to the _____. The whole process of depolarization and repolarization takes less than _____ to occur at a given point on the axon.

13. What is the chemical mechanism that allows the cell to restore the original balance of ions so that it can keep having action potentials?

14. Does the action potential occur in all parts of the axon simultaneously? Explain.

15. What is a cell's threshold?

The speed with which an action potential can travel down an axon is affected by several factors.

16. Larger-diameter axons will conduct an action potential _____ than thinner ones. Another factor that affects the speed of conduction is the presence or absence of a(n) _____. In cells with this type of insulation, the action potential does not move smoothly along the axon but rather _____ from one _____ to the next. The fastest neurons in the nervous system can carry an action potential at about _____ meters per second.

7. How could it be that you feel the pressure of a pin-prick before you feel the pain of it?

Neurons are separated from one another (and from muscle or gland cells) by tiny gaps. Synaptic transmission is the nervous system's way of conveying information across those gaps by chemical means. The chapter deals first with fast synapses. (See Figure 5.7 on text page 139.)

18. Answer the following questions about structures involved in synaptic transmission.

   a. Synapses fall into two basic categories, _____ and _____, with _____ synapses being the best understood.

   b. The synaptic _____ is the tiny gap that separates the _____ membrane from the _____ membrane that it influences.

   c. The axon terminals of the presynaptic cell contain hundreds of minute globelike _____, which hold chemical _____.

   d. When a(n) _____ reaches the axon terminals, it causes the neurotransmitter to be released into the _____, where it then diffuses through the fluid to reach the postsynaptic cell.

19. In general, what metaphor describes how neurotransmitter molecules have their effect on the postsynaptic cell?

It is important to consider neural activity in terms of the information being sent. When the postsynaptic cell is another neuron, a necessary distinction is that between excitatory and inhibitory synapses. At each of these types of synapses, a different type of signal is sent to the postsynaptic neuron. The two types of signals are designed to produce opposite effects in the postsynaptic cell.

20. Explain the mechanism by which these two types of synapses influence the postsynaptic neuron.

   a. excitatory synapses

   b. inhibitory synapses

21. What kinds of chemicals serve as neurotransmitters at fast synapses?

22. Why is it important to remember that each neuron receives input from many different synapses, often involving many different neurons? What ultimately determines the rate of action potentials in the postsynaptic neuron?

23. How do slow synapses differ from fast synapses?

24. What is a neuromodulator?

25. What are some of the psychological functions of slow-acting transmitters in the brain?

26. Comment on the types of chemicals that serve as transmitters at slow synapses.

Methods of Mapping the Brain's Behavioral Functions   (pages 141–146)

CONSIDER these questions before you go on. They are designed to help you start thinking about this subject, not to test your knowledge.

How can brain function be studied in living human beings?

Are there different methods for studying animals?

READ this section of your text lightly. Then go back and read thoroughly, completing the Workout as you proceed.

To learn about the functions of various areas of the brain, it is necessary to have some means of studying the brain in living subjects—that is, subjects capable of behaving.

1. Define the following terms:

nucleus

tract

2. What is it about the pattern of organization of nuclei and tracts that allows us to speak of functional areas of the brain?

Researchers have a number of ways to study brain function in humans. One of the oldest involves people with existing brain damage.

3. How do researchers use the effects of existing brain damage to learn more about the localization of brain function?

A rather new approach temporarily alters normal brain activity.

4. What is TMS and how does it enable researchers to study localized brain function?

Some methods record brain activity electrically.

5. What is an electroencephalogram (EEG) and what kind of information can it provide?

Other, newer methods are based on the fact that increased brain activity in a given area increases blood flow to that area.

6. Answer the following questions about two of these imaging methods—PET and fMRI.

   a. What does PET stand for and how does it work?

b. What does fMRI stand for and how does this technique work?

c. How and why do PET and fMRI studies employ control conditions?

Researchers using nonhuman subjects can employ more invasive techniques.

7. A localized area of damage called a _____ can be created either electrically or chemically. A(n) _____ instrument is used to allow precise placement. A thin _____ is used to make a lesion electrically and a tiny tube called a _____ is used to make a lesion by introducing a chemical into the brain to destroy specific neurons. Usually the lesions are placed in _____ parts of the brain that are similar for all _____, including humans.

8. How else can an electrode or cannula inserted in an animal's brain be used for mapping the brain?

9. Microelectrodes can be used to _____ the activity of a single neuron. These can show correlations between the _____ of _____ and the animal's behavior.

Functional Organization of the Nervous System (pages 146–159)

CONSIDER these questions before you go on. They are designed to help you start thinking about this subject, not to test your knowledge.

How do messages get from your feet or eyes or tongue to your brain? from your brain to your fingers?

How does the nervous system make your heart pound when you are scared? or make you want to get something to eat?

What part or parts of the brain are involved when you feel anger or joy?

How does the nervous system manage complex movement such as that involved in walking or skating?

READ this section of your text lightly. Then go back and read thoroughly, completing the Workout as you proceed.

The incredible capabilities of the nervous system depend on its complex organization. One important aspect of its organization is the fact that it includes two separate but interacting hierarchies—a sensory perceptual and a motor control hierarchy. The nervous system is also divided into the central and peripheral nervous systems. In learning about the nervous system's organization, try to keep in mind the main functions of each structure and try to relate each structure to others you've studied. We will begin by looking more closely at the peripheral nervous system, which consists of all of the body's nerves. We can differentiate two categories of nerves. In all cases, the nerves exist in pairs, with one left and one right member.

1. A bundle of axons of sensory or motor neurons outside the central nervous system is called a(n) _____. (Be sure you understand the difference between a nerve and a neuron.)

2. Humans have _____ pairs of cranial nerves and _____ pairs of spinal nerves. Cranial nerves extend directly from the _____ and spinal nerves from the _____.

3. Are cranial and spinal nerves exclusively sensory or motor? Explain.

4. Sensory input from the eyes, ears, nose, and tongue reaches the brain via _____ nerves.

5. Define *somatosensation*. How does such sensory input reach the brain?

Motor neurons provide the final common path.

6. What did Sherrington mean by the "final common path"?

The motor portion of the peripheral nervous system can be divided into two subsystems that affect different types of structures.

7. What is the skeletal portion of the peripheral nervous system? the autonomic portion?

8. Skeletal motor neurons _____ activity in the skeletal muscles. In contrast, autonomic motor neurons typically _____ activity in the visceral muscles, which have their own built-in nonneural mechanisms for generating activity.

The autonomic portion of the peripheral nervous system can be further subdivided into two systems.

9. What does the sympathetic division do?

10. What does the parasympathetic division do?

11. When you are conversing comfortably with a friend, the _____ division is probably predominating. When you are viewing the climax of a suspenseful movie, the _____ division is probably predominating.

Now we will examine the various parts of the central nervous system, starting with the spinal cord and moving up to the anatomical top of the system, the cerebral cortex. One major function of the spinal cord is to connect the brain with the rest of the body, neurally speaking.

12. In what sense is the spinal cord a conduit?

13. What are ascending tracts? descending tracts?

14. How is the level of spinal cord injury related to the severity of the resulting deficit?

The spinal cord directly controls some reflexive behaviors independent of the brain. These behaviors are called spinal reflexes.

15. What is a flexion reflex and why is it useful? Is it a response to feeling pain? How do you know?

The spinal cord also contains pattern generators.

16. What are pattern generators, and what function do they serve?

Moving up from the spinal cord, we turn to the organization of the brain. All brain structures below the cerebral cortex are called subcortical structures. We will begin with those subcortical structures that lie nearest to the spinal cord—the brainstem and the thalamus. (See Figure 5.14 on text page 150.)

17. The parts of the brainstem are the

_____, _____,

and _____.

18. Compare the brainstem and spinal cord in terms of anatomy and functions.

19. Two kinds of reflexes organized by the medulla and pons are _____ reflexes and _____ reflexes.

20. Characterize the brainstem's control of movement by describing the behavior of an animal after its central nervous system is severed just above the midbrain.

21. Why is the thalamus considered a relay station?

Moving beyond the brainstem and thalamus, we come to the cerebellum and basal ganglia, both importantly involved in motor control. (See Figure 5.15 on text page 151.)

22. Answer the following questions about the cerebellum.

a. The name *cerebellum* means _____ in Latin, and this part of the brain is so called because of its appearance.

b. The cerebellum rests on the rear of the

_____.

c. Describe the most well-known function of the cerebellum. What happens when the cerebellum is damaged?

23. Answer the following questions about the basal ganglia.

a. The basal ganglia are located on each side of the _____.

b. How is their role in motor control complementary to that of the cerebellum?

24. How do the cerebellum and basal ganglia differ in the way they use sensory information to guide movement?

25. Are the cerebellum and basal ganglia utilized only for sequencing and timing muscle movements? Explain.

At the next level up are the limbic system and the hypothalamus. (See Figure 5.16 on text page 152.)

26. Answer the following questions about the limbic system.

  a. The term *limbic* comes from the Latin word for _____. It divides the _____ parts of the brain from the cerebral cortex.

  b. What is the general anatomical pattern of the limbic system?

  c. Two important structures within the limbic system are the _____ and the _____.

  d. In general, structures of the limbic system help to regulate basic _____ and _____.

  e. Comment on the limbic system's connections to the nose and to the basal ganglia.

  f. The _____, a structure in the limbic system, is critical to the formation of some kinds of memories and for keeping track of _____.

27. Where is the hypothalamus? Why is it so very important, and how does it accomplish its tasks?

The evolutionarily newest part of the brain lies at the top of the brain.

28. The Latin word _____ means "brain"; the Latin word _____ means "bark." Thus the term _____ refers to the "bark," or outer layer, of the brain.

29. In size, the cerebral cortex is the _____ part of the human brain, accounting for about _____ percent of the brain's entire volume. Much of its surface area lies deep in _____ and is thus not visible in an undissected brain.

30. The cerebral cortex is divided into left and right halves, or _____. In turn, each of these can be divided into four _____.

31. Identify the lobes of the brain in the drawing below. (See Figure 5.17 on text page 153.)

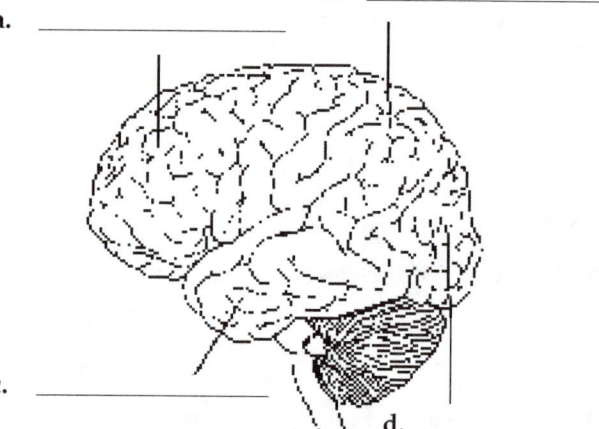

a. _____   b. _____

c. _____   d. _____

The cortex is also divided into three functional areas—primary sensory areas, the primary motor area, and association areas.

32. Identify the following different functional regions of the cortex by labeling the drawing below: primary sensory areas (including visual, auditory, and somatosensory areas) and primary motor areas. (Again see Figure 5.17.)

a. _____

b. _____

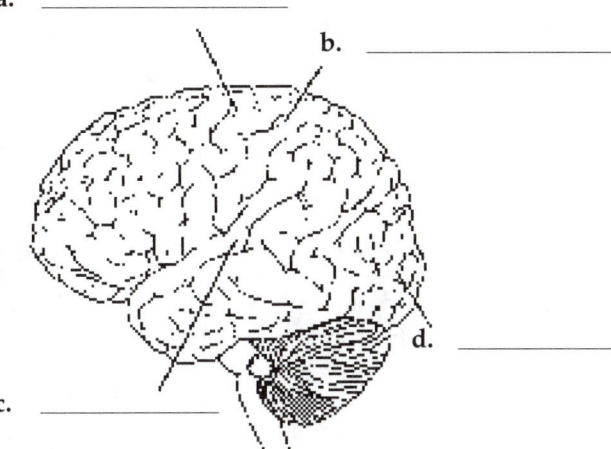

c. _____

d. _____

33. What are association areas, and what are their functions? How is the amount of association cortex in a given species related to the species' complexity? (See Figure 5.18 on text page 154.)

One way of approaching the complexities of the cortex is to think in terms of principles of organization, rather than physical divisions like right and left hemisphere.

34. What is the principle of topographic organization? Give one example to illustrate this principle.

35. Look at the maps of the somatosensory and primary motor areas of the cortex in Figure 5.19 on text page 155. Why do some body parts have greater representation than others? Why would species differ in terms of which body part has the greatest representation in these areas?

Now, let's concentrate on a more in-depth understanding of how the cortex is involved in motor control. (See Figure 5.20 on text page 156.)

36. The primary motor cortex, the basal ganglia, and the cerebellum are all involved in motor control. In what order do the structures exert their influence? How do we know?

37. Briefly describe evidence showing that the motor cortex is critical for making delicate movements.

38. What roles do the premotor area and other frontal lobe association areas play in motor control? How do we know?

39. What role in motor control is played by association areas in the parietal and temporal lobes?

Movement is behavior, whether it is something as dramatic and complex as a balance-beam routine or as subtle as a shift of the eyes. It is therefore worth understanding how the entire nervous system works to manage movement. This function of the nervous system also illustrates hierarchical control.

40. Figure 5.21 on text page 157 shows a functional hierarchy of movement control. Using this figure as an aid, describe what would be happening at the four levels of the hierarchy as a person thirsty after a long run spots a cool drink.

   a. at the first level (the top):

   b. at the second level:

   c. at the third level:

   d. at the fourth level:

41. Despite the elegance of a hierarchical explanation of nervous-system control over movement or some other activity, we do not have answers to all our questions. What type of question have we answered? What type of question have we not answered?

Assymetry of Higher Functions of the Cerebral Cortex   (pages 159–165)

CONSIDER these questions before you go on. They are designed to help you start thinking about this subject, not to test your knowledge.

Are the right and left hemispheres essentially the same in their functions?

How could we possibly study the hemispheres separately?

READ this section of your text lightly. Then go back and read thoroughly, completing the Workout as you proceed.

Even though the right and left hemispheres of the brain look like mirror images, their functioning is not the same in all regards.

1. Are the brain's two hemispheres isolated from one another? Explain.

2. In what ways are the hemispheres functionally symmetrical? functionally asymmetrical?

Split-brain studies provide some of the most compelling evidence for the functional differences between the hemispheres. These studies, done by Michael Gazzaniga and his colleagues, focus on individuals in whom the corpus callosum has been cut for medical reasons, thus effectively separating the hemispheres.

3. Describe a typical split-brain experiment and its results. Be sure to explain how the two hemispheres can be tested separately. (See Figures 5.23–5.24 on text pages 160–161.)

4. Are there individual differences in the right hemisphere's comprehension of language? Explain.

5. On what kinds of tasks is the right hemisphere superior?

10. How do modern theories account for the pattern of deficits seen in Broca's aphasia? in Wernicke's aphasia?

6. How do people who have had split-brain surgery manage in the everyday world?

Neuroimaging techniques now allow us to study the normal functioning of the brain. We no longer rely entirely on studies of people with brain damage.

11. Briefly describe a study of language that used PET scans. Did it support the classic view of the roles played by Broca's and Wernicke's areas?

7. What is the left brain interpreter and how is it related to Freud's theory of consciousness?

Effects of Experience on the Brain
(pages 165–169)

Much of our understanding of association areas specialized for language has come from studies of people with relatively localized brain damage.

CONSIDER these questions before you go on. They are designed to help you start thinking about this subject, not to test your knowledge.

8. A loss in language ability that results from brain damage is called _____.

Can experience affect the structure of the brain?

Is it true that blind people develop compensatory abilities? If so, is that reflected in brain differences?

9. Distinguish between Broca's (nonfluent) aphasia and Wernicke's (fluent) aphasia. Be sure to comment on both cause and effect.

Broca's aphasia

Is the brain of a new violin student organized the same as that of a virtuoso?

READ this section of your text lightly. Then go back and read thoroughly, completing the Workout as you proceed.

Wernicke's aphasia

As parts of a living system, neurons can be modified by experience. They can change in size, shape, excitability, and patterns of connections. Every day we establish new synapses and eliminate others by the millions.

1. What brain differences were found in rats raised in enriched, as compared with deprived, environments?

2. Did the different types of environments affect the brains of adult mice or only the brains of young mice?

3. Can the mammalian brain produce new neurons after birth? Explain.

Practice at a skill alters the brain in ways that support the performance of that skill.

4. Does practice at a given sensory discrimination task increases the number of neurons devoted to it? Is that true for people as well as other mammals?

5. How does the brain organization of a blind person differ from that of a sighted person?

6. Describe evidence that spatial learning can produce hippocampal growth.

Years ago, Donald Hebb proposed that some synapses grow stronger and more effective when pre- and post-synaptic neurons fire in immediate succession. Hebb's theory, which could help to explain classical conditioning and some other forms of learning, later received strong support from laboratory work on long-term potentiation, or LTP. (See Figure 5.28 on text page 168.)

7. Answer the following questions about long-term potentiation (LTP):
   a. How is it produced in the laboratory?

   b. How long does the potentiation last?

   c. What is the actual mechanism involved in LTP? In other words, what happens when LTP-inducing receptors on the postsynaptic membrane receive the transmitter they are primed for?

8. What question was addressed in research with "Doogie" mice? How was it addressed and what were the results?

How Hormones and Drugs Interact with the Nervous System   (pages 170–176)

CONSIDER these questions before you go on. They are designed to help you start thinking about the subject, not to test your knowledge.

What are hormones, and how do they affect the body's functioning?

How is the brain involved in hormonal effects?

How could a drug paralyze someone? affect someone's motor behavior? alter someone's mood?

What causes the unpleasant withdrawal symptoms associated with some drugs?

Given that the heart is part of a vast circulatory system and that its vessels are easier to see than nerves, it is not surprising that early theorists considered it the seat of thought, emotion, and behavioral control. In fact, the circulatory system does play a communications role within the body. It is, however, a much slower messenger system than the nervous system.

1. _____ are chemical messengers

    secreted into the blood to act on specific

    _____ tissues.

2. Hormones, dozens of which have been

    identified, are secreted not only by

    _____ glands but also by other

    organs such as the brain and stomach. (See

    Figure 5.30 on text page 170.)

3. How are hormones and neurotransmitters alike? How are they different?

4. Give two arguments to support the idea that hormones and neurotransmitters have a common evolutionary origin.

Hormones affect behavior in a variety of ways. They can influence growth, metabolism, and brain states that correspond with drives and moods.

5. Explain how sex hormones can have long-term effects by influencing growth.

6. Hormones can also have shorter-term effects. How do adrenal hormones such as cortisol help in times of stress?

The hormonal system is not independent of the nervous system. In fact, it would be reasonable to say that the brain is the master of the hormonal system. (Refer to Figures 5.32 and 5.33 on text pages 172 and 173.)

7. Why is the pituitary gland sometimes called the master endocrine gland? Where is it located?

8. Distinguish between the posterior and anterior lobes of the pituitary.

9. Briefly summarize a series of hormonal events that might occur in a frightening situation.

    a.

    b.

    c.

    d.

    e.

The blood can carry chemical messengers other than hormones that affect the body's tissues, sometimes dramatically.

10. How are drugs similar to hormones? How are they different?

11. Identify several different ways in which drugs can be introduced into the body. Why might one method be preferred in a given set of circumstances?

12. What is the blood-brain barrier? What kinds of substances can generally pass easily through this barrier?

Drugs can have a variety of effects by altering synaptic transmission. Most drugs used by psychiatrists and neurologists to affect mood or behavior work in this way.

13. List three ways that drugs can affect synaptic activity.

   a.

   b.

   c.

14. Explain how a lock-and-key analogy can help us to understand one of the modes of influence noted previously.

Drugs can influence behavior by affecting activity at any level of the behavior-control hierarchy.

15. What is curare? At what level of the hierarchy does it act? How does it have its effects?

16. What is L-dopa? What is it used to treat? Where in the hierarchy does it have its effects? Why isn't dopamine itself used?

17. What are psychoactive drugs? At what level of the hierarchy do they work? What can they affect?

Be sure to READ the Concluding Thoughts at the end of the chapter. Note important points in your Workout. Then consolidate your learning by answering the focus questions in the margins of the text.

After you have studied the chapter thoroughly, CHECK your understanding with the Self-Test that follows.

Self-Test 1

Multiple-Choice Questions

1. The neurons that carry messages from the central nervous system to, say, your right leg are classed as:

   a. sensory neurons.
   b. interneurons.
   c. motor neurons.
   d. skeletal neurons.

2. In some cases, a myelin sheath is wrapped around a neuron's:

   a. dendrites.   c. cell body.
   b. axon.   d. cell nucleus.

3. The hypothalamus regulates the body's internal environment by:

   a. influencing the autonomic nervous system.
   b. controlling the release of some hormones.
   c. affecting drive states such as hunger and thirst.
   d. doing all of the above.

4. The nervous system is made up of the _____ and the _____.

   a. skeletal motor system; autonomic nervous system
   b. central nervous system; peripheral nervous system
   c. peripheral nervous system; autonomic nervous system
   d. sympathetic nervous system; parasympathetic nervous system

5. An injury that severs the spinal cord will cause _____; the _____ the injury is, the more of the body it will affect.

   a. paralysis but not sensory loss; higher
   b. sensory loss but not paralysis; lower
   c. paralysis and sensory loss; higher
   d. sensory loss and paralysis; lower

6. A spinal animal's paw withdraws from a sharp pin even though the brain never receives pain signals because this behavior is based on:

   a. an ascending tract.
   b. a flexion reflex.
   c. cortical structures in the brain.
   d. subcortical structures in the brain.

7. Within the axon terminals are _____, which store the _____ needed for synaptic transmission.

   a. vesicles; neurotransmitter
   b. nodes; neurotransmitter
   c. vesicles; sodium
   d. nodes; sodium

8. The part of the brain regarded as a sensory and motor relay station is the:

   a. basal ganglia.
   b. cerebellum.
   c. limbic system.
   d. thalamus.

9. The part of the brain that plays a special role in the regulation of basic drives and emotions is the:

   a. limbic system.
   b. brainstem.
   c. cerebellum.
   d. corpus callosum.

10. Where are nerves found?

    a. only in the peripheral nervous system
    b. only in the brain
    c. only in the spinal cord
    d. in all parts of the nervous system

11. In the primary motor cortex, the amount of cortex devoted to each body part depends on the _____ of that body part.

    a. size   c. strength
    b. sensitivity   d. fineness of movement

12. During the depolarization phase of the action potential, _____ rush into the neuron.

    a. protein molecules   c. sodium ions
    b. potassium ions   d. chloride ions

13. A neuron's threshold is defined as the:

    a. strength of the action potentials that occur in that neuron.
    b. critical level of depolarization that must be reached before an action potential is triggered.
    c. number of action potentials that can take place in the neuron in a given unit of time.
    d. place on the neuron where action potentials begin.

14. The medulla, pons, and midbrain are all parts of the:

    a. limbic system.
    b. brainstem.
    c. thalamus.
    d. cerebellum.

15. Norepinephrine helps to illustrate the fact that:
    a. hormones target only one tissue each.
    b. hormones and neurotransmitters can be chemically identical.
    c. some hormones have their effects exclusively in the brain.
    d. neurohormones play a role in establishing the blood-brain barrier.

Essay Questions

16. Explain the process of synaptic transmission at fast synapses. How do excitatory and inhibitory synapses differ? What does it mean to say that the postsynaptic neuron integrates excitatory and inhibitory influences?

17. Name and describe three ways that brain function can be mapped in the human brain.

After you have assessed your understanding on the basis of Self-Test 1 and have tried to strengthen your preparation in any areas of weakness, GO ON to Self-Test 2.

Self-Test 2

Multiple-Choice Questions

1. The pituitary gland, located at the base of the brain:
   a. is often called the "master endocrine gland" because of its control over other glands.
   b. nevertheless operates independently of the brain.
   c. does not actually manufacture any hormones but does direct the movement of many hormones.
   d. exerts its effects on the brain but not on any other part of the body.

2. The most basic unit of the nervous system is a:
   a. lobe.   c. neuron.
   b. nerve.   d. tract.

3. In which type of neuron does stimulation come from a source other than neurons?
   a. motor neuron   c. sensory neuron
   b. interneuron   d. none of the above

4. When the neuron is inactive, the charge across the cell membrane is such that:
   a. the inside is about −70 millivolts relative to the outside.
   b. the inside is about −700 millivolts relative to the outside.
   c. the inside is about +70 millivolts relative to the outside.
   d. the inside is about +700 millivolts relative to the outside.

5. The sustained rhythmic movement of walking appears to be managed directly by:
   a. nuclei in the limbic system.
   b. pattern generators in the spinal cord.
   c. cranial nerves.
   d. the cerebellum.

6. Which of the following is part of the limbic system?
   a. pituitary   c. amygdala
   b. cerebellum   d. thalamus

7. Which part of the brain is considered a kind of computer or even a "little brain" that initiates and controls rapid movements?
   a. basal ganglia
   b. cerebellum
   c. frontal lobes
   d. brainstem

8. The cerebral cortex is divided into two _____ connected by _____.
   a. lobes; the corpus callosum
   b. hemispheres; the corpus callosum
   c. primary sensory areas; lobes
   d. association areas; tracts

9. Studies of people who have had split-brain surgery have taught us a great deal about:
   a. the limbic system.
   b. cortical involvement in movement.
   c. topographic organization in the cortex.
   d. the asymmetry of the higher functions in the cortex.

10. Which part of the nervous system directly mediates the body's physiologal response to a stressful situation by increasing heart rate, increasing blood pressure, releasing energy, and so on?
    a. excitatory nervous system
    b. sympathetic division of the autonomic system
    c. parasympathetic division of the autonomic system
    d. skeletal motor system

11. Sustained effects on a person's behavior can be produced by activity at _____ synapses.
    a. excitatory fast
    b. inhibitory fast
    c. slow
    d. peripheral

12. Experiments with rats and mice show that placing them in enriched (as compared with deprived) learning environments results in:
    a. no discernible differences in their brains.
    b. brain differences only if the experience occurs in infancy.
    c. thicker cerebral cortexes with more fully developed synapses.
    d. more numerous but smaller neurons in the cortex.

13. The brain and spinal cord together comprise the:
    a. autonomic nervous system.
    b. central nervous system.
    c. peripheral nervous system.
    d. sympathetic nervous system.

14. The chemicals that are produced by neurons and released by axon terminals into a bed of capillaries (rather than a synaptic cleft) are called:
    a. neurohormones.
    b. neurotransmitters
    c. neuromodulators
    d. psychoactive drugs

15. Curare is a drug that paralyzes by blocking postsynaptic binding sites in:
    a. muscle cells.
    b. nerves in the spinal cord.
    c. neurons in the cerebellum.
    d. neurons in the motor cortex.

Essay Questions

16. What is meant by hierarchical organization in the control of movement?

17. What is aphasia? How are Broca's and Wernicke's aphasia different in their symptoms? Briefly summarize modern theories about the two brain areas involved in these types of aphasia. Have studies involving PET scans clearly supported such theories?

Answers

Introduction AND *Neurons: Cells That Create the Mind*

1. neurons; 100; nerve; neurons; peripheral; central; brain; spinal cord

4. **a.** dendrites
   b. axon terminal
   c. cell body
   d. axon
   e. myelin sheath

5. action; axon; all; none; strength; rate

7. **a.** soluble protein molecules (A−), negative, internal only
   b. potassium ions (K^+), positive, greater internal concentration
   c. sodium ions (Na^+), positive, greater external concentration
   d. chloride ions (Cl^-), negative, greater external concentration

11. channels; sodium; concentration; electrical; positive; depolarization

12. repolarization; potassium; positively; inside; out; resting potential; one millisecond

16. faster; myelin sheath; skips; node; 100

18. **a.** fast; slow; fast
    b. cleft; presynaptic; postsynaptic
    c. vesicles; neurotransmitters
    d. action potential; synaptic cleft

Methods of Mapping the Brain's Behavioral Functions

7. lesion; stereotaxic; electrode; cannula; deeper (or more primitive); mammals

9. record; rate; action potentials

Functional Organization of the Nervous System

1. nerve

2. 12; 31; brain; spinal cord

4. cranial

8. initiate; modulate

11. parasympathetic; sympathetic

17. medulla; pons; midbrain

19. postural; vital

22. **a.** little brain
    b. brainstem

23. **a.** thalamus

26. **a.** border (or edge); evolutionarily older
    c. amygdala; hippocampus
    d. drives; emotions
    f. hippocampus; spatial location

28. cerebrum; cortex; cerebral cortex

29. largest; 80; folds

30. hemispheres; lobes

31. **a.** frontal
    b. parietal
    c. temporal
    d. occipital

32. **a.** motor
    b. somatosensory
    c. auditory
    d. visual

How Hormones and Drugs Interact with the Nervous System

1. Hormones; target

2. endocrine

Self-Test 1

1. **c.** (p. 134)

2. **b.** (p. 136)

3. **d.** (pp. 152–153)

4. **b.** (p. 134)

5. **c.** Severing the cord will cut through both ascending and descending tracts and will thus produce both sensory and motor deficits. The higher up in the cord the injury lies, the greater the number of spinal nerves that are cut off from the brain and thus the greater the area of the body affected. (p. 149)

6. b. The flexion reflex is an example of a spinal reflex. It is carried out independently of brain control. It makes adaptive sense that this defensive move should be handled by a spinal reflex since it can thus be accomplished faster, minimizing potential damage. (p. 149)

7. a. (pp. 138–139)

8. d. (p. 151)

9. a. (p. 152)

0. a. (p. 147)

1. d. (p. 154)

2. c. (p. 137)

3. b. (p. 138)

4. b. (p. 150)

5. b. (p. 170)

6. Synaptic transmission is the process through which a neuron sends a message to another cell, whether it be another neuron or a muscle or gland cell. When an action potential reaches the axon terminals of the "sending," or presynaptic neuron, it causes the release of the neurotransmitter from tiny vesicles in the axon terminals. The neurotransmitter acts as a chemical messenger that moves across the synaptic cleft, a tiny gap between the cells. The neurotransmitters at fast synapses are small and diffuse rapidly across this gap. When they reach the membrane of the "receiving," or postsynaptic, cell at a fast synapse, the molecules of the neurotransmitter are received at special receptor sites. The process works something like fitting a key (the neurotransmitter molecule) into a lock (the receptor site).

When the "key" fits into the "lock," the postsynaptic cell will contract if it is a muscle cell. If the postsynaptic cell is another neuron, the result is the opening of channels that allow ions to pass through, thus causing a change in the electrical balance across the cell's membrane. The direction of change depends on whether the synapse is excitatory or inhibitory. At an excitatory synapse, positively charged sodium ions enter the cell and slightly depolarize it, thus pushing it toward an action potential. At an inhibitory synapse, the entry of negatively charged chloride ions or the exit of positively charged potassium ions moves the cell farther away from the threshold level of depolarization needed to trigger an action potential, thus making one less likely. Since any given postsynaptic cell has many synapses, its rate of action potentials depends on the balance of activity at the various synapses. In other words, the neuron integrates the two types of inputs. (pp. 138–140)

17. An EEG (electroencephalogram) allows researchers to detect and amplify electrical activity from various areas of the brain. Electrodes placed on the scalp pick up the patterns of activity of many neurons just below the skull and computers can then be used to analyze the data.

TMS (transcranial magnetic stimulation) uses an electrical pulse to create a magnetic field just above the scalp. The field penetrates the skull at that location to temporarily inactivate or activate the neurons there. The resulting effect on behavior reveals something about the functional roles those neurons play.

In PET (positron emission tomography) scans, a radioactive substance is injected into the brain. Then the amount of radioactivity emitted from each portion of the brain is measured. This reveals the amount of blood flow in that area which is an index of the amount of neural activity there. The amount of activity in various areas while the subject is doing a specific task is compared against the amount of activity in these areas during a suitable control condition. (pp. 142–144)

Self-Test 2

1. a. (p. 172)

2. c. (p. 134)

3. c. Sensory neurons receive their input, directly or indirectly, from whatever type of sensory stimulation they are specialized to respond to. (p. 134)

4. a. (pp. 136–137)

5. b. Of course, the pattern generators exert their control under orders from the brain. You might say they are "deputized." (p. 149)

6. c. (p. 152)

7. b. (p. 151)

8. b. (p. 159)

9. d. (pp. 160–161)

10. b. (p. 148)

11. **c.** (p. 140)

12. **c.** (p. 165)

13. **b.** (p. 134)

14. **a.** (p. 171)

15. **a.** (pp. 174–175)

16. In hierarchical control, multiple behavior-control systems play a role in regulating behavior, each acting within a kind of chain of command. At the highest level of the hierarchy are systems involved in planning and motivation. Both cortical and subcortical structures are involved at the top levels of the hierarchy. These higher-level systems achieve their effects by acting upon the lower-level systems. At the lower levels are systems involved in refinement and actual execution of the planned behavior. (pp. 156–158)

17. Aphasia is any type of loss of language ability resulting from brain damage. Broca's and Wernicke's asphasia (also called nonfluent and fluent aphasia, respectively) are two categories of aphasia, each associated with characteristic patterns of language difficulty and each stemming from damage to a particular area of the brain.

    Damage to Broca's area, in the left frontal lobe, typically produces a tendency to speak in a labored way. The speech that the person with Broca's aphasia struggles to produce is generally telegraphic, that is, with short utterances containing mostly content words such as nouns and verbs. A person with Broca's aphasia who wanted to stop and sit under a tree with a friend might express that desire in a minimal form such as "Sit tree." Language comprehension is generally fairly good, but comprehension of grammatically complex sentences is impaired. A sentence in which the individual word meanings are not enough to convey the sentence meaning may not be understood correctly. For example, the pursued and the pursuer would not be clear in the statement "The woman chased the dog."

    A person with Wernicke's aphasia can speak with apparent fluency, but the speech is really only gibberish. It is full of articles, pronouns, prepositions, and nonsense words arranged in appropriate grammatical sequences, but has few content words such as nouns, verbs, and adjectives. The person with Wernicke's aphasia also has a serious deficit in understanding the words he or she hears. This kind of aphasia is associated with damage to Wernicke's area, located in the left temporal lobe.

    Contemporary theories propose that Broca's area is key for setting up master programs for fluent speech production and that Wernicke's area is involved in relating the sounds of words with their meanings as well as finding words needed to express specific meanings. Evidence from neuroimaging studies is not entirely consistent with these views. The neuroimaging research suggests that many left hemisphere areas may play a part in language usage. (pp. 162–165)

Mechanisms of Motivation and Emotion

READ the introduction below before you read the chapter in the text.

We can think of behavioral states as the slow-moving components of psychological life that help modulate and direct the fast-moving parts, such as thoughts, perceptions, and actions. This chapter examines the physiological bases of such states. One type of state—a motivational state or drive—is an internal condition that changes over time in a reversible way and orients an individual toward specific categories of goals, such as food, water, or a sexual partner. Some drives are designed to promote homeostasis, a constant state of internal conditions in the body. These are called regulatory drives. Other non-regulatory drives serve other purposes.

One important area of research has involved the discovery of systems in the brain that are responsible for reward. In fact, there are three interrelated components of reward—liking, wanting, and reinforcement—each with its own physiological basis. Understanding their functioning may help us to better understand the mechanisms of drug addiction and compulsive gambling, as well as natural drives such as hunger and sex.

Hunger, a regulatory drive, has been the subject of much research. Hunger and satiety are governed by an appetite control center in the hypothalamus. A number of internal signals, such as levels of hormones, blood glucose levels, and stomach distention, are acted upon by this center. External stimuli also play a role in appetite. Obesity, defined as a BMI (body mass index) of 30 or more, is influenced both by genes and culture.

Physiological psychology has also helped us to understand the sex drive, which is a non-regulatory drive. Hormones play a major role in the sex drive after puberty, although adult sexuality in humans is not strictly tied to hormones. Testosterone, popularly considered a strictly male hormone, is produced by both sexes and appears to be a key factor in the sex drive in women as well as in men. Sexual differentiation early in an individual's fetal development is due to testosterone's presence or absence. Factors that affect the prenatal hormonal environment may affect the individual's later sexual orientation, as well as the development of the brain and genitals.

One of the most important tools in sleep research has been the electroencephalogram, or EEG, which provides a crude picture of brain activity just beneath the skull. During the typical night's sleep, an individual goes through a well-ordered sequence of stages, each identifiable in part through the EEG pattern associated with it. Among the stages is REM sleep, so called because of the rapid back-and-forth eye movements that occur during this stage. It is during this stage that dreaming occurs. The body restoration theory and the preservation and protection theory both help to explain why sleep may have evolved. The first theory suggests that sleep is needed so that the body can recover from the day's wear and tear. The second suggests that sleep developed as a way for animals to conserve energy and to protect themselves at times of the day when activity would bring more risk than benefit. Sleep is an example of a circadian rhythm, an internally guided cycle that occurs on a 24-hour basis. Sleep deprivation affects performance on various tasks in a way that tracks levels of sleepiness. But the amount of sleep needed varies across individuals. At one extreme, nonsomniacs function normally on very little sleep. Like hunger and sex, sleep is governed by specific brain mechanisms.

Emotion is another type of state considered in this chapter. Emotion is a subjective feeling directed toward an object. Some of the central theoretical issues in the study of emotion concern the relationship between emotion and peripheral bodily changes. Some evidence suggests that the amount of physiological arousal we feel and even our facial expression may contribute to our emotional experience. Emotion also involves specific brain areas and mechanisms.

LOOK over the table of contents for this chapter in your textbook before you continue with your study.

Notice that there are focus questions in the margins of the text for your use in studying the material. The following chart lists which Study Guide questions relate to which focus questions.

Focus Questions	Study Guide Questions
Introduction and General Principles of Motivation	
1	1–4
2	5–6
3	7–8
4	9
5	10
6–7	11
8	12–13
9	14
10	15
11	16–18
Hunger: An Example of a Regulatory Drive	
12	1–2
13	3–4
14	5
15	6
16	7, 9–10
17	11–13
Sex: An Example of a Non-Regulatory Drive	
19	1–3
20	4–5
21	6–8
22	9–10
23	11–15
The Sleep Drive	
24	2–3
25	4–8
26	9–13
27	14
28	15
29	16
30	17
31	18–19
32	20–21
33	22
34	23
Foundations for Understanding Emotions	
35	1–2
36	3
37	4
38	5–6
39	7–8
40	9–10
41–42	11–15

The Integrated Study Workout

COMPLETE one section at a time.

Introduction AND *General Principles of Motivation*   (pages 179–189)

CONSIDER these questions before you go on. They are designed to help you start thinking about the subject, not to test your knowledge.

What does it mean to say you have a drive for something?

How can the pleasure we experience when a need is satisfied be explained physiologically?

What makes some people crave things that aren't good for them, like illicit drugs for example?

READ this section of your text lightly. Then go back and read thoroughly, completing the Workout as you proceed.

The term *motivation*, as used in psychology, refers to a host of factors, some internal and others external, that cause an individual to engage in particular behaviors at particular times. But this definition is really too broad to be theoretically useful. Psychologists who study motivation prefer more specific terminology.

1. Define *motivational state*. Give one example. What term is a synonym for *motivational state*?

2. How do psychologists determine when an individual is in a particular motivational state?

3. Define *incentive*. Give one example. What terms are synonyms for *incentive*?

4. How are drives and incentives related? Give an example to illustrate your point.

A drive is a hypothetical inner state. Efforts to understand such states physiologically are efforts to make the hypothetical more concrete. Some researchers, such as the physiologist Walter Cannon, described motivational states in terms of tissue needs.

5. Explain Cannon's concept of homeostasis. How, in Cannon's view, is homeostasis related to drives?

6. Briefly summarize some evidence suggesting that individuals behave in ways that fit their tissue needs.

The idea of homeostasis turned out to be more useful for understanding some drives than others.

7. Homeostasis is useful for explaining _____ drives, such as _____, which involve tissue needs. It cannot explain _____ drives such as _____.

One useful way to classify drives we share with other mammals is to categorize them in terms of their roles in promoting survival and reproduction.

8. Name and briefly describe five types of mammalian drives:

a.

b.

c.

d.

e.

9. How might we explain the universal human drives for art, music, and literature?

Since reward is a crucial concept in motivational psychology, a deeper analysis of what constitutes reward and how reward mechanisms work is necessary.

10. Discuss the interrelated meanings of reward: liking, wanting, and reinforcement.

11. What did Olds and Milner learn about reward pathways in the brain? Be sure to mention the medial forebrain bundle and the nucleus accumbens.

12. Which component of reward depends on the neurotransmitter dopamine? What is the evidence?

13. What neurotransmitter is involved in the "liking" component of reward? What is the evidence?

14. What other crucial role does dopamine play in reward? What is the evidence?

15. How can an understanding of the brain's reward system help to explain the following?
   a. drug addiction

   b. compulsive gambling

Today, physiological psychologists generally think of drives in terms of brain states.

16. Explain the central-state theory of drives. What is a central drive system?

17. Describe the characteristics a set of neurons must have to serve as a central drive system.

18. What characteristics of the hypothalamus make it a suitable hub of many central drive systems?

Hunger: An Example of a Regulatory Drive
(pages 189–195)

CONSIDER these questions before you go on. They are designed to help you start thinking about this subject, not to test your knowledge.

What internal factors cause a person to feel hungry?

What causes some people to become obese? What factors make it difficult for them to lose excess weight?

READ this section of your text lightly. Then go back and read thoroughly, completing the Workout as you proceed.

Though natural selection has equipped us with both a hunger drive and satiety mechanisms, the latter are not as strong as the former. That was fine in the evolutionary past, but may present problems for many people now.

1. In what way do hunger and satiety involve feedback control?

2. What is the arcuate nucleus and what role does it serve? Be sure to mention two classes of neurons there.

The central nervous system structures involved in hunger are sensitive to a variety of signals, though none by itself exerts total control.

3. List four types of signals that contribute to short-term regulation of appetite.

   a.

   b.

   c.

   d.

4. Comment further on a specific hormone called PYY.

5. What is the role of leptin in long-term appetite control? Could leptin be the anti-obesity drug many are hoping for? Why or why not?

6. Discuss the role of sensory stimuli in appetite control.

Many people weigh much more than they would like to. One aim of research on the motivational state of hunger has been to explain obesity.

7. How is obesity related to our evolutionary history and current environment?

8. Based on a 1999–2000 survey, _____ percent of people in the United States are obese and _____ percent are overweight, based on their BMI (or _____ _____ _____).

9. What primarily determines weight differences within a culture—genes or environment? Support your answer.

10. How do the Pima Indians illustrate the importance of environmental factors (including culture) on body weight?

Once a person has gained too much weight, it can be difficult (but not impossible) to shed the excess pounds.

11. How does weight loss affect basal metabolism? How does that affect further efforts to take off pounds?

12. How do most people who are successful at reducing their weight manage to do it?

13. Summarize expert advice for people who want to maintain a lower weight.

Sex: An Example of a Non-Regulatory Drive
(pages 195–201)

CONSIDER these questions before you go on. They are designed to help you start thinking about this subject, not to test your knowledge.

Does the sex drive work very differently in men and women? in humans and animals?

What is the basis of sexual orientation?

READ this section of your text lightly. Then go back and read thoroughly, completing the Workout as you proceed.

The sex drive has also received a great deal of attention from psychologists. Just as with hunger, most of the research has been conducted on laboratory animals. Because humans differ from other animals in both social and biological aspects of motivation, care must be taken in generalizing research findings to hu-

mans. However, humans do have something in common with other mammals in terms of basic physiological mechanisms. For example, sex hormones affect the sex drive in humans and other mammals by influencing the brain.

1. What two types of influences do sex hormones have?

Puberty marks a great increase in sex hormone production in humans as well as in other mammals. These hormones have activating effects.

2. At puberty, males have increased amounts of _____, which is produced by the _____. Females have increased levels of _____, produced by the _____.

3. Both sexes also produce _____ in the _____ glands beginning at about 6 years old. Early sexual feelings and attractions, which begin at about age _____ in both boys and girls, are due to the hormone _____. This hormone increases up to the mid-_____, then stabilizes at adult levels.

4. Castration, the removal of the male's _____, and thus the main supply of _____, causes a _____ in the sex drive in male animals. The implantation of a testosterone crystal in the _____ area of the hypothalamus _____ their sex drive.

5. Is testosterone critical for maintaining the sex drive in men? Explain.

5. What is the menstrual cycle? What is the estrous cycle?

7. Removal of the ovaries in most nonhuman female mammals causes the _____ of the sex drive; subsequent administration of estrogen (or estrogen and progesterone) _____ the sex drive. At least in rats, the _____ in the female plays a role analogous to that of the medial preoptic area in males. In comparison with most other female mammals, female monkeys and apes are generally _____ (less/more) dependent on ovarian hormones for their sex drive, with copulation being possible throughout the _____ cycle. They are still most likely to seek copulation at _____ when female hormone levels are high.

In human females, sex drive is even more independent of the hormonal cycle. Research has not produced clear evidence that there is *any* consistent relationship between the two.

8. Which hormones play a larger role in women's sex drive? How do we know?

Testosterone also plays a critical differentiating role. The presence or absence of testosterone has major influences before an individual's birth.

9. Describe the role of testosterone in producing prenatal sexual differentiation.

10. Why is a male rather than a female hormone critical to this early sexual differentiation?

The roots of sexual orientation are not fully understood, but research has begun to provide partial answers—and more questions.

11. About 2%–5% of _____ and 1%–2% of _____ are exclusively homosexual. Bisexuality is _____ (more/less) common and seems to occur more often in _____ (men/women).

12. Is sexual orientation due primarily to social learning? Support your answer.

13. Are there brain correlates of sexual orientation?

14. Is there a genetic contribution to sexual orientation? How might the prenatal environment be involved?

15. What is the fraternal birth-order effect on male homosexuality?

The Sleep Drive   (pages 201–212)

CONSIDER these questions before you go on. They are designed to help you start thinking about the subject, not to test your knowledge.

What is sleep? Is it just a kind of "suspended animation" in which nothing much is going on?

How can psychologists learn anything about sleep, given that the sleeping person is, well, asleep?

How much do people differ in the amount of sleep they need?

What is dreaming, and why does it happen? Does everyone do it?

READ this section of your text lightly. Then go back and read thoroughly, completing the Workout as you proceed.

Sleepiness is a drive, since people will go to some trouble to achieve sleep and experience pleasure as they do.

1. Is sleep a regulatory drive? Explain.

Because sleep involves little overt behavior that can be used to infer internal processes, scientists have developed ways to tap more subtle behavioral and physiological information. One of the most important tools at their disposal has been the EEG. (See Figure 6.12 on text page 202.)

2. What is the electroencephalogram (EEG), and what is it measuring?

3. For each of the following EEG patterns, note the frequency and amplitude of the waves and when each is likely to occur.
   a. alpha waves

b. beta waves

c. delta waves

The EEG follows a regular sequence of changes in sleeping person. The changes are used by researcher to divide sleep into four stages.

4. The brief transitional stage between waking and sleeping is called _____ sleep. As a person moves from stage 2 to stage 4, sleep becomes successively _____. At the same time, other physiological indices of arousal such as heart rate and muscle tension

   _____.

5. After getting to stage 4 sleep, a person _____ through stages 3 and 2 in a rapid _____ of sleep. A new stage of sleep occurs called REM or _____ sleep.

6. In what sense are there conflicting indicators o arousal during REM sleep (emergent stage 1 sleep)?

7. Stages 2, 3, and 4 are collectively referred to as _____ sleep.

8. A person goes through _____ sleep cycles in a typical night. A cycle consists of a progressive deepening of sleep, then progressive lightening, followed by _____

sleep. Each cycle lasts about _____ minutes. (Less/More) _____ time is spent in deep sleep with each successive cycle.

Dreams and other forms of mental activity occur during sleep.

9. What is a true dream? When do such dreams occur?

0. Does everyone dream? What is the evidence?

1. What is the content of dreams, generally speaking?

2. What is sleep-thought and when does it occur? How does it differ from daytime thought?

3. Are sleeping people completely unresponsive to environmental events?

One of the mysteries that has interested not just scientists but people in general is why we have developed a need for sleep. Researchers have offered two possible explanations for the evolution of sleep.

14. Explain the preservation and protection theory, and present two types of evidence that support it. How might this theory explain the typical 8-hour nighttime sleep pattern of adult humans?

15. Explain the body-restoration theory, and present evidence that supports it.

Other theories have been advanced to explain the specific function of REM sleep.

16. Expand on each phrase below to present the basic theory related to it and supporting evidence.
   a. maintenance of brain circuits

   b. consolidation of new memories

17. What is the side effect theory of dreams? Does that mean dreams are necessarily meaningless?

Most students have at some time or other experienced sleep deprivation, perhaps in studying for an exam or finishing a paper. (I hope that is not your current circumstance.) Of course, individual sleep needs vary.

18. Describe a nonsomniac. How does nonsomnia compare with insomnia?

19. What are the effects of extended sleep deprivation in people with a normal sleep drive?

Just as the hunger and sex drives are regulated by neurons in the brain, so too is sleep. Sleep is not, as researchers once believed, a state that the brain enters when external stimulation is low. After all, we sometimes sleep with considerable stimulation around us and sometimes fail to sleep when stimulation is minimal. One useful way to think of sleep is to see it as a biological rhythm.

20. A rhythmic change occurring on roughly a 24-hour cycle even without external cues is called a(n) _____ rhythm.

21. Where is the biological clock that controls this biological rhythm for sleep? How do we know?

22. How is this hypothalamic clock reset each day? What is a practical application of this fact?

23. What are the roles of the following nuclei?
    a. ventrolateral preoptic nucleus of the hypothalamus

    b. nuclei in the posterior hypothalamus and pon[s]

Foundations for Understanding Emotions
(pages 212–222)

CONSIDER these questions before you go on. They are designed to help you start thinking about the subject, not to test your knowledge.

Is emotion "all in the head," or does it have something to do with activity in the rest of the body, as well?

Sometimes people who are feeling a little blue are tol[d] they will feel happier if they make themselves smile Does this make any sense?

READ this section of your text lightly. Then go back and read thoroughly, completing the Workout as you proceed.

Emotion, though a pervasive experience in life and a relatively pervasive topic is psychology, has prove[d] hard to define.

1. How does the text define emotion?

2. Clarify the following terms that are either part o[f] the definition above or are related terms:
    a. feeling

    b. object

c. mood

7. Describe Schachter's theory of emotion. How is it like James's theory? How does it differ?

3. Briefly describe Platchik's model for classifying emotion. How was it developed? Is it generally accepted as correct?

8. What laboratory evidence did Schachter provide to support his view?

4. Make a case for this statement: Emotions are adaptive.

Depending on the stimulus and on your reaction to it, you may lower your eyebrows in anger or lift the corners of your mouth in a smile. Paul Ekman asked whether facial expressions can contribute to emotion.

9. What evidence suggests that "putting on" a particular facial expression can affect felt emotion?

f a police car pulls up behind you as you drive down the highway, its lights flashing and spinning, you will probably have more than a cognitive awareness of the event. Among other things, your heart may pound and your muscles may tense. These changes are part of the physiological response to emotional stimuli.

5. Define the term *peripheral changes* as it applies to the psychology of emotion. Give some examples.

10. What findings indicate that facial feedback may produce bodily states similar to those associated with the emotion depicted?

Psychologists have sought to understand the role that peripheral changes play in emotional feelings.

Emotion depends not just on peripheral processes, of course, but also on the brain, which not only produces the bodily changes but is responsible for experiencing the emotion.

6. What position did William James take on this issue? Was his theory based on experimental data? Does evidence available now support it?

11. Where is the amygdala and what is its role in emotion? How does it carry out this function through two separate routes?

More than 70 years later, Stanley Schachter developed a theory of emotion similar to James's.

12. Describe what happens to emotional responsiveness when the amygdala is removed or damaged.

13. Is the amygdala equally involved in all sorts of emotions?

14. How does the amygdala's role help to explain why emotions are often irrational and hard to control?

15. What rule does the prefrontal cortex play in emotion? What evidence suggests that the left and right prefrontal cortices frontal lobes may be specialized for different emotions?

Be sure to READ the Concluding Thoughts at the end of the chapter. Note important points in your Workout. Then consolidate your learning by answering the focus questions in the margins of the text.

After you have studied the chapter thoroughly, CHECK your understanding with the Self-Test that follows.

Self-Test 1

Multiple-Choice Questions

1. Which of the following is *not* a sex hormone found in humans?

   a. testosterone
   b. estrogen
   c. DHEA
   d. Hey, you can't fool me—all of the above ar human sex hormones.

2. According to Walter Cannon, tissue needs produc drives, which in turn produce behaviors that wi restore:

   a. a central drive system.
   b. motivational states.
   c. incentive.
   d. homeostasis.

3. An example of a non-regulatory drive is the driv for:

   a. food.   c. both **a** and **b**.
   b. sex.   d. neither **a** nor **b**.

4. A brain structure that is the hub of many centra drive systems is the:

   a. brainstem.   c. thalamus.
   b. cerebellum.   d. hypothalamus.

5. The medial forebrain bundle and the nucleus ac cumbens are essential to the rewarding effects of

   a. food.
   b. copulation.
   c. novel objects to explore.
   d. all of the above and more.

6. The term *motivational state* is synonymous with:

   a. emotion.   c. incentive.
   b. drive.   d. reward.

7. According to research described in the text, th hormonal changes that accompany a woman' menstrual cycle:

   a. cause her to experience peak sex drive during menstruation.
   b. cause her to experience a dramatically in creased sex drive about the time of ovulation.
   c. cause her to experience an absence of sex driv during menstruation.
   d. have relatively little, if any, effect on her se drive.

8. Dopamine is the neurotransmitter essential to the _____ of reward.

   a. wanting component
   b. liking component
   c. wanting *and* liking components
   d. wanting *and* reinforcement components

9. The electroencephalogram, or EEG, is a gross measure of _____ and has proved especially useful in studying _____.
   a. electrical activity in the brain; sleep
   b. electrical activity in the brain; hunger
   c. electrical activity in an individual neuron; sleep
   d. electrical activity in an individual neuron; hunger.

10. Which stage of sleep is associated with REM?
    a. stage 1
    b. emergent stage 1
    c. stage 2
    d. stage 4

11. PYY is a hormone that causes a _____ in the appetite for food.
    a. short-term increase
    b. short-term decrease
    c. long-term increase
    d. long-term decrease

12. Joyce sleeps only two hours per night on a regular basis because she doesn't feel the need for more. Joyce is:
    a. an insomniac.
    b. a nonsomniac.
    c. severely sleep-deprived.
    d. all of the above.

13. If you read research showing that extreme physical exercise is typically followed by lengthier, deeper sleep, you could correctly note that this supports the _____ theory of sleep.
    a. body restoration
    b. preservation and protection
    c. side-effect
    d. REM

14. The _____ assesses the emotional significance of stimuli.
    a. hypothalamus
    b. pons
    c. amygdala
    d. occipital cortex

15. Peripheral feedback contributes to emotional experience, according to:
    a. James.
    b. Schachter.
    c. both a and b.
    d. none of the above.

Essay Questions

16. What is obesity? Explain two factors that may predispose a person to become and stay obese.

17. Discuss hormonal effects on the human sex drive after puberty. Be certain to deal with both the male and the female sex drive.

After you have assessed your understanding on the basis of Self-Test 1 and have tried to strengthen your preparation in any areas of weakness, GO ON to Self-Test 2.

Self-Test 2

Multiple-Choice Questions

1. A thirsty fan at a football game waits in line for a soft drink. In this example, the fan's thirst is a(n) _____ and the soft drink is a(n) _____.
   a. reinforcer; incentive
   b. incentive; drive
   c. drive; incentive
   d. motivational state; drive

2. Research suggests that the prefrontal cortex is:
   a. not involved in emotion as was once thought.
   b. responsible for immediate unconscious assessment of emotional stimuli.
   c. essential for the full conscious experience of emotions.
   d. involved in emotional responses for women but not men.

3. In a normal night's sleep, one sleep cycle typically takes _____ minutes.
   a. 30   c. 90
   b. 60   d. 120

4. In the area of sex, a basic difference between humans and other species is that:
   a. humans are much more stereotyped in their sexual behavior.
   b. the sex drive of human females is not limited to a specific time in their hormonal cycle.
   c. humans are not sexually differentiated as a result of prenatal hormones.
   d. the human sex drive typically is unaffected by the absence of sex hormones.

5. The _____ nucleus in the _____ serves as an appetite-control center.
   a. suprachiasmatic; basal ganglia
   b. suprachiasmatic; hypothalamus
   c. arcuate; basal ganglia
   d. arcuate; hypothalamus

6. Injections of the hormone testosterone:
   a. will fail to restore the sex drive in men who have been castrated or who produce abnormally low levels of the hormone.
   b. lead to distortions of sexual orientation in heterosexual women.
   c. will be rejected by the immune systems of women because testosterone is an exclusively male hormone.
   d. will increase the sex drive in women who are experiencing low sex drive due to removal of the adrenal glands.

7. Large regular brain waves with a frequency of 8 to 13 cycles per second are called:
   a. alpha waves.   c. delta waves.
   b. beta waves.   d. REMs.

8. The hormone leptin contributes to _____ control of appetite; current research suggests that injections of it _____ help most obese people lose weight.

a. short-term; would
b. short-term; would not
c. long-term; would
d. long-term; would not

9. Knowing what you do about the brain's reward systems, you should expect that the administration of dopamine-blocking drugs will:
   a. cause animals who have learned to lever-press for food to stop their lever-pressing and eating behaviors.
   b. want food more, like it less, and yet work for it at the same level as before.
   c. help an animal learn faster how to obtain food by pressing a lever.
   d. cause animals who have learned to lever-press for food to exhibit this behavior at unusually high rates.

10. Prenatal differentiation of human males and females depends on the presence or absence of:
    a. estrogen.
    b. testosterone.
    c. dopamine.
    d. DHEA.

11. The sleep cycle can be reset through carefully timed:
    a. exposure to bright fluorescent light.
    b. changes in temperature.
    c. alterations in diet.
    d. mild electrical shocks.

12. True dreams occur during _____ sleep.
    a. deep   c. stage 2
    b. REM   d. stage 3

13. The circadian clock is located in a specific nucleus in the:
    a. pons.   c. hypothalamus.
    b. cerebral cortex.   d. medulla.

14. Induced facial expressions (such as a smile or frown) can produce corresponding changes in:
    a. felt emotion only.
    b. physiological response only.
    c. both felt emotion and physiological response.
    d. self-reports of emotion, but these have been shown to arise solely from subject expectations.

15. A set of neurons in which activity constitutes a drive is a:
    a. central drive system.
    b. motivational state.
    c. limbic system.
    d. homeostatic regulator.

Essay Questions

6. What is the function of sleep? Offer evidence for any theories that you present.

17. What are peripheral changes associated with emotion? What role do they play in felt emotion? Present the views of two theorists.

Answers

Introduction AND *General Principles of Motivation*

7. regulatory; hunger; nonregulatory; sex

Hunger: An Example of a Regulatory Drive

8. 31; 65; body mass index

Sex: An Example of a Non-Regulatory Drive

2. testosterone; testes; estrogen; ovaries

3. DHEA; adrenal; 10; DHEA; teens

4. testes; testosterone; decrease; medial preoptic; restores

7. elimination; restores; ventromedial area of the hypothalamus; less; hormonal; ovulation

11. men; women; more; women

The Sleep Drive

4. stage 1; deeper; decline

5. returns; lightening; rapid eye movement

7. non-REM

8. four or five; REM; 90; Less

20. circadian

Self-Test 1

1. **d.** (p. 196)

2. **d.** (p. 181)

3. **b.** Non-regulatory drives are those whose purpose is other than to maintain internal bodily conditions within certain limits. In other words, non-regulatory drives exist for nonhomeostatic purposes. (p. 182)

4. **d.** (p. 190)

5. **d.** (p. 184)

6. **b.** (p. 179)

7. **d.** (p. 198)

8. **d.** (p. 185)

9. **a.** (pp. 202–203)

10. **b.** (p. 203)

11. **b.** (p. 191)

12. **b.** (p. 209)

13. **a.** (pp. 206–207)

14. **c.** (p. 220)

15. **c.** (pp. 215–217)

16. Obesity is a condition in which a person has a BMI (body mass index) of 30 or more. Although it is possible for people to overcome the tendency to be obese, a number of factors make it difficult. One such factor is that weight loss lowers basal metabolism so the body needs fewer calories to maintain itself and any additional calories are stored as fat. Obese individuals also may be strongly influenced by hereditary factors. Evidence from adoption studies shows that adopted children resemble their biological parents more than their adoptive parents where weight is concerned. If the biological parents were obese, then the individual is fighting against his or her genetic makeup in attempting to attain a lower body weight. (pp. 193–195)

17. The hormone testosterone appears to be important for maintaining the sex drive in both men and women. Men who have been castrated or who produce abnormally low amounts of testosterone will show a decline in the sex drive and sexual behavior, though they will often not lose the drive entirely. If they receive injections of testosterone, their sex drive will be restored. At least in the case of noncastrated men with abnormally low levels of testosterone, injections specifically affect the desire for sex, not the ability to carry out sexual behavior.

    In women, the sex drive also appears to depend on some minimum level of testosterone in the body. Unlike females of other species, a woman's sex drive is not tied directly to cyclic fluctuations in female hormones such as estrogen. A woman whose ovaries have been removed will generally experience no decline in sex drive. However, a woman whose adrenal glands have been removed, and who therefore is producing no testosterone, will often experience a decline in sex drive. As with men, treatment with testosterone restores the sex drive in such women. (pp. 197–198)

Self-Test 2

1. c.   Remember that the drive, or motivational state, is the condition of the individual that causes the individual to orient toward some goal. The incentive is the external stimulus toward which motivated behavior is directed. (pp. 179–180)

2. c.   (p. 221)

3. c.   (p. 203)

4. b.   (p. 198)

5. d.   (p. 190)

6. d.   (p. 198)

7. a.   (p. 202)

8. d.   (p. 192)

9. a.   (p. 185)

10. b.   (pp. 198–199)

11. a.   (p. 211)

12. b.   Sleep thought, a type of mental activity different from true dreaming, occurs during non-REM sleep (p. 204)

13. c.   (p. 211)

14. c.   (p. 217)

15. a.   (p. 188)

16. There are two major theories on the functions of sleep. The body restoration theory suggests that sleep is needed for the body to recover physically after a day of wear and tear. Several lines of evidence support this notion. One is the fact that sleep really is a time of rest in which the muscles are relaxed, the metabolic rate is slowed, and growth hormone, which promotes body repair, is secreted at a higher level. Also, prolonged total sleep deprivation in rats led to a breakdown in tissues and eventually to death.

    The preservation and protection theory is also supported by several different kinds of evidence. The theory states that sleep came about in evolution to conserve energy and to keep an animal relatively safe during that part of a 24-hour period when activity would be more risky than beneficial. Evidence for this theory comes primarily from comparing different species. For example, the theory helps to make sense of the fact that variations in sleep time between species correspond to feeding habits and ways of achieving safety. Animals who need to spend large amounts of time getting food and who are too big to hide easily during sleep do not sleep much. Animals who get all the food they need easily and who can sleep in a safely hidden place sleep for a large proportion of a 24-hour period. This theory also helps to explain when members of a species tend to sleep, as well as for how long. For example, species that need visual information to find food tend to be awake in daylight hours and asleep at night. (pp. 205–210)

7. A pattern of physiological changes occurs in connection with many emotions. The particular changes involved vary from individual to individual and from emotion to emotion, but may include such things as changes in heart rate, breathing rate, and blood pressure; diversion of blood from one set of tissues to another; increased muscle tension; and facial expressions of emotion. These peripheral changes are commonly thought by nonexperts to follow emotion, but major theorists have suggested that they precede the experience of emotion and contribute to it.

James's peripheral feedback theory suggests that emotion—the subjective feeling we have—is simply our awareness of the bodily changes we experience. Schachter's theory proposes that emotion is a product both of the peripheral changes we experience and of an emotionally significant stimulus that causes us to interpret these changes in emotional terms. According to this theory, the greater the changes, the more intense the emotion we experience. (pp. 215–219)

Smell, Taste, Pain, Hearing, and Psychophysics

chapter 7

READ the introduction below before you read the chapter in the text.

Sensation occurs when a physical stimulus produces physiological responses in the sensory organs and brain that lead to a subjective, psychological experience of that stimulus. Perception is the more complex organizing and meaningful interpreting of sensory information, though the boundary between sensation and perception is blurry.

Sensations, in the form of sights, sounds, tastes, smells, and so on, are necessary for us to know about the world around us and even about our own bodies. Our various sensory systems actually have much in common. For example, all need certain types of neural structures: receptors, which respond directly to the stimulus; sensory neurons, which carry sensory information to the central nervous system; and still other neurons in the brain that process sensory information in particular ways. Processes common to all of our senses include transduction (responding to a physical stimulus with electrical changes that can trigger neural impulses), coding (preserving information about the stimulus in patterns of neural activity), and adaptation (altering sensitivity to a stimulus with continued stimulation or lack of stimulation).

Smell is a chemical sense, with receptors designed to respond to the molecules of many different odorants. The human sense of smell is very useful and also quite sensitive. Smell receptors are distributed throughout the olfactory epithelium in the nose. Neural signals travel from these receptors to glomeruli in the olfactory bulb of the brain. Major pathways lead from there to the limbic system and hypothalamus, which may help to explain the powerful effect of smell on emotion and motivation. Other important destinations for output from the olfactory bulb allow fine distinctions between odors and conscious experience of odors. Smell plays a significant role in our experience of flavor. In many animal species, pheromones provide a means of communicating with other members of the same species via smell. The evidence is not so clear for humans.

Taste, too, is a chemical sense. To be tasted, molecules must be dissolved in saliva and stimulate appropriate receptor cells in the taste buds, most of which are found on the tongue. Current research suggests that there are five basic taste sensations and five corresponding types of taste receptors: sweet, salty, sour, bitter, and umami.

Taste evolved to guide our food choices toward beneficial foods and away from harmful substances, such as poisons. Many harmful substances are experienced as bitter, and bitter foods are generally experienced as unpleasant and thus rejected. Women and young children are more sensitive to bitter taste. Bitter sensitivity increases in women during early pregnancy to provide greater protection to the vulnerable fetus.

Pain is a body sense we may at times wish we didn't have; yet it is one with real survival value. The receptors for pain are the sensory neurons themselves, which have sensitive free nerve endings. There are two types of pain-sensory neurons, called C fibers and A-delta fibers. Different aspects of the pain experience are associated with different brain areas. The gate-control theory helps to explain pain and its inhibition. Pain relief may come from a number of natural sources, including endorphins, acute stress, and even our beliefs. The body also enhances pain at times, however.

Sound waves—vibrations in the air or some other medium—are the stimuli that initiate auditory responses in the ear. The chapter explains both the nature of sound waves and the workings of the human ear. Emphasis is placed on a structure called the cochlea, which is located in the inner ear, because it is in this coiled structure that transduction takes place. Two types of deafness—conduction deafness and sensorineural deafness—can occur, each resulting from a different type of malfunction in the ear. The basilar membrane, a structure in the inner ear, is the focus of theories of pitch perception; both the pattern and timing of its movement contribute to our ability to discriminate among pitches. Differences in timing and amplitude of the sound waves reaching the right and left ears help us to localize sounds.

The chapter concludes by introducing several questions addressed by the field of psychophysics, which attempts to relate characteristics of the stimulus to aspects of the resulting subjective experience. For example, one psychophysical question is: How weak can a stimulus be and still be detected? This question concerns the absolute threshold. Psychophysics has been a fruitful area for those who appreciate mathematical precision in their answers.

LOOK over the table of contents for this chapter in your textbook before you continue with your study.

Notice that there are focus questions in the margins of the text for your use in studying the material. The following chart lists which Study Guide questions relate to which focus questions.

The Integrated Study Workout

COMPLETE one section at a time.

Introduction AND *Overview of Sensory Processes* (pages 225–230)

CONSIDER these questions before you go on. They are designed to help you start thinking about this subject, not to test your knowledge.

How can psychologists study a person's sensations, given that they're completely private experiences?

Are there really only five senses?

The eyes are certainly necessary for sight and the ears for hearing, but does seeing actually take place in the eyes? or hearing in the ears?

How can the wonderful smell of fresh coffee seem so vivid at first but become barely noticeable after a short while?

READ this section of your text lightly. Then go back and read thoroughly, completing the Workout as you proceed.

The term *sensation* refers both to our elementary psychological experience of a stimulus, such as a light or sound, and to the basic physiological processes that allow us to respond to the stimulus. Sensation, and the kinds of questions scientists ask about it, can be more clearly understood if the process is broken down into three classes of events.

1. Indicate the three types of events involved in sensation by filling in the diagram below.

_____ → _____

→ _____

2. The text states that the sensory experience reflects the physical stimulus but is also a very different thing from the stimulus. Explain this statement.

We have more than five senses, but specifying a particular number would be arbitrary. Though each is unique in important ways, all senses have some things in common. For example, all depend on certain types of anatomical elements, which carry out particular types of functions. The senses also have some basic processes in common.

3. Name the three types of physiological structures common to all senses, and briefly state their respective functions.

> Structure   Function

a.

b.

c.

4. Define the following sensory processes and give a specific example of each.
   a. transduction

b. receptor potential

c. coding (qualitative and quantitative)

d. sensory adaptation

5. In what part(s) of the sensory system does sensory adaptation take place?

Smell (pages 230–235)

> *CONSIDER these questions before you go on. They are designed to help you start thinking about this subject, not to test your knowledge.*

How sensitive is the human sense of smell?

Why are smells able to provoke powerful emotions and drives?

> *READ this section of your text lightly. Then go back and read thoroughly, completing the Workout as you proceed.*

Both smell and taste are specialized to respond to chemical molecules. Though keener in many other species, the sense of smell in humans is actually quite sensitive and very useful. Smell is handled by the olfactory system. It also plays a significant role in motivation and emotion. (See Figure 7.3 on text page 231.)

1. Note two facts that underscore the sensitivity of human smell.

b.

c.

2. The stimuli for smell are _____ that _____. The _____ contains the sensitive terminals of about _____ olfactory sensory neurons. Each of these terminals contains many _____ sites capable of binding the molecules of specific odorants.

3. What happens when an odorant molecule binds to a receptor site? In other words, how does transduction take place?

4. How do quantitative and qualitative coding take place in the olfactory system?

5. The axons of the sensory neurons pass into the _____ in the brain, where they synapse with other neurons in structures called _____. Each one of these structures receives input from only one of the _____ types of sensory neurons but from several _____ neurons of that type.

6. Where does output from the glomeruli go in the brain, and why are these pathways important?

a.

The senses of taste and smell are more closely linked than many people realize.

7. How is it possible to smell food in the mouth?

8. Describe evidence that smell contributes significantly to the experience of flavor.

9. Are there age and/or sex differences in sensitivity to smell? Explain.

Obviously, we are capable of recognizing other people by their faces and by their voices, but what about recognizing them by their odor?

10. Can humans identify other people by their smell? Support your answer.

11. What evidence suggests that smell may play a role in human mother-infant bonding?

12. What is the major histocompatibility complex (MHC)? How and why might it affect mating preferences in mice? Is there evidence of the same preference pattern in humans?

In many species, smell is the basis of a communications system. A specific chemical called a pheromone is released by an animal to influence the behavior or physiology of other members of its species.

13. What is the vomeronasal organ found in most mammalian species? How does it function differently from the main olfactory epithelium?

14. Summarize the current state of research on human communication by means of pheromones.

Taste (pages 236–239)

CONSIDER these questions before you go on. They are designed to help you start thinking about this subject, not to test your knowledge.

What makes some foods taste sweet and others salty or bitter?

How many types of taste sensations are there?

What is the evolutionary value of taste?

READ this section of your text lightly. Then go back and read thoroughly, completing the Workout as you proceed.

Some species walk on their taste receptors and others carry them all over their bodies, but in humans, they are found exclusively in the mouth—mainly on the tongue, but also on the roof of the mouth and in the opening of the throat. The taste receptors are organized somewhat like the segments of an orange in spherical structures called taste buds. There are 50–150 receptor cells in each of the thousands of taste buds in a person's mouth. (See Figure 7.6 on text page 236.)

1. What is necessary for a substance to be tasted?

2. What constitutes transduction in the sense of taste? Is it the same for all types of receptors? Explain.

3. Western taste researchers formerly believed that there were four basic taste sensations corresponding to four types of taste receptors. Each type of receptor was named after the type of sensation it produces when activated. Those four tastes receptors were:

_____   _____

_____   _____

4. Why do we now believe there are five basic types? What is the fifth?

5. Where is the primary taste area in the cerebral cortex and how is it organized?

Taste evolved to guide our eating behavior—drawing us to some substances and away from others. Generally speaking, we find salty, sweet, and umami tastes pleasant, and sour and bitter tastes unpleasant. The text presents an evolutionary perspective on the rejection of bitter-tasting foods. It also points out that learning can override this tendency, allowing us to eat some foods that are safe and nutritious though bitter-tasting—like brussels sprouts or spinach.

6. Explain why we may experience so many chemically diverse substances as bitter? How and why might this ability have evolved?

7. Which categories of people are especially sensitive to bitter tastes? Why might this be the case?

Pain   (pages 239–244)

CONSIDER these questions before you go on. They are designed to help you start thinking about this subject, not to test your knowledge.

The usefulness—and the pleasures—of senses such as taste and hearing are obvious, but why should pain exist?

Is there a sense organ for pain? Where does this type of sensation originate?

Why might a person who has been badly injured not feel pain until later?

Can our beliefs affect pain?

READ this section of your text lightly. Then go back and read thoroughly, completing the Workout as you proceed.

Pain is a biologically useful and highly motivating, though generally unwanted, type of sensation. It is a body sense that is related to other somatosenses such as the senses of touch and temperature.

1. Comment on each of the following aspects of pain:
   a. pain as "body" sense

   b. pain as emotion

   c. pain as drive

2. What is some dramatic evidence of the evolutionary value of pain?

Pain receptors are actually sensory neurons, with special receptive endings, not separate cells. (See Figure 7.8 on text page 240.)

3. Pain neurons have sensitive terminals called

   _____, which are found in

   _____ from which pain is sensed.

4. Distinguish between C fibers and A-delta fibers. Indicate the types of stimuli that activate them, and specify the type of pain associated with each.
   a. C fibers

   b. A-delta fibers

As with other senses, pain depends not only on specialized peripheral neurons but also on specialized areas of the brain. (See Figure 7.9 on text page 241.)

5. Describe the type of pain experience associated with each brain area listed below and (where possible) the evidence that supports that association.
   a. somatosensory cortex

   b. cingulate cortex and insular cortex in the limbic system

   c. prefrontal lobe of the cortex

6. The fact that the experience of pain does not always come from pain receptors is illustrated by an experience called _____.

The very same pain stimulus doesn't always produce the same level of pain. Ronald Melzack and Patrick Wall proposed the gate-control theory to explain the extent to which pain will or will not be felt. The theory is well supported by physiological evidence.

7. Explain the basic premise of the gate-control theory. (See Figure 7.10 on text page 243.)

Because pain was designed to serve a protective function—by alerting us to physical damage or disease and motivating us to behave in certain ways—the body has mechanisms to enhance pain.

8. How and why does illness produce a general increase in pain sensitivity?

9. How and why does injury lead to a localized increase in pain sensitivity?

The periaqueductal gray (PAG) in the midbrain is a major center for pain inhibition.

10. Describe the role of the PAG in pain reduction. What happens to pain levels when the PAG is stimulated electrically?

11. How do morphine and other opiates reduce pain?

12. What are endorphins and how do they act to reduce pain?

Nature has also provided us with several psychologically mediated mechanisms of pain reduction.

13. Describe the phenomenon of stress-induced analgesia.

14. Describe evidence suggesting that stress-induced analgesia is mediated at least partly by endorphins.

15. Can pain be reduced through the power of belief or faith? Explain.

16. What do endorphins have to do with placebo-induced pain reduction?

Hearing   (pages 245–254)

CONSIDER these questions before you go on. They are designed to help you start thinking about this subject, not to test your knowledge.

Where in the ear does the neural response to sound occur?

What causes deafness? Why does a hearing aid help some people with impaired hearing and not others?

What makes some sounds high, such as those of a piccolo, and others low, such as those of a tuba? What makes them loud or soft?

READ this section of your text lightly. Then go back and read thoroughly, completing the Workout as you proceed.

As in every sensory system, hearing is specialized to respond to a particular type of stimulation. To understand this sense, you must understand the nature of its stimulus—sound waves. (See Figure 7.11 on text page 245.)

1. Sound occurs when an object produces _____ of the air or some other medium, which can be described in terms of _____ with a given height and rate of movement.

2. We experience the intensity, or _____, of the sound (measured in _____) as _____.

3. The rate at which a sound wave travels is called its _____ and is measured in units called _____. This aspect of the sound stimulus corresponds to what we hear as _____. Humans hear sounds varying from 20 up to _____.

4. Most natural sounds are more complex than a(n) _____ tone, which is a constant-frequency wave of vibration that can be described as a sine wave. Natural sounds include vibrations at several _____ at once.

To understand the sense of hearing, you must also know something about the parts of the ear. The ear is commonly divided into three major sections, each with its own functions. (See Figure 7.12 on text page 247.)

5. The outer ear, which consists of the _____ and the _____, is separated from the middle ear by the _____, which is also called the _____. The function of the outer ear is to _____ sound inward.

6. The middle ear contains the _____ (more specifically called the _____, _____, and _____), which essentially transfer vibration from the eardrum to the much smaller _____ window. The middle ear's main function is to increase the _____ that sound waves exert on the inner ear.

7. Identify and describe the following parts of the inner ear. (See Figures 7.13 on text page 248.)

    a. cochlea

    b. basilar membrane

    c. hair cells

    d. tectorial membrane

    e. auditory nerve

8. Briefly describe the process of transduction in the inner ear.

Two types of deafness can occur, each stemming from a different physiological problem.

9. What problem underlies conduction deafness? Is there any help for this problem? Explain.

10. What problem underlies sensorineural deafness? What kind of device can help this problem? How much help can the best devices provide?

A major task for scientists studying sensation is to understand how the nervous system codes various aspects of the stimulus. In the study of hearing, interest has centered on how frequency is coded to produce the experience of pitch. A key idea is that of the traveling wave.

11. How does the ear code various frequencies to allow pitch perception, according to Georg von Békésy? (See Figure 7.14 on text page 250.)

12. Has subsequent research confirmed Békésy's hypothesis? What has been revealed about the inner row of hair cells?

13. Explain how Békésy's traveling-wave hypothesis partially accounts for asymmetry in auditory masking. (See Figure 7.15 on text page 251.)

14. How does his hypothesis fit with the fact that aging reduces sensitivity to higher frequencies more than to lower frequencies?

15. Explain how the timing of activity in the basilar membrane plays a role in pitch perception of sounds below about 4000 Hz.

Information delivered to the brain by auditory sensory neurons receives extensive processing in the auditory cortex.

16. What does it mean to say that neurons in the primary auditory cortex are tonotopically organized? Is the arrangement totally determined by heredity?

Imagine you were hiking and heard a threatening rattle. It would certainly be a good idea not to come closer to that sound source. Our ability to discern where sounds are coming from is clearly important—so important that we are born with it. It even helps in ways that may not be obvious, such as mentally separating the conversation we want to listen to from the other conversations at a restaurant.

17. Localization of sounds depends in large part on the relative _____ of the sound waves reaching the two ears. Sound from a source directly in front of us will be received _____ by the two ears, but sound coming from slightly farther to the left will arrive at the _____ ear sooner than it will arrive at the other ear, with the difference ranging from a few to about 700 _____.

18. Describe neurons in a way station of the auditory system that might respond differentially based on such timing differences.

Beyond the primary auditory area, the cortex contains neurons specialized for analyzing patterns of auditory input. It is these patterns that allow us to extract meaning from sounds despite variations in pitch or loudness, for example.

19. Briefly, what are some of these cortical neurons specialized to respond to?

Our auditory system, under some circumstances, creates the compelling impression that we have heard something that was not physically present.

20. Describe the phenomenon of phonemic restoration. Why might the auditory system produce this effect?

Psychophysics   (pages 255–260)

CONSIDER these questions before you go on. They are designed to help you start thinking about this subject, not to test your knowledge.

What's the smallest amount of light a person can see? the smallest amount of sound a person can hear?

Are any general psychophysical relationships pretty much the same for everyone? Or is everyone so different that a scientific law would be impossible to establish?

Why does changing lighting from a 50- to a 100-watt bulb make a bigger difference in brightness than changing from a 150- to a 200-watt bulb?

READ this section of your text lightly. Then go back and read thoroughly, completing the Workout as you proceed.

Psychophysics involves the relationship between physical characteristics of a stimulus and the psychological experiences that it produces. The physical characteristics of the stimulus can be measured directly but experience must be measured indirectly, generally by asking subjects to make some sort of judgment. One major psychophysical question is: What is the weakest stimulus that can be detected in a particular sensory system, for example, vision?

1. What does the term *absolute threshold* refer to?

A second question asked by psychophysicists is: How different must two stimuli be in order to be noticeably different?

2. What is a difference threshold, or jnd?

3. Express Weber's law as a formula, defining each element. Now state the same law verbally. Give an example to illustrate the law.

Another major interest in psychophysics has been the way sensation increases with increasing stimulus intensity. Gustav Fechner in the nineteenth century and S. S. Stevens in the twentieth century both produced elegant mathematical descriptions of this relationship.

4. On what theoretical unit did Fechner base his law? What important assumption did he make about this unit?

5. State Fechner's law mathematically. According to Fechner, to what is the magnitude of the sensory experience proportional?

6. Why is it useful that the law involves a logarithmic relationship?

Stevens went on to do what Fechner believed could not be done: He tested the validity of Fechner's work experimentally.

7. Describe the subject's task in Stevens's method of magnitude estimation.

8. If Fechner's law were correct, what relationship should Stevens have found in his subjects' magnitude estimations? What did he find instead?

9. What kind of mathematical relationship best describes Stevens's results?

10. Is the exponent (p) greater or less than 1 for most of the various types of stimuli Stevens investigated? When p is less than 1, does a given increase in stimulus intensity produce equal sensory effects at the high and low ends of the scale? Explain. What about cases in which p is greater than 1?

11. Why did Stevens think nature would produce senses that follow power laws?

12. What advantage does Stevens's law offer compared with Fechner's law?

Be sure to READ the Concluding Thoughts at the end of the chapter. Note important points in your Workout. Then consolidate your learning by answering the focus questions in the margins of the text.

After you have studied the chapter thoroughly, CHECK your understanding with the Self-Test that follows.

Self-Test 1

Multiple-Choice Questions

1 The basic sequence of events in sensation is (1) physical stimulus → (2) physiological response → (3) sensory experience. Psychophysics is concerned with:

   a. only 2.
   b. the relationship between 1 and 3.
   c. the relationship between 2 and 3.
   d. the relationships among 1, 2, and 3.

2. There is a limited number of basic taste sensations and types of receptors. They are:

   a. sweet, salty, and sour.
   b. sweet, salty, sour, and umami.
   c. sweet, salty, sour, bitter, and umami.
   d. sweet, salty, sour, bitter, and creamy.

3. The main function of the ear's ossicles is to:

   a. simplify sound waves so as to reduce the processing needed.
   b. decrease the pressure of sound waves before they reach the delicate inner ear.
   c. increase the pressure that incoming sound waves place on the inner ear.
   d. lower the frequency of incoming sound waves to reduce wear and tear on the auditory nerve.

4. Békésy found that high-frequency sounds cause:

   a. the basilar membrane to vibrate equally over its whole length.
   b. the basilar membrane to vibrate maximally near its proximal end (near the oval window).
   c. the basilar membrane to vibrate maximally near its distal end (farthest from the oval window).
   d. the two ends of the basilar membrane to vibrate more than the middle.

5. Conduction deafness occurs when the _____ become(s) rigid.

   a. basilar membrane   **c.** hair cells
   b. tectorial membrane   **d.** ossicles

6. Which of the following statements is true of stress-induced analgesia?

   a. It is at least partially the result of endorphins in the brain.
   b. It is purely psychological and unrelated to physiological mechanisms of pain.
   c. It has not been found to occur under controlled laboratory conditions.
   d. It occurs in humans but not in other animals.

7. Sally smells a great cup of coffee being delivered to her table. The transduction necessary for that sensory experience to take place occurs in her:

   a. vomeronasal organ.
   b. olfactory bulb.
   c. glomeruli.
   d. olfactory epithelium.

8. Glomeruli are located:

   a. in the olfactory epithelium.
   b. in the olfactory bulb.
   c. on the tongue and soft palate.
   d. in the vomeronasal organ.

9. Jaclyn wonders why she can barely detect the perfume she puts on in the morning once a couple of hours has passed. You explain that it's due to:

   a. qualitative coding.
   b. adaptation.
   c. transduction.
   d. a placebo effect.

10. Bitterness sensitivity is greater in:

   a. men than in women.
   b. women than in men.
   c. old people than in younger adults.
   d. adults than in young children.

11. The amplitude of a sound is:

   a. a dimension of psychological sensation rather than of the physical stimulus.

b. related to what the hearer experiences as loudness.

c. the rate at which the sound waves are traveling.

d. measured in units called hertz.

12. Which of the following is true of pain receptors?

a. They are the same ones used for touch and temperature.

b. They are found only in the skin and joints.

c. They are specialized endings of the pain sensory neurons.

d. They are short, thick neurons with special encapsulated endings.

13. Research on mice has shown that they prefer to mate with opposite-sex mice that:

a. smell most like themselves.

b. smell most different from themselves.

c. have the least amount of body odor.

d. have the greatest amount of body odor.

14. The strong association we experience between smells and emotional/motivational states is supported anatomically by connections between the:

a. vomeronasal organ and the somatosensory cortex.

b. vomeronasal organ and the amygdala.

c. glomeruli and the limbic system and hypothalamus.

d. glomeruli and the frontal lobes.

15. Suppose that in a room with 20 lit candles, we must add 2 to get a jnd. How many would Weber's law say we have to add to a set of 100 candles to get a jnd?

a. 2

b. 5

c. 10

d. 20

Essay Questions

16. What are three different aspects of our conscious pain experience? With which brain areas are they associated?

17. What is the phonemic restoration effect and what does it illustrate about hearing?

After you have assessed your understanding on the basis of Self-Test 1 and have tried to strengthen your preparation in any areas of weakness, GO ON to Self-Test 2.

Self-Test 2

Multiple-Choice Questions

1. The PAG (periaqueductal gray):

a. serves to inhibit pain when activated.

b. is responsible for localizing pain.

c. reduces pain when it is inhibited.

d. gives pain its motivational and emotional facets.

2. The process by which a receptor cell produces electrical changes in response to a physical stimulus is called:

a. sensory adaptation.

b. coding.

c. perception.

d. transduction.

3. Each of the glomeruli receives olfactory input from _____ of the _____ types of olfactory sensory neurons.

a. all; 400   **c.** all; 75

b. one; 400   **d.** one; 75

4. A higher tone cannot mask a lower tone very effectively because:

a. the basilar membrane vibrates more intensely for lower tones than for higher ones.

b. the area of the basilar membrane that responds to high tones is completely separate from the area that responds to low tones.

   c. the part of the basilar membrane that responds to low tones extends well beyond the part that responds to higher tones.

   d. our ears are insensitive to higher frequencies.

5. Which of the following demonstrates the fact that pain does not always originate from stimulation of pain receptors?

   a. belief-induced analgesia

   b. gate-control theory of pain

   c. endorphins

   d. phantom-limb pain

6. The major histocompatibility complex is used by mice to help them "sniff out" potential mates that are:

   a. most genetically different from themselves.

   b. most genetically similar to themselves.

   c. maximally receptive to sex at a given time.

   d. already carrying the offspring of another mouse.

7. Which category of taste receptors is key to avoiding the ingestion of harmful substances:

   a. sweet.   c. umami.

   b. bitter.   d. salty.

8. Pain is:

   a. one of the somatosenses.

   b. an emotion.

   c. a drive.

   d. all of the above.

9. In the sensory system for pain, A-delta fibers are:

   a. relatively fast-conducting.

   b. activated by chemical changes in damaged tissue.

   c. associated with diffuse, lasting pain.

   d. the receptive endings for C fibers.

10. Pauletta feels refreshed and happy whenever she smells freshly-mown grass. Her emotional response to the smell stimulus involves activity in these parts of her olfactory system (in order):

   a. glomeruli, olfactory bulb, limbic system

   b. olfactory epithelium, limbic system, temporal cortex

   c. olfactory bulb, olfactory epithelium, prefrontal cortex

   d. olfactory epithelium, glomeruli, limbic system

11. Results of research done on human mothers and their newborn babies suggest that:

   a. the mothers generally could not identify their own babies based on smell alone.

   b. the infants showed no sign of recognizing their mothers based on smell alone.

   c. smell is critical to mother-infant bonding.

   d. bonding between mothers and infants involves odor among a number of other stimuli.

12. The _____ is (are) found in the inner ear and contain(s) the _____.

   a. cochlea; ossicles

   b. basilar membrane; cochlea

   c. cochlea; basilar membrane

   d. ossicles; tympanic membrane

13. Which of the following allows us to calculate the jnd for a given stimulus magnitude?

   a. Fechner's law   c. Stevens's law

   b. Weber's law   d. none of the above

14. The function of the outer ear is to:

   a. vibrate in response to incoming sound waves.

   b. transduce sound.

   c. increase the frequency of incoming sound waves.

   d. funnel soundwaves inward.

15. Which law relates sensory magnitude to stimulus magnitude in a way that compresses large physical changes down to smaller sensory changes?

   a. Fechner's logarithmic law

   b. Stevens's power law

   c. both a and b

   d. neither a nor b

Essay Questions

16. Describe the theoretical concepts necessary to explain the full range of our ability to discriminate pitch.

17. What are endorphins? How do they have their effect? What evidence suggests that they are involved in stress-induced analgesia?

5. pinna; auditory canal; eardrum; tympanic membrane; funnel

6. ossicles; hammer; anvil; stirrup; oval; pressure

17. timing; simultaneously; left; microseconds

Self-Test 1

1. **b.** (p. 255)

2. **c.** (p. 237)

3. **c.** (p. 247)

4. **b.** Békésy found that the effects of sounds of various frequencies differ in the total area of the basilar membrane stimulated and in the place of maximal vibration. For example, low sounds produce vibration in a larger portion of the membrane and also produce peak vibration nearer the distal tip. (pp. 249–250)

5. **d.** (p. 248)

6. **a.** (pp. 243–244)

7. **d.** Since the receptors for smell are located in the olfactory epithelium, transduction necessarily occurs there. (p. 230)

8. **b.** And the olfactory bulb is in the brain. (p. 231)

9. **b.** (p. 229)

10. **b.** (p. 238)

11. **b.** Amplitude is the physical dimension of sound related to the psychological dimension of loudness. Frequency is the physical dimension of sound related to the psychological dimension of pitch. (pp. 245–246)

12. **c.** (p. 240)

13. **b.** (p. 234)

14. **c.** (p. 231)

15. **c.** Weber believed that the amount that must be added to the original stimulus to produce a jnd was a constant proportion of the original stimulus. So, if we had to add 2 to 20, the proportion would be 1/10. This proportion would also apply to 100 candles. Thus, we would need to add 1/10 of 100, or 10. (p. 256)

Answers

Introduction AND *Overview of Sensory Processes*

1. physical stimulus; physiological response; sensory experience

Smell

2. molecules; evaporate; olfactory epithelium; 6 million; receptor

5. olfactory bulb; glomeruli; 400; thousand

Taste

3. sweet, salty, sour, bitter

Pain

3. free nerve endings; all parts of the body

6. phantom-limb pain

Hearing

1. vibrations; waves

2. amplitude; decibels; loudness

3. frequency; hertz; pitch; 20,000 hertz

4. pure; frequencies

16. Our psychological experience of pain involves several different aspects. The immediate emotion and motivation we feel to escape the pain depends on the limbic system, specifically the cingulate cortex and the insular cortex. Our ability to perceive the sensation of pain in the first place is due to the somatosensory cortex which is located in the parietal lobe. A third aspect of pain is cognitive in nature. We may worry about the future or about the meaning of the pain. The prefrontal lobes are essential to this aspect of pain experience. (pp. 240–241)

17. The phonemic restoration effect is basically an auditory illusion. Richard Warren found that if he spliced out a phoneme (an individual vowel or consonant sound) from a word in a sentence and replaced it with noise, subjects believed they could hear the missing phoneme even after listening repeatedly. The missing sound subjects think they hear can be manipulated by the surrounding phonemes and the meaning of the sentence. Subjects will hear something that fits. This effect illustrates the fact that sensory input is processed and even modified for the purpose of extracting meaning. (pp. 253–254)

Self-Test 2

1. **a.** The PAG, when it is activated, blocks the progress of pain messages at the point where they would enter the central nervous system. (p. 242)

2. **d.** (p. 228)

3. **b.** But each glomerulus receives input from thousands of sensory neurons of that single type. (p. 231)

4. **c.** One tone masks another when the wave it sets up in the basilar membrane interferes with the wave set up by the masked tone. Higher tones affect only the near portion of the basilar membrane. Therefore, they cannot disrupt the distal area of the membrane as it responds to low tones. (pp. 249–250)

5. **d.** (p. 241)

6. **a.** (p. 234)

7. **b.** (p. 238)

8. **d.** (p. 239)

9. **a.** Alternatives **b** and **c** describe C fibers, not A-delta fibers. (p. 240)

10. **d.** (pp. 231–234)

11. **d.** (p. 233)

12. **c.** (p. 247)

13. **b.** (p. 256)

14. **d.** (pp. 246–247)

15. **c.** However, only Stevens's power law preserves the constancy of stimulus ratios. (pp. 256–257)

16. Two kinds of theories of pitch discrimination are necessary. Békésy's traveling-wave theory suggests that sounds produce traveling waves in the basilar membrane, with different frequencies traveling different distances and having maximal effects in different areas. The waves produced by high frequencies create maximal vibration in the near, or proximal, portion of the basilar membrane and travel no farther. Lower frequencies produce waves that travel farther and peak toward the distal end. The brain can then interpret sounds as higher or lower depending on the location of the most rapid firing. For sounds below 4000 Hz which includes most human speech, the *timing* of the activity in the basilar membrane also determines the pitch we hear. Basically, frequency of firing in the auditory neurons will match the frequency of the incoming stimulus. (pp. 249–252)

17. Endorphins are chemicals produced by the body that play an important role in pain reduction. They behave much like drugs such as morphine. In fact they are so named because they are *endogenous, morphine*-like substances. We believe endorphins reduce pain by stimulating the PAG, a site also responsive to morphine. Activation of the PAG inhibits pain signals at the point where they enter the central nervous system. Endorphins are also thought to act in the spinal cord and lower brain stem where pain neurons enter. Experimental evidence that endorphins mediate the phenomenon of stress-induced analgesia comes from a study of rats that were shocked and were then shown to be insensitive to pain for a short time after. Rats that had been given a drug that blocked either the action or release of endorphins did not show any such analgesic effect of stress. (pp. 242–244)

The Psychology of Vision

chapter 8

READ the introduction below before you read the chapter in the text.

The discussion of vision begins with a description of the basic workings of the eye. The retina, the part of the eye that includes the receptor cells capable of responding to light, contains two types of visual receptors—rods and cones—each underlying a kind of visual subsystem with particular strengths and weaknesses. The rods enable us to see in very dim light, but we must rely on the cones to see color and fine detail.

Color vision involves neural mechanisms that code information provided by the light stimulus. It is the wavelength of light that color vision depends on. Three types of photoreceptors are differentially sensitive to the various wavelengths. Color vision also involves an opponent process (push-pull) mechanism that causes some phenomena not explainable otherwise.

The next section concerns our ability to see form and pattern. It begins by discussing how the visual system enhances contrast for sharper vision and how the brain processes information about visual features. It concludes by presenting evidence for two visual pathways in the brain— a "what" pathway for identifying objects and a "where" pathway for locating objects. At the most elementary level of the stimulus are primitive parts called features, such as lines, angles, or color. The chapter introduces work by several theorists who focus on different levels of form. Ann Treisman, for example, concentrates on the early process of detecting and combining simple features. Gestalt theorists emphasize whole forms. Wholes can even influence the perception of parts through a process called unconscious inference. This is a top-down process in which the brain tries to figure out what it is experiencing—in this case, what it is seeing—based on neural activity in higher areas of the brain. Top-down processes interact with bottom-up processes that bring in stimulus information.

A primary goal of the visual system is to recognize objects—to permit us to know whether we're seeing a bird, a teacup, or a bridge. Beyond the primary visual cortex are two anatomically and functionally different visual pathways. The "what" pathway is critical to identification of objects. The "where-and-how" pathway is necessary for locating objects in space and guiding interaction with them. Object recognition appears to involve a level of form intermediate between features and wholes. Irving Biederman has advanced a theory about recognizing objects based on such component parts. Context and even movement can affect object recognition.

The chapter then turns to the three-dimensional perception of objects. We use various cues to help us make determinations about depth and size. For example, binocular disparity—the slight difference in the views our two eyes receive—is a major cue to depth. In general, the closer an object is, the more different the two views will be. Many other depth cues are available to us. Some can even be used to create the impression of depth in a two-dimensional scene such as a painting. In some cases, the study of spatial aspects of perception has progressed by means of studying visual illusions. For example, psychologists have gained a better understanding of how we perceive size by studying errors in judgment. A case in point is the moon illusion, in which the moon looks much larger near the horizon than high in the sky, even though the size of the retinal image cast by the moon remains the same. Theorists try to explain this and other systematic errors in spatial perception not just to uncover the reasons for the illusions but to reveal something about the normal mechanisms of perception. Unconscious inference is a major theoretical concept in this area of research.

LOOK over the table of contents for this chapter in your textbook before you continue with your study.

Notice that there are focus questions in the margins of the text for your use in studying the material. The following chart lists which Study Guide questions relate to which focus questions.

Focus Questions	Study Guide Questions
Introduction and How the Eye Works	
1	1
2–4	2–4
5	5–9
6	10
Seeing Colors	
7	1
8	2
9	3
10	4
11	5–8
12	9–10
13	11
Seeing Forms and Patterns	
14	1–2
15	3–4
16	5–7
17	8–9
18	10–13
19	14–16
20	17–18
21	19–20
22	21
Recognizing Objects	
23	2
24	3–5
25–26	6–8
27–28	9–11
29	12
30	13
Seeing in Three Dimensions	
31	1
32	2
33	3
34	4–5
35	6
36	7
37	8–10

The Integrated Study Workout

COMPLETE one section at a time.

Introduction AND How the Eye Works
(pages 263–268)

CONSIDER these questions before you go on. They are designed to help you start thinking about this subject, not to test your knowledge.

Which part of the eye is able to respond to light? What do the other parts do?

When you enter a dark, crowded movie theater, you may be unable to see the bucket of popcorn in your hand; yet, moments later, you see well enough to find an unoccupied seat. Why is that?

READ this section of your text lightly. Then go back and read thoroughly, completing the Workout as you proceed.

Most species—even single-celled organisms—have some light sensitivity because such sensitivity is highly adaptive. But the rudimentary photoreceptors of, say, an earthworm are a far cry from the refined visual system of a human being.

1. How might eyes like ours have evolved?

Some parts of the eye are designed for responding to light with neural signals. Others are designed for focusing the light on the cells that are light sensitive.

2. Match the parts of the eye with their descriptions. (See Figure 8.1 on text page 264.)

_____ A doughnut-shaped ring of muscle fibers that opens or closes to control the amount of light entering the eye

_____ Transparent tissue at the front of the eye with a curved surface that begins to focus incoming light

_____ A thin membrane at the back of the eye's interior that contains vision receptors

a. pupil
b. retina
c. cones
d. lens
e. fovea
f. rods
g. iris
h. cornea
i. optic nerve

____ A hole that admits light into the eye

____ A structure that carries visual information from the eye to the brain and causes a blind spot where it leaves the eye

____ A tiny retinal area specialized for high visual acuity

____ A flexible structure that can become rounder or flatter to focus on objects at different distances

____ Type of receptor cell that permits sharply focused color vision in bright light

____ Type of receptor cell that permits vision in dim light

3. Briefly describe the process of transduction in vision.

Rods and cones underlie two separate but coordinated systems that together allow us to see over an enormous range of light intensities.

4. Describe the difference between these two systems by filling in the table that follows.

	Rods (scotopic vision)	Cones (photopic vision)
Sensitivity to light		
Acuity		
Color vision capability		
Distribution over retina		

In light adaptation, the eyes become less sensitive; in dark adaptation, they become more sensitive. This is due primarily to changes in the photochemicals inside rods and cones and shifting between rod and cone vision.

5. When do we undergo light adaptation? dark adaptation?

6. What happens to the photochemicals in rods and cones in bright light?

7. State one reason that cones are more sensitive than rods in bright light.

8. What happens to the photochemicals in rods and cones in darkness?

9. In what sense is dark adaptation a two-part process? (See Figure 8.5 on text page 267.)

Rods and cones send information on to bipolar cells, which in turn send information on to ganglion cells. The axons of ganglion cells form the optic nerve.

10. Using the concept of neural convergence, explain how the increased sensitivity and reduced acuity of rods are really two sides of the same coin. (See Figure 8.6 on text page 268.)

Seeing Colors   (pages 268–275)

CONSIDER these questions before you go on. They are designed to help you start thinking about this subject, not to test your knowledge.

How do we see color? Why are some people color-blind?

Why does mixing blue and yellow paint yield green?

READ this section of your text lightly. Then go back and read thoroughly, completing the Workout as you proceed.

The world we see is full of color. Our experience of color depends on the wavelengths of light reaching our eyes. An object absorbs some wavelengths from the light falling on it and reflects others, depending on its pigments. With vision as with hearing, it is necessary to understand the nature of the stimulus for which the sense is specialized.

1. Light, a form of _____ energy, can be thought of in terms of particles called _____. It can also be thought of in terms of _____, which provides the most useful perspective for understanding vision, especially color vision. Light varies in _____ from about 400 to 700 nanometres (nm). _____ light contains all visible wavelengths (and some that are not visible).

2. Answer the following questions about subtractive color mixing. (See Figure 8.8 on text page 270.)

   a. Subtractive color mixing involves mixing

      _____.

   b. Under what circumstances would the mixture appear green?

3. Answer the following questions about additive color mixing. (See Figure 8.9 on text page 270.) Also spend some time studying the standard chromaticity diagram in Figure 8.10 on text page 271.)

   a. Additive color mixing involves mixing

      _____.

   b. State the three-primaries law of color vision.

   c. State the law of complementarity.

   d. Why do we say that these two laws represent psychological, not physical, facts?

Two theories—the trichromatic and opponent-process theories—have been advanced to explain the behavioral and physiological aspects of color vision.

4. Explain the trichromatic theory developed by Thomas Young and later by Hermann Helmholtz. How well does this theory fit with the discovery of three types of cones? (See Figure 8.11 on text page 272.)

5. What is a dichromat?

6. Why is the most common type of dichromat more likely to be male than female?

7. What colors will a red-green color-blind person find hard to distinguish? Why? What is the prevalence of this disorder?

8. How does human color vision compare with that of cats and dogs? of birds?

The trichromatic theory of color vision doesn't explain everything as nicely as it does the three primaries law and certain types of color blindness.

9. What observation was Ewald Hering trying to explain with his opponent-process theory of color vision? What was Hering's explanation?

10. How does the opponent-process theory explain the complementarity of afterimages?

11. Are the trichromatic and opponent-process theories considered to be contradictory? Explain.

Seeing Forms and Patterns   (pages 276–286)

CONSIDER these questions before you go on. They are designed to help you start thinking about this subject, not to test your knowledge.

How does the brain process the signals it receives from the eye to give us such incredibly detailed and subtle views of the world?

Since the typical visual scene is full of many parts—lines, curves, textures—how do we know what goes with what?

Can anything other than the "objective facts" of a stimulus affect the way we perceive it?

READ this section of your text lightly. Then go back and read thoroughly, completing the Workout as you proceed.

Our visual system is designed to provide us with the information we need to survive. That entails the ability to identify objects. Though the fact that objects may differ in color or brightness helps, we also need information about contour to identify objects around us.

1. Define the term *contour*.

Contour is so important that the visual system enhances contrast to " sharpen" contours for us.

2. What is lateral inhibition and how does it serve to enhance contours? (See Figures 8.15 and 8.16 on text pages 276 and 277.)

We can think of the objects we see in terms of their elementary features, such as lines, curves, angles, movement, color, and so on. Using cats and monkeys as subjects, Hubel and Wiesel studied feature detectors in the primary visual area of the cortex. (See Figure 8.17 on text page 277.)

3. What was the basic procedure used by Hubel and Wiesel?

4. What did they discover about the preferential responding of neurons in the primary visual cortex? What has subsequent research added to their findings?

Of course, features must not only be detected. The visual system must also determine how various features fit together. Anne Treisman theorized about how they are picked up and integrated.

5. What is the essence of Treisman's feature-integration theory?

6. Name the two stages in Treisman's theory.

   stage 1: _____

   stage 2: _____

7. Distinguish between serial and parallel processing. When is feature processing serial and when is it parallel, according to Treisman? (See Figure 8.18 on text page 278.)

8. Describe the pop-out phenomenon that offers evidence supporting Treisman's theory. Be sure include not just anecdotal evidence but evidence from controlled experiments. (See Figure 8.19 o text page 279.)

9. What are illusory conjunctions, and why do the occur, according to Treisman? Describe the case of a man who was especially prone to them.

Gestalt psychologists were among those who took strong stand on the nature of perception in the earl twentieth century, and their influence has lasted. The emphasized the holistic nature of perception.

10. The Gestalt psychologists are responsible for well-known saying: "The whole is different from the sum of its parts." Explain this statement. Tr to produce an example that illustrates the point.

11. The German word *gestalt* means _____

    _____

12. Would Treisman and the Gestalt theorists neces sarily disagree? Explain.

Gestaltists believed that we tend innately to see certain principles of grouping to organize what we see.

3. Identify the following principles of grouping by writing the correct term in the blank provided. (See Figure 8.20 on text page 281.)

_____ **a.** Elements closer to one another are grouped together as part of the same object.

_____ **b.** When lines cross, line segments are put together perceptually so that smooth, unbroken lines are formed.

_____ **c.** Stimuli are perceptually organized in ways that maximize symmetry, simplicity, and predictability.

_____ **d.** Gaps in a form's border are ignored.

_____ **e.** Like objects are grouped together, separate from unlike objects.

_____ **f.** Stimuli moving in the same direction at the same rate are seen as part of a single object.

The Gestalt psychologists also pointed out our tendency to automatically divide a scene into a more important part (the object to which we attend) and a less important part (the background). (See Figures 8.21 and 8.22 on text page 282.)

14. The object to which we attend is called the _____, while the rest of the scene is the _____.

15. This automatic process is guided by certain cues in the stimulus. For example, _____ is a cue that will cause a surrounded form to be seen as the _____ and the surrounding form as the _____.

16. When cues are insufficient, figure and ground may exchange roles, sometimes at the will of the perceiver. This is what occurs in _____ figures.

The visual system's orientation toward whole, organized patterns and objects is so strong that we may perceive wholes where they do not physically exist.

17. In the visual stimulus above, you may see a white triangle even though there is no continuous edge outlining this "triangular" area. This phenomenon is called _____.

18. How is this type of phenomenon explained by way of unconscious inference?

19. What are illusory lightness differences?

20. Can illusory lightness differences be adequately explained in terms of simple lateral inhibition? How might unconscious inference explain the effect?

21. Distinguish between top-down and bottom-up control processes. In which category would unconscious inference fall?

Recognizing Objects   (pages 286–292)

CONSIDER *these questions before you go on. They are designed to help you start thinking about this subject, not to test your knowledge.*

How do we decide whether the object we're looking at is a tree, a trumpet, or a teapot?

Does anything other than the object itself affect the process of identifying it?

READ *this section of your text lightly. Then go back and read thoroughly, completing the Workout as you proceed.*

Most of us have normal visual perception. And most of us take our ability to recognize objects for granted.

1. What is object recognition?

Ungerleider and Mishkin proposed an influential theory suggesting that visual processing areas outside the primary area are organized along two rather distinct pathways or streams—a "what" pathway and a "where" pathway. The "where" pathway is called the "where-and-how" pathway in the text because of more recent discoveries about its functions.

2. Briefly characterize and locate the two pathways. (See Figure 8.28 on text page 287.)

3. What is visual agnosia? Where is the damage that produces this type of deficit?

4. Distinguish between the following forms of visual agnosia.

   a. visual form agnosia

   b. visual object agnosia

5. How does the existence of these two forms of visual agnosia shed light on the visual perception of an object?

6. What could D.F. do despite having severe visual form agnosia due to damage in the "what" pathway? What does that indicate?

7. What abilities are disrupted by damage in the "where-and-how" pathway?

8. How are the two visual pathways normally related?

rving Biederman's theory of object recognition proposes that there is a level of structure between the kind of primitive features that Treisman has studied and whole, real-world objects like faces, houses, or flowers. Using components at this intermediate level of form helps to simplify the job of perception, according to Biederman.

9. Explain the basic idea behind Biederman's recognition-by-components theory.

10. Define the term *geons*. What role do they play in perception?

11. Briefly describe two pieces of evidence that support Biederman's theory.

The identification of objects is also affected by context and even by the object's movement.

12. Explain how context can contribute to top-down processes in object recognition.

13. Summarize Gunnar Johansson's research on the role of stimulus movement in perception.

Seeing in Three Dimensions   (pages 292–300)

CONSIDER these questions before you go on. They are designed to help you start thinking about this subject, not to test your knowledge.

Why does a person who has the use of only one eye, perhaps because of blindness or having to wear an eyepatch, find it harder to perceive depth?

Why is the experience of depth partly missing in paintings, photographs, and movies? On the other hand, what allows them to give as much of an impression of depth as they do?

Can the eye be fooled in judging such things as size?

READ this section of your text lightly. Then go back and read thoroughly, completing the Workout as you proceed.

As modern psychologists have attempted to understand how we manage to perceive the visual world, they have found Helmholtz's nineteenth-century notions about unconscious inferences consistently valuable.

1. Briefly refresh your memory about the concept of unconscious inference.

The retina directly represents only two dimensions—an up-down dimension and a side-to-side dimension. Where do we get the information that allows us to see depth? The answer lies in a variety of depth cues that fall into two categories—binocular cues and monocular cues. Binocular cues require both eyes, but monocular cues are available even when we're depending on one eye.

2. Define the following two binocular depth cues, making sure to note which is more important.

   a. eye convergence

   b. binocular disparity

3. What is stereopsis? How is this ability exploited to create illusions of depth in a stereoscope?

Motion parallax is an important monocular depth cue that is present only when one is moving through real three-dimensional space.

4. Define motion parallax in general terms. Now describe a specific scene in which a person has a clear experience of motion parallax and a consequent sense of depth.

5. How is motion parallax similar to binocular disparity?

Unlike motion parallax, most monocular depth cues can help to convey a sense of depth in the two-dimensional realm of pictures. Monocular cues that function in this way are called pictorial cues for depth.

6. Name the monocular due represented in each of the following descriptions. (See Figure 8.37 on text page 296.)

   _____ a. A tree appears closer to the horizon than the house it shades and thus looks farther away.

   _____ b. Railroad tracks appear to get closer and closer together with increasing distance.

   _____ c. The bricks in a campus sidewalk look smaller, more densely packed together and less defined the farther away they are.

   _____ d. A person sees a car and a billboard and, because the retinal image of the car is bigger, the car appears closer.

   _____ e. A vase in the middle of a table is partially hidden by a hat, so we see the hat as being closer to us.

   _____ f. A photograph shows two people side-by-side. The eyes of one appear deep-set, sunken in shadow whereas the other has eyes that appear to protrude with only a hint of shadow.

The perception of an object's size is closely related to the perception of distance.

7. What is size constancy? How can distance cues sometimes play a part in promoting or interfering with size constancy? (See Figures 8.39 and 8.40 on text page 297.)

Psychologists have often tried to understand size perception by seeking to explain size illusions. One proposed explanation for a number of size illusions is that we unconsciously process depth cues that then lead us to erroneous conclusions—a view known as depth-processing theory.

8. Briefly describe the following size illusions or draw a rough sketch of each, as you prefer. (See various illustrations on text pages 298 and 299.)

   a. Müller-Lyer illusion

b. Ponzo illusion

Be sure to READ the Concluding Thoughts at the end of the chapter. Note important points in your Workout. Then consolidate your learning by answering the focus questions in the margins of the text.

c. moon illusion

After you have studied the chapter thoroughly, CHECK your understanding with the Self-Test that follows.

Self-Test 1

Multiple-Choice Questions

9. How does the depth-processing theory explain the following illusions?
   a. Ponzo illusion

   b. Müller-Lyer illusion

   c. moon illusion

1. Anne Treisman has proposed that there are two different steps in feature processing—first _____ and then _____.
   a. feature detection, which involves parallel processing; feature integration, which involves serial processing
   b. feature detection, which involves serial processing; feature integration, which involves parallel processing
   c. feature integration, which involves parallel processing; feature detection, which involves serial processing
   d. feature integration, which involves serial processing; feature detection, which involves parallel processing

2. In the retina, _____ synapse on _____, which in turn synapse on _____.
   a. rods; cones; ganglion cells
   b. rods and cones; ganglion cells; bipolar cells
   c. rods and cones; bipolar cells; ganglion cells
   d. ganglion cells; rods and cones; the optic nerve

10. Why is the depth-processing theory problematic as an explanation of those illusions? How do proponents defend the depth-processing explanation?

3. A biologist watches a group of twenty penguins moving toward the water for feeding. The group then splits into two groups, some moving to the left and some moving to the right. What Gestalt principle helps the biologist to perceive that there are two groups now instead of one?
   a. good continuation   **c.** good form
   b. similarity   **d.** common movement

4. In _____, figure and ground may switch roles.
   a. the Ponzo illusion
   b. illusory contours
   c. a reversible figure
   d. illusory conjunctions

5. Mark has suffered brain damage in a car accident. He now can manage to draw the shape of an object shown to him but can't identify the object. Mark appears to suffer from:
   a. visual form agnosia.
   b. visual object agnosia.
   c. damage to the "where-and-how" pathway.
   d. lateral inhibition.

6. Cells in the retina produce neural responses initiated by light, while the rest of the eye is designed primarily to:
   a. form an image on the retina.
   b. filter incoming light.
   c. transduce light.
   d. separate light into different wavelengths.

7. Which of the following is true of dark adaptation?
   a. It involves reduced sensitivity with increased time in the dark.
   b. It involves changes in cones as well as rods.
   c. It depends primarily on chemical changes in ganglion cells.
   d. It is due to the breakdown of photopigments in cones.

8. If we simultaneously view pictures of the same object taken from slightly different angles, looking at one picture with the left eye and the other with the right eye, we may see the object in depth. Our ability to perceive depth in this case depends on:
   a. occlusion.   c. binocular disparity.
   b. eye convergence.   d. pictorial cues.

9. When you're riding through the countryside, telephone poles appear to move by at a pretty fast clip; trees some distance from the road move more slowly; and hills in the distance pass by more slowly still. This experience is a product of:
   a. binocular disparity.
   b. linear perspective.
   c. occlusion.
   d. motion parallax.

10. The Ponzo and Müller-Lyer illusions are illusions of _____ that have been fairly well (but not perfectly) explained by _____ theory.
    a. color; depth-processing
    b. color; recognition-by-components
    c. size; depth-processing
    d. size; recognition-by-components

11. Which of the following statements is true of people with red-green color blindness?

    a. They may be completely unaware that they have defective color vision.
    b. They are more likely to be female than male.
    c. They have a defective or missing blue cone.
    d. They can distinguish only colors in the red-to-green part of the spectrum.

12. Circumscription is a major cue that helps us to:
    a. divide a scene into figure and ground.
    b. perceive depth.
    c. see color in bright illumination.
    d. avoid susceptibility to size illusions.

13. We tend to ignore gaps in the border of a form. The Gestalt psychologists called this tendency:
    a. good continuation.
    b. closure.
    c. proximity.
    d. similarity.

14. The notion that color vision is mediated by three different types of receptors is known as:
    a. the law of complementarity.
    b. the three-primaries law.
    c. additive color mixing.
    d. trichromatic theory.

15. Hubel and Wiesel showed visual stimuli to cats and monkeys while recording electrical activity in individual cells of their visual cortex. They were interested in discovering how the visual system accomplishes:
    a. transduction.
    b. adaptation.
    c. feature detection.
    d. depth perception.

Essay Questions

16. Present Biederman's recognition-by-components theory of object recognition. Cite one type of evidence in support of the theory.

7. What is the meaning of the Gestalt psychologists' statement that "the whole is different from the sum of its parts"? What is the status of the *whole* in the Gestalt conception of object perception?

After you have assessed your understanding on the basis of Self-Test 1 and have tried to strengthen your preparation in any areas of weakness, GO ON to Self-Test 2.

Self-Test 2

Multiple-Choice Questions

1. Eye convergence is:
   a. a monocular depth cue in which lines move closer together, thus giving an appearance of depth.
   b. a binocular depth cue in which we unconsciously rotate the eyes inward as we focus on an object.
   c. poorer for closer objects than for more distant ones.
   d. the most powerful binocular depth cue available to us.

2. If the time to locate a target increases in direct proportion to the number of distractors, this indicates that the perceiver is:
   a. doing serial processing, that is, attending to one item at a time.
   b. doing parallel processing, that is, attending to all items at the same time.
   c. doing parallel processing, that is, attending to one item at a time.
   d. doing serial processing, that is, attending to all items at the same time.

3. The Gestalt psychologists believed that we automatically and immediately perceive:
   a. features.
   b. whole patterns and objects.
   c. components.
   d. sometimes a, sometimes b, sometimes c.

4. When you see a highway sign for a deer crossing, the deer symbol is immediately perceived as the object of interest while the rest of the sign appears to exist as merely a backdrop behind the symbol. This exemplifies:
   a. illusory conjunctions.
   b. illusory contours.
   c. the figure-ground relationship.
   d. relative size.

5. In Biederman's theory of object perception, geons are:
   a. primitive features.
   b. complex whole shapes such as flowers and faces.
   c. basic geometric forms that can be combined to create more complex forms.
   d. irregular, almost random shapes.

6. Human color vision depends on _____ designated as red, _____, and _____.
   a. cones; blue; green.
   b. cones; yellow; blue.
   c. rods; blue; green.
   d. rods; yellow; blue.

7. Hubel and Wiesel discovered cells in the primary visual cortex that are maximally responsive to:
   a. bars or edges at specific orientations.
   b. roughly circular spots of light at specific locations on the retina.
   c. simple shapes such as circles and triangles.
   d. whole complex forms.

8. Which of the following statements is true of depth perception?
   a. It is possible only with two eyes.
   b. It is possible with one eye, but better with both eyes.
   c. It is equally good with both eyes or with just one.
   d. None of the above is true.

9. The wavelength of visible light ranges from about:
   a. 20 to 20,000 nm.   c. 100 to 1000 nm.
   b. 400 to 700 nm.   d. 700 to 1400 nm.

10. Which of the following statements regarding size perception is true?
    a. When we are dealing with familiar visual objects such as a car, a telephone, or a person, our previous knowledge of the object's size surprisingly plays no part in size perception.
    b. We can accurately judge the size of objects, familiar or unfamiliar, with or without cues to the object's distance.
    c. We judge size directly from the size of the retinal image, with a larger image meaning a larger object and a smaller image meaning a smaller object.
    d. We can perceive the size of even familiar objects incorrectly if distance cues mislead us.

11. Which of the following is better explained by the opponent-process theory than by the trichromatic theory of color vision?
    a. the three-primaries law
    b. red-green color blindness
    c. the complementarity of afterimages
    d. all of the above

12. Where in the visual system does transduction occur?
    a. ganglion cells   c. rods and cones
    b. optic nerve   d. lens

13. The "where-and-how" pathway of the visual system is found in the occipital lobe and the ___ lobe.
    a. prefrontal   c. parietal
    b. frontal   d. temporal

14. The trichromatic and opponent-process theories of color vision:
    a. are contradictory and have both been proved wrong by recent physiological data.
    b. are contradictory and only trichromatic theory is supported by physiological data.
    c. are contradictory and only opponent-process theory is supported by physiological data.
    d. are complementary and both have been supported by physiological data.

15. The visual system uses lateral inhibition in the retina to:
    a. reduce contrast.
    b. preserve exact levels of physical contrast.
    c. exaggerate contrast.
    d. accomplish all of the above under different levels of illumination.

Essay Questions

16. Compare rods and cones in terms of acuity and sensitivity. Explain how the concept of neural convergence can be used to help account for these differences.

17. What is motion parallax? Is it a monocular or binocular cue?

Answers

How the Eye Works

2. g; h; b; a; i; e; d; c; f

Seeing Colors

11. electromagnetic; photons; waves; wavelength; White

2. a. pigments

3. a. colored lights

Seeing Forms and Patterns

6. stage 1: feature detection; stage 2: feature integration

1. organized shape *or* whole form

3. **a.** proximity, **b.** good continuation, **c.** good form, **d.** closure, **e.** similarity, **f.** common movement

4. figure; ground

5. circumscription; figure; ground

6. reversible

7. illusory contours

Seeing in Three Dimensions

6. **a.** position relative to the horizon
   b. linear perspective
   c. texture gradient
   d. relative image size for familiar objects
   e. occlusion
   f. differential lighting of surfaces

Self-Test 1

1. **a.** According to Treisman, serial processing (as compared with parallel processing) is indicated when the time it takes to find a target increases proportionally with the number of distractors. (pp. 278–279)

2. **c.** Photoreceptors (rods and cones), bipolar cells, and ganglion cells essentially make up three different layers of the retina. (p. 267)

3. **d.** (p. 281)

4. **c.** (p. 282)

5. **b.** (p. 287)

6. **a.** (p. 264)

7. **b.** Dark adaptation involves increasing sensitivity with time in the dark. Improvement involves changes in cones but most improvement results from changes in the rods. (p. 266)

8. **c.** (p. 293)

9. **d.** Motion parallax and binocular disparity are somewhat related, but motion parallax arises because the two eyes of a stationary perceiver occupy different positions. Also note that motion parallax as described in the question could be experienced monocularly. (p. 295)

10. **c.** (p. 298)

11. **a.** People who are red-green color-blind are generally male because of the nature of the genetic transmission of the defect. Red-green color-blind people are one type of dichromat. The defective or missing cone is either a red or a green one; its absence produces abnormalities in the way these people see colors in the red-to-green part of the color spectrum. But because visual experience is private, they cannot compare their color vision directly with that of normal individuals and thus may not realize there is a problem. (pp. 272–273)

12. **a.** (p. 282)

13. **b.** (p. 281)

14. **d.** The three-primaries law is about color matching and is evidence for the trichromatic theory. (p. 272)

15. **c.** (p. 278)

16. Biederman suggests that when we recognize a three-dimensional object, we do so by first accomplishing an intermediate goal—the organization and recognition of simpler three-dimensional components. We then use the arrangement of those component shapes to recognize the whole object. Biederman argues that using a finite set of shapes such as these components simplifies the job of object recognition. The components, which he calls geons, function somewhat like an alphabet of form. Combining a few geons gives us a recognizable form just as combining a few letters gives us a recognizable word. One type of evidence for the theory is the existence of people with visual agnosias. These include people with visual form agnosia and visual object agnosia. People with visual form agnosia basically can't perceive the geons of an object. People with visual-object agnosia can perceive geons but can't combine them to recognize objects. (pp. 289–291)

17. When Gestalt psychologists said, "the whole is different from the sum of its parts," they meant something is added. The whole cannot be reduced to a catalog or a "line-up" of parts. It is an organization of those parts into a pattern or form that causes something new to emerge. In fact, the Gestalt psychologists believed the whole that is created by the arrangement of parts is the first thing we see when we perceive an object. To them, it is the primary—the most important—thing. They believed we are biologically designed to be

able to perceive incoming information in simple, holistic ways. Their principles of grouping were an attempt to specify the bases for this organized perception. (pp. 280–281)

Self-Test 2

1. **b.** The other binocular depth cue—binocular disparity—is much more important. (p. 293)

2. **a.** This makes sense because, for example, it takes twice as long to check 10 items serially (one item at a time) as it does to check 5. If parallel processing were being used, all 5 or all 10 items would be checked simultaneously and the number of items would not affect processing time. (p. 279)

3. **b.** (p. 280)

4. **c.** (p. 282)

5. **c.** (p. 289)

6. **a.** (p. 272)

7. **a.** (pp. 277–278)

8. **b.** It is possible with one eye, but without binocular disparity, we are lacking a powerful cue to depth. (pp. 292–293)

9. **b.** Remember that the visible spectrum is just a small part of the entire electromagnetic spectrum. (p. 268)

10. **d.** (p. 297)

11. **c.** (p. 274)

12. **c.** (pp. 264–265)

13. **c.** (p. 288)

14. **d.** (p. 275)

15. **c.** (pp. 276–277)

16. Rods are more sensitive than cones, but cones have higher acuity than rods do. Different levels of neural convergence help to produce both the sensitivity and the acuity difference. Neural convergence occurs when receptor cells feed information to a smaller number of sensory neurons. If many photoreceptors feed information to a single ganglion cell (which is done via bipolar cells) there is high convergence. This is typical of rods. By contrast, if only one or a few receptors feed information to a single ganglion cell, there is little or no convergence. This is typical of cones. With high convergence, a single ganglion cell will benefit from the combined sensitivity of a number of receptors. However, it will also lose acuity for the following reason. If only one receptor is feeding information to each ganglion cell, as with most cones, the distinct spatial layout of the stimulus can be preserved. For example, if ganglion cell X responds, it had to get its stimulation from receptor A. If there is high convergence, however, the ganglion cell's firing doesn't "tell" the brain as much about what spatial location on the retina was the source of that stimulation. So, a great deal of spatial detail is lost. (pp. 266–268)

17. Motion parallax is a depth cue that depends on the viewer's movement through space. As the viewer (specifically the viewer's eyes) move sideways relative to those things being viewed, the image of an object that is nearer changes more rapidly than that of an object farther away. For example, as a person walks down a city sidewalk, the parking meters that line the sidewalk appear to go past faster than the cars parked across the street; and the cars seem to move through the person's view faster than the trees in the park behind the cars. The smaller the amount of change in the view from moment to moment (that is, the slower the view seems to be changing) the farther away the object appears to be. Motion parallax is the most powerful of the monocular cues. (pp. 295–296)

Memory and Consciousness

chapter 9

READ *the introduction below before you read the chapter in the text.*

Memory holds a central place in cognitive psychology. All of our cognitive activities, such as reasoning, understanding, perceiving, planning—and indeed most of our physical activities, such as speaking, playing sports, or driving—depend on memory. The most influential and widely accepted theory of memory, the modal model, proposes that memory consists of sensory memory, working memory, and long-term memory, each with its own characteristics and functions. The model also describes control processes, which handle information within stores or transfer information from one store to another.

Sensory memory is the first component of the memory system in which incoming information is registered. It holds a good deal of information, but very briefly. Each sensory system has its own sensory store. Visual sensory memory, also called iconic memory, and auditory sensory memory, also called echoic memory, have received the most study.

A large array of stimuli are available to us at any given moment in the sensory stores but only some can be sent on to working memory via the control process called attention. Studies show that we can successfully focus attention on some incoming information, with the information not selected being barely noticed or recalled. However, we also monitor that unselected stream of information for potentially significant stimuli and can turn our attention to them. We can improve our attentional capacity with practice, but sometimes practicing a skill can cause it to become not only automatic but obligatory, as in the Stroop effect. Recent research has shed light on brain mechanisms underlying attentional phenomena.

Working, or short-term, memory is the component of memory in which conscious thought occurs. It is the main "workplace" of the mind. Information enters from either sensory or long-term memory. Working

memory is itself thought to consist of several components. Baddeley proposed that these are the phonological loop, the visuospatial sketch pad, and the central executive. Neuroimaging studies have shown that perceptual tasks, such as checking for a detail on a picture, may involve the same brain areas as purely mental tasks that are analogous, such as checking for a detail on a mental picture.

Long-term memory is the more permanent large-scale repository of knowledge. Information is stored there through the control process known as encoding. Long-term memory for information is best achieved through elaboration, which involves thinking about the information. Memory can be made more efficient through various organizational strategies. For example, by packaging information so that each item is a larger unit called a chunk, we can fit more information into memory. Techniques involving visualization, such as the mental walk, which visually associates to-be-remembered information with familiar places, can also help.

Retrieval is the process of accessing information in long-term memory. The effectiveness of retrieval cues depends on mental associations and the organization of long-term memory. As the chapter makes clear, remembering is not just the passive replaying of some sort of mental "tape." Rather, it is a constructive process in which retrieved information is pieced together and inferences are drawn. This constructive nature of memory is adaptive, but it also opens the door to potential distortion.

While the modal model described at the beginning of the chapter works well for explicit memory, it is not so useful for implicit memory. Explicit memory involves making the remembered information consciously available. Implicit memory, in contrast, influences perception, thought, or behavior without the stored information itself entering consciousness. Evidence for the existence of these two broad classes of memory—explicit and implicit—includes findings from neuropsychological research. Neuropsychological evidence also supports the difference between working memory and long-term memory as well as different types of explicit memory.

LOOK over the table of contents for this chapter in your textbook before you continue with your study.

Notice that there are focus questions in the margins of the text for your use in studying the material. The following chart lists which Study Guide questions relate to which focus questions.

The Integrated Study Workout

COMPLETE one section at a time.

Introduction AND *Overview: An Information-Processing Model of the Mind*   (pages 303–307)

CONSIDER these questions before you go on. They are designed to help you start thinking about this subject, not to test your knowledge.

What is memory?

How is it that a person can remember some information for a lifetime and forget other information seconds after acquiring it?

Are there different forms of memory?

How is memory related to consciousness?

READ this section of your text lightly. Then go back and read thoroughly, completing the Workout as you proceed.

Before outlining the theoretical model of memory that organizes most of the chapter—and most research on memory—the text clarifies some terms.

1. How is memory related to learning?

2. How is the term *consciousness* defined in the text?

The dominant theory of memory since the 1960s—the modal model of the mind—proposes that memory is made up of several interacting components. The model has led to intensive study of those proposed components, of their interactions, and of the very idea that memory is actually divided in such a fashion. Keep in mind as you study that the model is just that—a model—not reality itself. (See Figure 9.1 on text page 304.)

3. Broadly defined, what is memory?

4. What is a model in the context of cognitive psychology?

5. The term *modal* in "modal model of memory" simply means _____.

6. The three components of memory (or memory stores) proposed by the modal model are _____, _____, and _____ memory.

7. The modal model characterizes each component in terms of its _____, _____, and _____.

8. In general terms, what do control processes do? What are some specific examples?

9. Describe the nature and function of each of the memory stores. Be certain to make clear the differences among them.
   a. sensory memory

   b. working memory

   c. long-term memory

Information can move from one store to another by means of specific control processes.

10. Label each of the following with the control process being described:

   _____ a. is the control process that moves information from working memory into long-term memory.
   _____ b. is the control process that moves information from long-term memory into working memory.
   _____ c. is the control process that moves information from the sensory memory into working memory.

11. Why must attention restrict the flow of information?

12. Is encoding generally deliberate?

13. What do we commonly call retrieval? Is it deliberate or automatic?

Attention: The Portal to Consciousness
(pages 307–314)

CONSIDER these questions before you go on. They are designed to help you start thinking about this subject, not to test your knowledge.

What happens to the information we are not paying attention to?

Why do we have sensory memory?

Can we improve our attentional abilities?

READ this section of your text lightly. Then go back and read thoroughly, completing the Workout as you proceed.

We need the attentional system to accomplish two things. In a world full of stimuli, we need to focus attention on those that are relevant at present. But we must also be able to monitor the other stimuli rather than shutting them out entirely because we may need to or want to shift our attention to something in that category in the next moment.

1. Describe the general model of attention presented in the text. (See Figure 9.2 on text page 308.) Be sure to explain preattentive processing.

Psychologists have learned a good deal about focusing attention and ignoring irrelevant information from studies of selective listening. The typical experiment on selective listening is one in which a subject hears two tape-recorded messages at the same time and is asked to shadow one.

2. Describe the cocktail-party phenomenon.

3. What is shadowing?

4. According to early experiments, what affects the ease of shadowing? And what do people notice about the unattended message? Be specific.

Studies of selective viewing have provided findings analogous to those of selective-listening studies.

5. Describe a selective-viewing study and its results.

Sensory memory, which holds a brief trace of incoming sensory information, allows attention to be turned to stimuli that seem important. Auditory sensory memory is called echoic memory.

6. How might a typical experiment on echoic memory be done? What would the results likely show?

7. How are such results related to the finding that people generally noticed their own names in the unattended voice in a selective-listening study?

8. Is there corresponding evidence for iconic memory (visual sensory memory)? Provide evidence.

Some of the most practical findings in research on attention concern the effects of practice on our ability to process information.

9. What did a study involving video games demonstrate about this matter?

The existence of priming helps to emphasize a serious defect in the modal model—its failure to consider *unconscious* effects of sensory input.

10. What is priming?

11. Describe an experiment that provides evidence for priming of concepts in long-term memory without conscious awareness of the priming stimuli.

12. How might priming serve us in everyday life?

Though automatic, unconscious processing has obvious advantages, the Stroop interference effect illustrates a major disadvantage. In the Stroop technique, subjects are shown a series of stimuli, including color names, each printed in a particular ink color. For example, the word "blue" might be printed in red ink. (See Figure 9.6 on text page 313.)

13. Describe the subject's task in a Stroop experiment.

14. When are subjects slowest at performing that task?

15. What disadvantage of automaticity is illustrated by the Stroop interference effect? In other words, what causes the effect?

Advances in methods for studying the intact brain, such as fMRI, have permitted recent research on the brain mechanisms of attentive and preattentive processing.

16. What kind of brain activity occurs during unconscious, preattentive analysis of stimuli?

17. What effect does attention seem to have at a neural level?

18. Which brain areas have been found to be responsible for attentional shifts?

Working Memory: The Active, Conscious Mind
(pages 315–318)

CONSIDER these questions before you go on. They are designed to help you start thinking about this subject, not to test your knowledge.

If someone were to say a string of 11 digits to you, could you remember the string exactly?

When you are mentally repeating a phone number you've just looked up, what is happening in your memory?

What is a mental image? When we "look at" a mental picture of, say, our living room, is that anything like actually looking at our living room?

READ this section of your text lightly. Then go back and read thoroughly, completing the Workout as you proceed.

Just as memory in general is thought to involve separate but interacting components, so too is working memory thought to consist of such components. Alan Baddeley has proposed an influential theory of working memory that consists of three components—the phonological loop, the visuospatial sketch pad, and the central executive.

1. The phonological loop is responsible for

   _____ by means of

   _____.

2. Define *the span of short-term memory.*

3. Baddeley suggests that such measures as digit or word span are actually measuring the span of the phonological loop of working memory. Describe evidence that the span of short-term memory is related to subvocal repetition.

4. In everyday life, how might we utilize the phonological loop of working memory?

In working memory, we also deal with mental pictures of various kinds.

5. The visuospatial sketch pad is responsible for holding and potentially manipulating

   _____ and _____

   information.

6. Give three examples of tasks in which you might depend on the visuospatial sketch pad. Make sure at least one example is original and not from the text.

7. How did Stephen Kosslyn show that there is some similarity between examining a visual image and examining an actual picture? (See Figure 9.7 on text page 316.)

Neuroimaging studies and studies of people with specific types of brain damage have helped us to understand how mental performance of a task (such as subvocal speech) is like actual overt performance of the task (speech).

8. What do neuroimaging studies and cases of brain damage show about the brain areas involved in mental rehearsal of words?

9. Describe two types of evidence that the "what" and "where" visual pathways are also involved in mental imagery tasks.

Though most of this section has focused on the other two components of working memory, the central executive is extremely important.

10. The central executive is thought to be responsible for

    _____

    and _____.

    (Refer back to text page 315 if necessary.)

11. Which area of the brain is critically involved in the activity of the central executive component? How do we know?

Encoding Information into Long-Term Memory
(pages 319–326)

CONSIDER *these questions before you go on. They are designed to help you start thinking about this subject, not to test your knowledge.*

Why don't we remember everything we've ever noticed or thought about?

How can we improve our memory performance?

In what ways is an expert's memory different from a novice's?

READ *this section of your text lightly. Then go back and read thoroughly, completing the Workout as you proceed.*

One of the most interesting areas of research on memory—and one especially relevant to students—concerns the kind of processing that can help to encode information into long-term memory.

1. Have you had experiences like Edmund Sanford's that suggest repetition is just not enough to produce long-term memory? Explain.

2. The process by which information is held in short-term memory for a time is _____ rehearsal. The process of encoding information into the long-term store involves _____ rehearsal. Some of the most effective activities to accomplish the latter are _____, _____, and _____.

3. What is elaboration (or elaborative rehearsal)? What is its immediate goal? What is its "bonus" effect?

4. Briefly summarize three examples of experimental evidence from the laboratory and school settings that show that elaboration is valuable.

a.

b.

c.

5. How does your textbook author recommend you approach studying?

Organizing information—which requires elaboration, of course—is a useful strategy for increasing the effectiveness of memory. It helps to create connections among items that would otherwise be separate.

6. What is chunking? How and why is it related to memory efficiency?

7. How does chunking help to explain experts' outstanding memory for information in their particular field? Be sure to use the concept of long-term working memories.

8. What is hierarchical organization? Does this type of organization improve long-term memory performance? Explain.

Visualization has also been found to be an important aid to long-term memory.

9. Can visualization help us remember verbal information? Support your answer.

10. Why might visualization help?

11. What is the memory technique called the mental walk? Which possible explanation for the value of visualization does it support?

Evidence for the reality of distinctions between working- and long-term memory and between explicit and implicit memory is available from neuropsychological studies.

12. Who is H. M., and how does his case support a clear distinction between working and long-term explicit memory?

13. What evidence indicates that the hippocampus and nearby temporal-lobe structures are involved in encoding explicit long-term memories? What have neuroimaging studies shown about the role of certain areas of the prefrontal cortex?

14. Distinguish between anterograde and retrograde amnesia.

15. What does the time-graded nature of retrograde amnesia tell us about long-term memories?

Retrieving Information from Long-Term Memory   (pages 326–333)

CONSIDER these questions before you go on. They are designed to help you start thinking about this subject, not to test your knowledge.

What kinds of cues can help us to probe our memories most effectively?

Can a memory be altered by information learned later? For example, could an attorney's misleading questions affect a witness's memory of an accident?

READ this section of your text lightly. Then go back and read thoroughly, completing the Workout as your proceed.

Somehow we are more likely to complain about the occasional failures of our memories than to applaud the frequent successes. Psychologists have tried to discover some of the reasons underlying those failures—the kind we tend to notice, such as the outright inability to retrieve desired information, as well as the less detectable cases of distortion in memory.

1. How are associations, priming, and retrieval cues essential to our ability to access long-term memories when we want them?

Who was your first-grade teacher? What is one of your favorite books? How many times have you read it? What does the word *stirrup* mean? What countries border France? Our long-term memories allow us to answer innumerable questions, skip from topic to topic, make sensible associations, and much more. Retrieval cues are apparently critical to our ability to gain access to long-term memories. And the associative organization of memory is critical to the effectiveness of retrieval cues. Some of the basic principles of association were originally proposed by Aristotle.

2. State Aristotle's principle of association by contiguity. What can it help to explain?

3. What was Aristotle's principle of association by similarity? What can it help to explain?

4. Describe William James's views on the roles of contiguity and similarity in the organization of memory.

A common way of portraying the mind's vast, organized store of knowledge is a network in which concepts are linked. (See Figure 9.12 on text page 328.)

5. What led Allan Collins and Elizabeth Loftus to develop their model? Briefly describe the model.

6. Why is the term *spreading activation* used to describe the model?

7. Why does elaborative rehearsal aid later retrieval? Briefly describe an experiment that supports this view.

8. How does context affect memory? Is this adaptive? How can you use this knowledge in your own life?

Remembering is an active, rather than a passive, process. It is not like replaying a tape recording or even like reading words we have written down.

9. Explain what it means to say that memory entails construction. What are some of the consequences of memory's constructive nature?

10. Identify the following:

_____ **a.** one's general mental representation or concept of a class of object, scene, or event that one uses to recognize and understand examplars of that class

_____ **b.** a schema that involves the organization of events in time rather than objects in space

11. We might very well have _____ to represent such events as football games, final exams, and vacations. We might represent such concepts as continents, dogs, furniture, and vehicles in _____.

12. Briefly describe how Frederick Bartlett used "The War of the Ghosts" to illustrate the power of culture-specific schemas on memory.

Suggestion and imagination may sometimes become factors in memory construction.

13. How can this cause eyewitness testimony to result in injustices?

14. What are some factors that can increase the likelihood of people "retrieving" or believing false memories?

15. How did Elizabeth Loftus and J. C. Palmer show that the construction of memories can be affected by information acquired after the original experience?

Some studies appear to show that strong suggestion can cause some people to "remember" childhood events—such as getting lost in a mall or spilling the punch at a wedding—that never happened.

16. What did Loftus and Pickrell find in their study?

17. How did experiments show that deliberately imagining an event can make subjects more likely to report that it actually happened?

18. How are source confusion and social pressure thought to be involved in instances of remembering things that never occurred?

Multiple Memory Systems: Beyond the Modal Model   (pp. 333–338)

CONSIDER these questions before you go on. They are designed to help you start thinking about this subject, not to test your knowledge.

Can knowledge in memory affect our perception or thought only if it becomes conscious?

Isn't there something fundamentally different about memory for the meaning of the word "dance" and memory for how to dance? Why is it that we can sometimes fail to recall someone's phone number verbally and yet can quickly dial the number?

READ this section of your text lightly. Then go back and read thoroughly, completing the Workout as you proceed.

As mentioned earlier, though the modal model accounts well for many memory phenomena, it falls short when we consider memory that does not involve the conscious mind. (Examine Figure 9.15 on text page 334.)

1. Label the following types of memory.

   a. _____ is memory in which the remembered information enters consciousness. It is also called _____ memory.

   b. _____, on the other hand, involves previously acquired information that affects behavior or thought without itself entering consciousness. It is also called _____ memory.

2. How are the two types of memory assessed?

3. How do implicit and explicit memories differ in terms of their context-dependence?

There are two types of explicit memory differentiated by cognitive psychologists.

4. Describe each of the following:
   a. episodic memory

   b. semantic memory

5. Can an episodic memory become a semantic memory? Explain.

Implicit memory can also be subdivided.

6. List three types of implicit memory, and define them as necessary.

7. How do some experiments with artificial grammars illustrate the implicit nature of rule-based procedural memories?

8. Why is priming considered implicit?

9. How might priming be important in everyday life?

Some of the evidence for multiple, distinct memory systems comes from studying people with brain damage. Recall the material from earlier in the chapter about H. M. and others with temporal-lobe amnesia.

10. Are the hippocampus and nearby temporal-lobe structures critical for creating or using implicit memories? Support your position with evidence.

There is also neuropsychological evidence suggesting that episodic and semantic memory involve different neural systems.

11. What does a disorder called developmental amnesia reveal about the role of the hippocampus in episodic as compared with semantic memory?

12. What evidence suggests that the prefrontal cortex is more critical to episodic than to semantic memory?

13. How might the role of the prefrontal cortex in episodic memory help to explain such diverse issues as childhood amnesia, age-related memory declines, and human self-awareness?

Be sure to READ the Concluding Thoughts at the end of the chapter. Note important points in your Workout. Then consolidate your learning by answering the focus questions in the margins of the text.

After you have studied the chapter thoroughly, CHECK your understanding with the Self-Test that follows.

Self-Test 1

Multiple-Choice Questions

1. According to the modal model of memory, memory is made up of a(n):
   a. attentive memory, short-term memory, and long-term memory.
   b. sensory memory, working memory, and short-term memory.
   c. sensory memory, working memory, and long-term memory.
   d. episodic memory, procedural memory, and semantic memory.

2. A brief, picturelike trace of a visual stimulus is held in _____ memory.
   a. episodic
   b. implicit
   c. echoic
   d. iconic

3. Information passes into working memory from:
   a. short-term memory.
   b. sensory memory.
   c. long-term memory.
   d. both **b** and **c**.

4. The span of short-term memory is probably really measuring the capacity of:
   a. the central executive.
   b. the visuospatial sketch pad.
   c. procedural memory.
   d. the phonological loop.

5. Studies of selective listening and viewing have typically found that subjects can later report:
   a. absolutely nothing about the unattended material.
   b. at best some physical characteristics of the unattended material.
   c. only the meaning of the unattended material.
   d. none of the above, since selective listening and selective viewing have virtually opposite patterns of results.

6. Suppose you have been introduced to a friend of a friend, and you repeat that person's name in your mind over and over with no elaborative processing. This approach is most likely to serve as:
   a. maintenance rehearsal.
   b. encoding rehearsal.
   c. chunking.
   d. echoic memory.

7. Suppose that Stroop stimuli, such as the word *red* printed in green ink, are presented to a variety of

subjects. Who among the following should be *most* susceptible to the Stroop effect in this case?

a. a normal adult reader of English

b. a young child who is just beginning to read English

c. a Chinese person who speaks English but does not read it

d. a normal adult reader of English who is looking at the stimuli with her head tilted 90 degrees to the side

8. A woman chooses a secret PIN number for using her bank's cash machines. She remembers the number, 111621, as 11 (the month of her birth), 16 (sweet sixteen), and 21 (the age of majority). This woman is using _____ to enhance her memory performance.

a. episodic memory   **c.** chunking

b. implicit memory   **d.** context

9. The mental walk, a method that aids memory performance, depends on:

a. visualization.

b. chunking.

c. hierarchical organization.

d. none of the above.

10. "What is a meal?" is a question that requires you to access _____ memory. "What did you have for lunch yesterday?" is one that requires you to get information from _____ memory.

a. semantic; episodic   **c.** implicit; explicit

b. episodic; semantic   **d.** explicit; implicit

11. According to the Collins and Loftus network model of memory organization, hearing the word *table* facilitates subsequent recognition of *chair* through the process of:

a. visualization.

b. elaborative rehearsal.

c. spreading activation.

d. procedural memory.

12. Suppose a subject is given a list of words for later recall. Next to each word is another word, which the subject is simply asked to read. One of the words to be recalled is *jam* and the word beside it is *strawberry*. Considering what you know about context, association by contiguity, and retrieval what would make the best retrieval cue for *jam* at recall time?

a. trouble

b. traffic

c. strawberry

d. All of the above would be equally effective.

13. Frederick Bartlett asked subjects to listen to "The War of the Ghosts" and later retell the story from memory. He found that subjects:

a. had excellent memory for the story, retelling it in the very same terms in which they heard it.

b. distorted the story in accordance with their own culture-based schemas.

c. used their schemas to accurately relate the meaning of the story in different words.

d. could not retain any aspect of the story.

14. Dr. England presents subjects with a word printed on a card that has a colored border. Their task is to give an example of the category indicated by the word. He finds that when the card says "fruit" and has a yellow border, they are more likely to say "banana" than if the card has a blue or red border. This illustrates:

a. the Stroop effect.

b. iconic memory.

c. priming.

d. visualization.

15. Neuropsychological studies have provided evidence suggesting that:

a. there really is no distinction between working and long-term memory.

b. implicit and explicit memories are encoded by way of different neural structures.

c. episodic and semantic memories are encoded through the same neural mechanisms.

d. both **a** and **b** are true.

Essay Questions

16. Distinguish between explicit and implicit memory, giving examples of each. Present one piece of evidence to support the reality of this distinction.

17. What is the visuospatial sketchpad? Does what happens there have any relation to perceptual processing? If so, provide evidence.

After you have assessed your understanding on the basis of Self-Test 1 and have tried to strengthen your preparation in any areas of weakness, GO ON to Self-Test 2.

Self-Test 2

Multiple-Choice Questions

1. Which of the following statements regarding sensory memory is true?
   a. Apparently, only vision and hearing have sensory-memory systems.
   b. We are generally conscious of iconic memory.
   c. Information in the visual sensory store is still in visual form.
   d. Maintenance rehearsal can help to keep information in sensory memory longer.

2. People with temporal-lobe amnesia show deficits in _____ but not _____ memory, which suggests that only the former depends on the _____.
   a. implicit; explicit; hippocampus
   b. explicit; implicit; hippocampus
   c. implicit; explicit; hypothalamus
   d. explicit; implicit; hypothalamus

3. Which of the following is considered the seat of conscious thought?
   a. long-term memory
   b. short-term memory
   c. working memory
   d. both b and c, which are two names for the same memory component

4. According to Baddeley, what refreshes information in the phonological loop, helping us to hold the information there longer?
   a. coordination with the visuospatial sketch pad
   b. subvocal repetition
   c. attention
   d. retrieval

5. Encoding is the control process that:
   a. maintains information in working memory.
   b. maintains information in sensory memory.
   c. transfers information from sensory to working memory.
   d. transfers information from working to long-term memory.

6. Which of the following statements concerning rehearsal is true?
   a. Maintenance rehearsal is the best means of accomplishing encoding.
   b. Maintenance rehearsal and encoding rehearsal are one and the same.
   c. Elaborative rehearsal is accomplished unconsciously.
   d. Elaborative rehearsal promotes encoding better than repetition does.

7. Gail routinely greeted her professors by name when she met them on campus. But when she encountered one of them at the movies, she couldn't think of the person's name. In fact, she wasn't quite sure if it was the same person. What could best explain this?
   a. context differences
   b. chunking
   c. schemas
   d. temporal-lobe amnesia

8. Source confusion is thought to be a major cause of
   a. developmental amnesia.
   b. false memories.
   c. nondeclarative memories.
   d. all of the above.

9. The process by which the labile form of long-term memory becomes solid is called:
   a. priming.
   b. spreading activation.
   c. networking.
   d. consolidation.

10. If you were to study by outlining a chapter using several levels of headings, from more general to more specific, you would be using _____ to aid your memory.

a. consolidation
b. the mental walk
c. memory construction
d. hierarchical organization

11. A type of schema that organizes events in time rather than objects in space is called a(n):

a. script.   c. episodic memory.
b. procedural memory.   d. network model.

12. The role of the prefrontal cortex in episodic memory can help to explain:

a. childhood amnesia.
b. why aging causes declines in episodic memory sooner than semantic memory.
c. the uniquely human capacity for self-awareness.
d. all of the above.

13. Which of the following is a type of explicit memory?

a. episodic memory
b. nondeclarative memory
c. sensory memory
d. memories produced by classical conditioning

14. What kind of information in your memory allows you to be a skillful dancer?

a. procedural   c. semantic
b. declarative   d. episodic

15. Priming is based on a type of _____ memory.

a. explicit.   c. working
b. procedural   d. implicit

Essay Questions

16. What is the span of short-term memory? How does chunking affect the amount of information that can be held in short-term memory? How can it help long-term memory?

17. Explain Aristotle's concepts of association by contiguity and association by similarity. Give examples of each. Is the notion of mental associations still important in modern theories of memory organization? Explain.

Answers

Overview: An Information-Processing Model of the Mind

5. standard

6. sensory; short-term or working; long-term

7. function; capacity; duration

10. encoding; retrieval; attention

Working Memory: The Active, Conscious Mind

1. holding verbal information; subvocal repetition

5. visual; spatial

10. coordinating mental activities; bringing new information into working memory from the sensory and long-term stores

Encoding Information into Long-Term Memory

2. maintenance; encoding; elaboration; organization; visualization

Retrieving Information from Long-Term Memory

10. a. schema, b. script

11. scripts; schemas

Multiple Memory Systems: Beyond the Modal Model

1. **a.** Explicit memory; declarative
   b. Implicit memory; nondeclarative

Self-Test 1

1. **c.** (p. 304)

2. **d.** (p. 310)

3. **d.** Information coming in from the outside world passes through sensory memory before it can be transferred to working memory. Information in long-term memory must enter working memory to be consciously processed. For example, to think about an event that happened to you last week or to form a mental image of a friend's face, you must process information from the long-term store in working memory. Remember that working memory is also called short-term memory. (pp. 305–306)

4. **d.** (p. 315)

5. **b.** However, the unattended information is processed preattentively. (pp. 308–309)

6. **a.** Elaborative rehearsal is much more likely to help you remember the name long-term. (p. 319)

7. **a.** (p. 313)

8. **c.** (p. 321)

9. **a.** (p. 323)

10. **a.** (p. 334)

11. **c.** Spreading activation can help to explain priming. (p. 328)

12. **c.** Since "strawberry" is part of the learning context and occurs contiguously with it, you should expect it to be the best retrieval cue. (p. 328)

13. **b.** (p. 330)

14. **c.** (pp. 311–312)

15. **b.** Neuropsychological research has suggested that all of the distinctions mentioned in the alternatives (working and long-term memories, implicit and explicit memory, and episodic and semantic memories) have some physiological basis. (pp. 336–337)

16. Explicit memory is memory in which the remembered information enters consciousness. It is tested by asking a person to recall or report the information of interest. Explicit memory is well accounted for by the modal model. Implicit memory involves stored information that can influence behavior or cognitive processes without entering consciousness. Episodic memory, such as your memory for the last movie you saw, is a type of explicit memory. Procedural memory, such as your knowledge of how to drive a car, would be considered an example of implicit memory. One kind of evidence for the distinction comes from amnesic patients like H. M. who cannot create new long-term memories of the explicit type but can create new implicit ones. (pp. 333–334)

17. According to Baddeley's model, working memory consists of three separate but interacting components—the phonological loop, the central executive, and the visuospatial sketchpad. The visuospatial sketchpad is used for holding and actively processing visual and spatial information. We know there is a similarity between the processing of a mental image and the corresponding action performed on a current visual stimulus. Kosslyn, for example, showed that we scan a mental image much as we do a visual stimulus. Brain research also supports this idea. For example, a man with brain damage in the "what" pathway lost much of his ability to visualize the shapes of familiar objects as well as to see the shapes of objects in front of him. (p. 316)

Self-Test 2

1. **c.** (p. 310)

2. **b.** In fact, this offers neuropsychological evidence that the implicit/explicit distinction is genuine. (p. 336)

3. **d.** (p. 305)

4. **b.** (p. 316)

5. **d.** (p. 319)

6. **d.** (pp. 319–320)

7. **a.** (p. 329)

8. **b.** (p. 332)

9. **d.** (p. 325)

10. **d.** (p. 322)

11. **a.** (p. 330)

12. **d.** (pp. 336–337)

13. **a.** The other type of explicit memory is semantic memory. (p. 334)

14. **a.** (p. 335)

15. **d.** (p. 335)

16. The term *span of short-term memory* refers to the number of pronounceable items that can be held in short-term memory at one time and repeated back after a brief delay. Even though the number of items that can be held stays roughly the same, the effective capacity of short-term memory can be improved by increasing the amount of information packed into each item. This is called chunking. For example, the letters *c, i, a, f, b, i* could be remembered not as six individual letters but as two familiar acronyms—CIA and FBI. With this method, it is possible to dramatically improve memory performance. Chunking is a way of organizing information and often requires elaboration. As such, it is very effective in promoting the encoding of information into long-term memory. Chunking also seems to be a consequence of becoming an expert. Expert chess players, for example, can reproduce a briefly displayed layout of a chess game better than people less experienced at chess. This ability is attributed to the fact that they could chunk meaningful combinations of pieces on the board. When a random layout of chess pieces was shown, in which no such meaningful combinations would be likely, experts did essentially no better than other players. (pp. 315, 321–322)

17. Aristotle suggested that memory is organized in terms of associations. An association exists between two pieces of stored information if the thought of one tends to evoke the thought of the other. Association by contiguity occurs when information is associated because of co-occurrence in a person's experience. For example, dentists might be associated with drills for this reason because the two have been experienced together (that is, contiguously) in the past. Association by similarity is involved in those cases of association based on some shared property. For example, bathtubs and oceans might be associated because both contain water. The idea of mental associations is still central to modern theories of memory organization, such as the Collins and Loftus network model. (pp. 327–328)

Reasoning and Intelligence

chapter 10

READ the introduction below before you read the chapter in the text.

A major function of the human intellect involves reasoning. Analogies, which depend on the perception of similarities, are a primary foundation for reasoning. They are commonly used in scientific reasoning; in judicial thinking, political thinking and persuasion; and in tests of reasoning ability, as well as in everyday thought. Inductive reasoning entails reasoning from specific facts or observations to general conclusions. Research on inductive reasoning has identified several kinds of biases.

Deductive reasoning involves reasoning from premises that are assumed to be true to a conclusion that logically follows from them. Again, there are biases that are common in deductive reasoning. For example, people often pay too much attention to the concrete content of the problem and not enough to the logical structures. Research suggests that people who reason successfully on deductive problems often use visual imagery to aid their thinking. Insight is often required to solve a problem, which entails seeing it in a new light. Becoming stuck in a way of viewing the problem that does not work is called mental set. Deliberately looking for new ways to perceive the problem can help, as can a playful or happy frame of mind.

Both one's culture and one's language can affect thought. For example, non-Westerners do not look at Western-style logic problems in the same way as do Westerners. East Asians take a more holistic approach to problems than Westerners do. An issue in the study of language and thought is linguistic relativity, the notion that thought may be shaped and even limited by the language of the thinker. For example, mathematical thinking has been found to be related to the way a given language represents numerical concepts in words. Language can also affect the way we think about our three-dimensional world. It can even affect our tendency to think in sexist ways.

Chapter 10 continues with a discussion of intelligence testing. The testing methods most familiar today were pioneered by Alfred Binet. Binet developed his test to identify schoolchildren who were not thriving in the French educational system. Performance on IQ tests, not surprisingly, is moderately predictive of school performance but can to some extent predict job performance and even longevity.

One major question about the nature of intelligence is whether it consists of a single mental ability or different abilities. A statistical method called factor analysis has been applied to the pattern of scores on different subsets of intelligence tests. With this technique, Charles Spearman found evidence of both a general intelligence, which he called g, and a number of specific types of intelligence. Raymond Cattell proposed that g itself actually had two aspects, not just one. He called these two aspects fluid intelligence and crystallized intelligence. Researchers looking for the properties of the mind that underlie general intelligence have considered mental speed, working memory capacity, and what Robert Sternberg calls mental self-government.

The chapter next explores the nature-nurture debate regarding intelligence, explaining the central concept of heritability. Heritability and environmentality are complementary concepts; both terms are used to refer to the degree to which genetics (or environmental factors) are responsible for the variation in IQ (or some other trait) seen in a given population. Unfortunately, there have been significant misunderstandings and misuses of the concept of heritability. In particular, it has been inappropriately used to try to explain average IQ differences between racial or cultural groups, such as that between American blacks and whites, as genetic in origin. Much evidence favors environmental explanations of such differences. For example, the social status of involuntary minorities is associated with essentially equivalent deficits in IQ measurements for such groups in various parts of the world. When that status no longer holds, the deficit in IQ scores disappears.

LOOK over the table of contents for this chapter in your textbook before you continue with your study.

Notice that there are focus questions in the margins of the text for your use in studying the material. The following chart lists which Study Guide questions relate to which focus questions.

Focus Questions	Study Guide Questions
Introduction and How People Reason I: Analogies and Induction	
1	1–3
2	4–5
3	6
4	7
5	8
6	9
7	10
8	11
How People Reason II: Deduction and Insight	
9–10	1–4
11	5
12	6–7
13–14	8–12
15	13–14
Effects of Culture and Language on Thought	
16	1–3
17	4–6
18	8
19–20	9–11
21	12
22	13
The Practice and Theory of Intelligence Testing	
23	2–3
24	4–6
25	7–9
26	10–13
27	14–16
28	17–19
29	20
30	21–22
31	23–25
32	26
33	27
Genetic and Environmental Contributions to Intelligence	
34	1
35	2–5
36–37	6–11
38	12–13
39	14
40	15
41	16–18
42	19
43	20

The Integrated Study Workout

COMPLETE one section at a time.

Introduction AND *How People Reason I: Analogies and Induction*   (pages 341–348)

CONSIDER these questions before you go on. They are designed to help you start thinking about this subject, not to test your knowledge.

Are human beings really capable of being logical?

Do we tend to make certain types of mistakes in our reasoning or are our errors just random?

How can we improve our reasoning?

READ this section of your text lightly. Then go back and read thoroughly, completing the Workout as you proceed.

The perception of similarities is fundamental to many psychological processes, including analogical reasoning and inductive reasoning.

1. What do psychologists typically mean by the term analogy?

2. Give an example of an analogy that proved helpful to a scientist of historical note.

3. Is analogical reasoning common among scientists? among nonscientists reasoning about physical systems? Support your answer.

4. Give an example of analogies being used for persuasion in judicial or political matters.

5. When are analogies misleading?

6. Describe the use of analogies for testing reasoning ability.

Psychologists seek to understand how people *typically* reason, not to describe ideal logic. In fact, they have found that humans are not ideal logic machines whether they are engaging in inductive reasoning or deductive reasoning (covered in the next section).

7. Inferring a new principle or proposition from specific facts or observations is called

_____ or _____.

8. How does availability bias thinking?

9. What is confirmation bias? Give an example of how it has been demonstrated in experiments.

10. Could confirmation bias occur because it is adaptive in daily life? Explain.

11. How does the predictable-world bias affect people's thinking and behavior? Use an example from die-tossing games to illustrate.

How People Reason II: Deduction and Insight
(pages 348–355)

CONSIDER these questions before you go on. They are designed to help you start thinking about this subject, not to test your knowledge.

When you try to solve a deductive reasoning problem do you try to picture it in your head? Is that useful?

Why do we sometimes get stuck on a problem and then have an "aha!" experience that leads to a sudden solution?

READ this section of your text lightly. Then go back and read thoroughly, completing the Workout as you proceed.

Psychological research has also focused on deductive reasoning.

1. Deciding logically that a given conclusion inevitably follows from premises that are accepted as true is called _____ reasoning.

2. Describe the following types of problems typical of those psychologists use to study deductive reasoning:

   a. series problem

   b. syllogism

3. Does research suggest that people solve deductive-reasoning problems through formal, abstract logic? Explain.

4. What is some evidence that we are biased to consider content rather than logic in deductive reasoning problems? How does this represent a bias toward induction?

A crucial element in solving a complex deductive reasoning problem is how we represent the relevant information.

5. Are diagrams and Euler circles useful? How so?

6. How do people accomplish deductive reasoning in the view of Phillip Johnson-Laird?

7. Is there evidence that visual imagery is important to deductive reasoning?

The purpose of reasoning is, of course, to solve problems. Some problems are solved only through insight.

8. Define the term *insight problem*.

9. Give an example of an insight problem and its solution below.

Habits are often helpful results of learning, but they can sometimes set up barriers to effective problem solving.

10. Define the concept of mental set, and show how it applies to a specific problem.

11. Define the type of mental set known as functional fixedness.

12. Is it helpful to deliberately look at the problem materials differently?

3. Can a lighthearted mood help to overcome mental set?

4. How does Barbara Fredrickson explain such effects? How does your text's author explain them?

Effects of Culture and Language on Thought
(pages 355–362)

CONSIDER these questions before you go on. They are designed to help you start thinking about this subject, not to test your knowledge.

Do people from different cultures reason differently? Can the language we speak affect our thoughts or make some thoughts more likely than others? Can sexist language, such as the use of *man* to refer generically to all humans, promote sexist thinking?

READ this section of your text lightly. Then go back and read thoroughly, completing the Workout as you proceed.

The majority of psychological research on reasoning has been done in Western cultures. Cross-cultural differences can affect performance on Western-style logic problems.

1. Are Westerners or non-Westerners more likely to stick with concrete experiences when faced with a logic problem?

2. How do unschooled non-Western people tend to approach classification problems? How do Westerners generally approach them?

3. Is this cross-cultural difference a matter of ability or a matter of preference?

4. Describe some differences in perception and memory between Westerners and East Asians. What experimental results support this view?

5. How can such differences affect reasoning?

6. What might underlie such cultural differences?

Language allows us to span distance, time, and the limitations of our personal experience. It is the means by which people communicate, by which cultures are developed and passed on. It is a foundation for much of our thought. Psychologists and others have theorized about the relationship between language and thought for many years.

7. What did Vygotsky mean by the term verbal thought?

8. What is suggested in the theory of linguistic relativity proposed by Edward Sapir and Benjamin Whorf? In what form is this theory generally accepted today?

Linguistic relativity may help to explain cultural differences in spatial reasoning and math ability.

9. Explain the difference between an egocentric and an absolute frame of reference. (Look at Figures 10.7 and 10.8 on text pages 358 and 360.)

10. Some languages lack the words needed to use an egocentric frame of reference. How do speakers of such languages differ from speakers of other languages?

11. How do the Piraha illustrate an obvious effect of language on mathematical thinking?

12. How might language differences account for the superior mathematical performance of Asian children compared with American and European children? What evidence supports this explanation?

The possibility exists that we can deliberately affect our thinking by altering our language. That idea provides part of the motivation for the attempt to eliminate certain sexist constructions in the English language. An example of such a construction is the use of *man* to mean both humans in general and human males in particular.

13. Describe research showing that such generic use of the term *man* or *he* does, in fact, affect thinking.

The Practice and Theory of Intelligence Testing
(pages 362–371)

CONSIDER these questions before you go on. They are designed to help you start thinking about this subject, not to test your knowledge.

How did intelligence tests originate?

What underlying mental qualities cause one person to score higher than another on intelligence tests?

Can performance on intelligence tests really predict anything about performance outside the testing room?

READ this section of your text lightly. Then go back and read thoroughly, completing the Workout as you proceed.

Historically, there have been different approaches to the study and measurement of intelligence, each with its own view of what intelligence is.

1. What is the general definition of intelligence presented in the text?

Both Francis Galton in England and Alfred Binet in France were major figures in early efforts to understand and measure intelligence. But today's intelligence tests can be traced back to the pioneering work of Binet.

2. How did Galton conceive of intelligence?

3. How did Galton try to measure intelligence and how did his approach to measurement turn out? Was that the last word on the subject?

4. What was Binet's notion of intelligence?

5. Why was the Binet-Simon Intelligence Scale originally developed?

6. What kinds of items did Binet and Simon include on their test? How were items selected? Were the kinds of items used consistent with the purpose of the test? Explain.

In North America, the first widely used intelligence test was a modification of the Binet and Simon scale. It was called the Stanford-Binet Scale because the work was conducted at Stanford University.

7. What are the most common individually administered intelligence tests? Are they related to Binet's test?

8. What kinds of subtests are used on the WAIS-III?

9. What is an IQ and how is it derived?

Psychologists in the field of intelligence testing must ask themselves whether their tests provide useful and trustworthy information—that is, whether they really tell us about a person's intelligence.

10. The extent to which a test measures what it is supposed to measure is its _____.

11. How well do IQ scores correlate with school grades?

12. What evidence suggests that IQ can help to predict on-the-job performance? Does it predict equally well across all occupations?

13. Can IQ predict longevity? Explain.

Scientists have long debated the essential nature of intelligence, an issue that also affects the measurement of intelligence. Does it make sense to summarize a person's intelligence with a single number? Or does this misrepresent something as complex as the intellect? The answer depends on whether one believes intelligence to be unitary, a collection of separate abilities, or some combination of the two. An important tool for studying the structure of intelligence is factor analysis, a method invented by Charles Spearman.

14. What did Spearman refer to as g? What suggested to him that g existed?

15. According to Spearman and his followers, what does every mental test measure?

16. How does Spearman's g relate to the approach used in standard intelligence tests such as the Wechsler tests?

Raymond Cattell, a student and colleague of Spearman, developed his own modified version of Spearman's theory of intelligence. He distinguished between two kinds of general intelligence.

17. Define the following two terms of g.
　a. fluid intelligence (g_f)

　b. crystallized intelligence (g_c)

18. Describe two types of evidence that led Cattell to make this distinction.

19. Cattell noted that _____
intelligence depends on _____
intelligence.

What really underlies general intelligence? One goal is to identify elementary cognitive correlates of intelligence. Many of the research findings in this area highlight the importance of mental speed, a notion that echoes Galton's idea of mental quickness.

20. Summarize evidence that general intelligence is correlated with mental speed.

21. Why might one think that working-memory capacity underlies differences in intelligence?

22. Why would we expect working-memory capacity to be related to mental speed? What evidence supports this idea?

Other researchers have explored individual differences more complex than variables like mental speed.

23. What does Sternberg mean by "mental self-government"?

24. In related thinking, the mind's central executive is thought to be the basis of intelligence. What does this mean and what is some evidence for it?

25. Why and how does Sternberg think people can increase their intelligence?

26. Which part of the brain is crucial to mental self-government and fluid intelligence? Why do scientists believe this?

27. From an evolutionary perspective, what is general intelligence for?

Genetic and Environmental Contributions to Intelligence   (pages 372–380)

CONSIDER these questions before you go on. They are designed to help you start thinking about this subject, not to test your knowledge.

Is the variation in intellectual ability among individuals due more to nature or to nurture? How can we tell?

Are there average differences in IQ between racial or cultural groups? How could we interpret any such differences rationally?

READ this section of your text lightly. Then go back and read thoroughly, completing the Workout as you proceed.

The nature-nurture debate concerning intelligence began with Galton's theories about the hereditary basis of variations in intelligence. The essential question of nature versus nurture is often misunderstood, with one version being a reasonable question to ask and the other being absurd. To clarify the distinction between the reasonable question and the absurd one, consider the rectangle analogy presented in Figure 10.12 on text page 372.

1. State the essential nature-nurture question in its two forms as applied to the matter of intelligence.
   a. absurd version

   b. reasonable version

Heritability is the concept that scientists use to frame the nature-nurture question regarding intelligence or any other characteristic that varies among individuals. Like the nature-nurture question itself, the concept of heritability is often misunderstood. It is worth your time to be clear about it.

2. Define *heritability*.

3. Heritability can be expressed quantitatively by means of the heritability coefficient, abbreviated h^2. Fill in the terms in the formula below.

   $h^2 = $ _____ $ = $ _____

4. Give the heritability coefficient that would correctly describe each of the following situations.

    _____ **a.** None of the observed variance in the population is due to genetic differences.

    _____ **b.** Seventy percent of the observed variance in the population is due to genetic differences.

    _____ **c.** All of the observed variance in the population is due to genetic differences.

    _____ **d.** Forty percent of the observed variance in the population is due to environmental differences.

5. Logically, when we measure heritability, we are also measuring _____.

The study of twins has been a valuable avenue for estimating the heritability of IQ.

6. Why are twins particularly valuable subjects in the attempt to tease apart genetic and environmental contributions to IQ variation?

One approach to estimating heritability coefficients is to compare identical twins raised together with fraternal twins raised together. The rationale is that while both types of twins share an environment, identical twins have twice the genetic relatedness that fraternal twins have. The former are 100 percent related and the latter only 50 percent related, just like any other pair of biological siblings.

7. In general, how do IQ correlations between identical twins raised together compare with IQ correlations between fraternal twins raised together? What does this suggest about the heritability of IQ?

8. Is IQ heritability as estimated in these studies equal for children and adults? Explain.

9. How is a heritability coefficient estimated?

10. What is the average heritability coefficient found in twin studies prior to 1993? Overall, what do studies suggest about the source of IQ variance in children? in adults?

11. Are fluid and crystallized intelligence equally heritable?

Many studies of IQ correlations show that the effect of a shared family environment has only a temporary effect on IQ. A direct method for addressing the impact of shared environment on IQ is to study biologically unrelated people who are adopted into the same home.

12. What is the IQ correlation for such individuals in childhood? in adulthood?

3. How might we explain the transient effect of a shared family environment on IQ?

4. What can intellectual involvement do for a person's intelligence and how is this related to personality? to one's occupation? Present evidence.

Heritability coefficients are legitimately applied only within the population studied. In general, the heritability estimates discussed so far came from white, North American or European populations in the upper two-thirds of the socioeconomic scale.

15. If heritability coefficients were estimated for the broadest range of the human population, how would those estimates compare with the ones just discussed?

One focus in IQ research has been average differences between racial or cultural groups. Though the difference between American blacks and whites has attracted particular attention, racial or cultural comparisons often show differences in average IQ.

16. What is the average difference in IQ points between blacks and whites in the United States?

17. Why doesn't it make sense to use heritability within groups to assess the reasons for differences between groups?

18. Present evidence that the black/white IQ difference represents cultural rather than genetic effects.

19. What is an involuntary minority and what is the impact of this social status on IQ? How might this effect occur?

20. Is there a historical trend in IQs? Describe the findings and explain their implications and possible causes.

Be sure to READ the Concluding Thoughts at the end of the chapter. Note important points in your Workout. Then consolidate your learning by answering the focus questions in the margins of the text.

After you have studied the chapter thoroughly, CHECK your understanding with the Self-Test that follows.

Self-Test 1

Multiple-Choice Questions

1. Karen is buying a lottery ticket today, so she puts on her yellow sweatshirt—the one she was wearing when she won $1000 last year. Karen is exhibiting:
   a. confirmation bias.
   b. a predictable-world bias.
   c. the availability bias.
   d. a mental set.

2. Asking whether an intelligence test really measures what it is supposed to measure is a question about the test's:
   a. reliability.   c. factor analysis.
   b. validity.   d. *g*.

3. The technique known as *factor analysis* is a powerful means of determining the _____ of intelligence.
   a. biological basis   c. degree
   b. evolutionary origins   d. major components

4. Fredricksen's broaden-and-build theory is designed to explain the value of _____ for perception, thought, and creativity.
   a. mental models   c. positive emotions
   b. analogies   d. linguistic relativity

5. Galton believed that intelligence was essentially _____ and sought to measure it through _____.
   a. biological and hereditary; mental quickness
   b. biological and hereditary; complex reasoning problems
   c. determined by environment; mental quickness
   d. determined by environment; complex reasoning problems

6. Which of the following has been suggested as a basis for *g*?
   a. mental speed
   b. mental self-government
   c. working memory capacity
   d. all of the above

7. Most modern intelligence tests are based on the work of:
   a. Binet.
   b. Galton.
   c. Spearman.
   d. Sternberg.

8. A person who reasons from the premises *All birds can fly* and *Chickens are birds* that *Chickens can fly* has:
   a. engaged in deductive reasoning.
   b. engaged in inductive reasoning.
   c. fallen prey to the availability bias.
   d. fallen prey to the confirmation bias.

9. Research subjects were either asked to decide whether an interviewee was an extrovert or whether the person was an introvert. The questions the subjects asked in their interviews revealed:
   a. an absence of any bias.
   b. a predictable-world bias.
   c. an availability bias.
   d. a confirmation bias.

10. Charles Darwin used selective breeding by horticulturists to help him understand natural selection. This illustrates the power of:
   a. deductive reasoning.
   b. availability.
   c. functional fixedness.
   d. analogies.

11. In general, _____ declines throughout adulthood.
   a. crystallized intelligence
   b. fluid intelligence
   c. neither a nor b
   d. both a and b

12. Comparison of African Americans and the Buraku in Japan suggests that black/white IQ differences in the United States are due to:
   a. poorer educational opportunities for blacks.
   b. the genetic endowment of the two groups.
   c. unfair testing.
   d. blacks' representing an involuntary minority.

13. The _____ plays a crucial role in mental self-government and fluid intelligence.
   a. prefrontal cortex
   b. parietal cortex
   c. temporal cortex
   d. thalamus

14. The personality trait called openness to experience is positively correlated with:
   a. fluid (but not crystallized) intelligence.
   b. crystallized (but not fluid) intelligence.
   c. both fluid and crystallized intelligence.
   d. creativity but not IQ.

5. The idea that language can affect thinking is known as _____ and is associated with _____.
   a. linguistic relativity; Binet
   b. linguistic relativity; Whorf and Sapir
   c. heuristic thought; Sternberg
   d. heuristic thought; Wechsler

Essay Questions

6. What is heritability? Why and how is heritability affected by the amount of environmental variation among the group (or population) being tested? How can heritability be high within two groups and yet not account for differences between those groups?

17. Describe Binet's conception of intelligence. How were his views consistent with his goals and methods in developing an intelligence scale?

After you have assessed your understanding on the basis of Self-Test 1 and have tried to strengthen your preparation in any areas of weakness, GO ON to Self-Test 2.

Self-Test 2

Multiple-Choice Questions

1. Given cross-cultural research, which of the following students is likely to pay most attention to background, context, and interrelationships in a perception and memory task?
   a. a Canadian student
   b. a student from the United States
   c. a Japanese student
   d. a Belgian student

2. Alfred Binet and Theophile Simon developed the Binet-Simon Intelligence Scale by trying out items similar to those found in schoolwork and:
   a. keeping only those that could be answered by about 50 percent of the children.
   b. making them easier or harder to accommodate children of different mental ages.
   c. dropping those that did not correlate well with simple measures of mental speed and sensory acuity.
   d. keeping only those that distinguished between children that teachers rated high and those that teachers rated low on classroom performance.

3. Cultural influences have led to a steady historical _____ in IQ with the greatest changes coming in tests of _____ intelligence.
   a. increase; fluid
   b. increase; crystallized
   c. decrease; fluid
   d. decrease; crystallized

4. IQ scores on standard intelligence tests are correlated with school grades:
   a. quite weakly.   c. almost perfectly.
   b. moderately.   d. not at all.

5. According to Raymond Cattell, mental ability derived directly from previous experience is classified as:
   a. crystallized intelligence.
   b. fluid intelligence.
   c. comprehension.
   d. irrelevant to a consideration of intelligence.

6. If an entire population were genetically identical, heritability in its members would:
   a. be zero.
   b. be 50 percent.
   c. be 100 percent.
   d. depend on the trait in question.

7. Twin studies published before 1993 suggest that the heritability of IQ averages is:
   a. .11   c. .73
   b. .48   d. .92

8. Researchers found that unschooled non-Western people:
   a. were unable to sort by taxonomic category as Westerners typically do.
   b. could sort by taxonomic category but preferred to sort in another way.
   c. typically sorted by taxonomic category just as Westerners do.
   d. could not sort at all unless they were given a set of categories.

9. A hypothesis consistent with Phillip Johnson-Laird's theory would be that college students reason better with syllogisms that are easier to:
   a. pronounce.
   b. visualize.
   c. state in terms of a mental set.
   d. combine into one sentence.

10. Carrie is nervous about boarding her flight to Denver because of a highly publicized plane crash the previous week. We could best explain her apprehension in terms of:
    a. mental set.   d. an analogy.
    b. availability bias.   c. confirmation bias.

11. People who speak languages that lack egocentric spatial terms generally have:
    a. much worse absolute spatial abilities.
    b. much better absolute spatial abilities.
    c. somewhat better deductive reasoning.
    d. somewhat better inductive reasoning.

12. Suppose a person going to a birthday party needs something to protect a carefully wrapped present from the rain but overlooks an unused plastic trash bag lying on the counter. This person has illustrated the problem of:
    a. functional fixedness.
    b. confirmation bias.
    c. a predictable-world bias.
    d. availability bias.

13. Imagine that a group of genetically diverse children from a variety of different backgrounds are randomly assigned to two school systems, one excellent and one poor. Differences in academic performance between the two school systems would be due primarily to:
    a. genetic variability among the children.
    b. variability in the backgrounds of the children.
    c. the different environments of the school systems.
    d. mental set.

14. The fact that East Asian children perform better than North American and European children in math at all levels of schooling appears to be due in part to:
    a. the fact that their native languages make the base-10 number system transparent.
    b. genetic factors that favor quantitative reasoning in these children.
    c. the tendency toward more holistic, less analytic reasoning in these children.
    d. all of the above

15. Juan decides that memory is like a tape-recorder and Armand figures that it is really like a sketchboard. They are both trying to:
    a. produce an analogy.
    b. reason deductively.
    c. create a syllogism.
    d. solve an insight problem.

Essay Questions

16. What is confirmation bias? Give an example from laboratory research.

17. What is deductive reasoning? Explain Phillip Johnson-Laird's hypothesis about why some people solve syllogisms better than other people. What evidence suggests that Johnson-Laird's hypothesis might be correct?

Answers

How People Reason I: Analogies and Induction

7. inductive reasoning; hypothesis construction

How People Reason II: Deduction and Insight

1. deductive

The Practice and Theory of Intelligence Testing

10. validity

19. crystallized; fluid

Genetic and Environmental Contributions to Intelligence

3. $h^2 = \dfrac{\text{variance due to genes}}{\text{total variance}} =$

$$\dfrac{\text{variance due to genes}}{\text{variance due to genes} + \text{variance due to environment}}$$

4. **a.** 0.00
   b. 0.70
   c. 1.00
   d. 0.60

5. environmentality

Self-Test 1

1. **b.** (p. 347)

2. **b.** (p. 366)

3. **d.** Factor analysis can help to reveal the essential makeup of intelligence in terms of general ability and component mental abilities. (p. 367)

4. **c.** (p. 354)

5. **a.** (p. 363)

6. **d.** (pp. 367–370)

7. **a.** (p. 363)

8. **a.** (pp. 348–349)

9. **d.** They tended to ask questions consistent with their starting hypothesis. (p. 346)

10. **d.** (p. 342)

11. **b.** Crystallized intelligence continues to increase past the age of 50, but fluid intelligence declines from early adulthood (ages 20–25) on. (p. 368)

12. **d.** (p. 378)

13. **a.** (p. 370)

14. **c.** (p. 376)

15. **b.** (p. 358)

16. Heritability, the central concept of nature-nurture debates, is the extent to which genetic differences in a group (population) of individuals can account for observed differences in some characteristic such as intelligence. Heritability is logically and necessarily influenced by the amount of environmental variation within the group. For example, suppose the members of a group were exposed to identical environments and still differed in some trait. We would have to assume that the differences were due to genetic variation. The reverse is equally true.

One can look at the formula for the heritability coefficient to see this point another way. This statistic essentially defines heritability as the amount of genetic variation divided by the amount of total variation (that is, genetic variation plus environmental variation—the only two possibilities). If environmental variation (variation being expressed statistically as variance) were nonexistent in a particular case, then the denominator would equal the numerator and thus heritability would be 1.00, the highest possible. The smaller the amount of environmental diversity, the higher the heritability coefficient will be; conversely, the greater the environmental diversity, the lower heritability will be.

Heritability can be high within groups and low or nonexistent between them if the individuals within a group have very similar environments and the two goups have different environments. In fact, heritability within groups tells us nothing about the causes of differences between those groups. (pp. 373–375)

17. Binet thought of intelligence as a collection of various higher-order mental abilities that are only loosely related to one another. He also emphasized the importance of the environment in shaping intelligence. In fact, his test was intended to identify children who were not benefiting as much as they should from schooling so that they could receive special attention and thereby increase their intelligence. The questions and problems on the test assessed memory, vocabulary, common knowledge, number usage, and other higher-level intellectual functions. Items were selected by pretesting on schoolchildren of various ages and comparing results with teachers' ratings of the children's classroom performance. Only items answered correctly by high-rated children more often than by low-rated children were retained. Both the nature of the items and their manner of selection made them consistent with Binet's goals and his concept of intelligence. (pp. 363–364)

Self-Test 2

1. **c.** (p. 356)

2. **d.** Binet realized the circular nature of this selection procedure but also saw the advantages of a single standard test that could be used on many different children in different circumstances. Further, since he was trying to produce a valid test of academic ability, he needed to compare it with an accepted measure of such ability. (p. 364)

3. **a.** (pp. 379–380)

4. **b.** (p. 366)

5. **a.** (p. 368)

6. **a.** Genetic variation can't explain variation on a trait if genetic variation doesn't exist! (p. 373)

7. **c.** (p. 374)

8. **b.** The Kpelle clearly had a different notion of what constituted intelligent behavior, since they would sort by taxonomic category only when they were asked to sort the way a stupid person would (p. 356)

9. **b.** (pp. 340–351)

10. **b.** (pp. 345–346)

11. **b.** (p. 359)

12. **a.** Mental set is a situation in which we have difficulty breaking free of existing habits of thought to find a solution. Functional fixedness is a special case of mental set in which a habit of thought makes it harder to think of using objects for unaccustomed purposes. (pp. 352–353)

13. **c.** (p. 372)

14. **a.** (pp. 360–361)

15. **a.** (p. 342)

16. Confirmation bias is the normal human tendency to look for confirmation rather than disconfirmation of a hypothesis. This is despite the fact that, logically, no amount of confirmation can prove a hypothesis true and that disconfirmation has the power to rule *out* a hypothesis. Peter Wason asked subjects to guess the rule that the experimenter was using to generate sequences of three numbers, such as 5-7-9. The subjects could test their hypotheses by generating sequences of their own and having the experimenter say whether they fit his rule or not. Subjects tended to generate sequences consistent with their own hypotheses rather than sequences that could tell them if the hypothesis was wrong. These people never correctly guessed the rule Wason was using. (pp. 346–347)

17. Deductive reasoning involves reasoning from premises assumed to be true to a conclusion that logically follows from them. It is often tested in logic problems such as syllogisms or series problems. An example would be "All fish are scaly (major premise); Cedric is a fish (minor premise); therefore, Cedric is scaly (conclusion)." In this

case, the conclusion does follow logically from the premises. Johnson-Laird suggested that people who solve deductive-reasoning problems successfully do so by creating and then examining a mental model, often in the form of a visual image. Research evidence to support this idea comes from fMRI studies showing greater activity in the right hemisphere (specialized for visuospatial tasks) than in the left (specialized for verbal processing) during deductive reasoning. Also, the ability to solve syllogisms is more strongly correlated with visual-spatial ability than with verbal ability. (pp. 348–351)

The Development of Thought and Language

READ the introduction below before you read the chapter in the text.

Chapter 11 explores the development of mental abilities during infancy and childhood. Babies are born with certain sensory and perceptual capabilities, which develop further during infancy—roughly the first 18 to 24 months of life. These abilities are exploited even by newborns as they seek to explore the world around them. Soon after birth, infants show an interest in controlling their environment and reveal a preference for novel over familiar stimuli. As they gain the ability to coordinate different parts of their bodies, such as eyes and hands, they actively examine objects.

Though they do not require adult encouragement to explore, infants begin at about 6 to 12 months to use social cues to guide their exploration. Even very young infants seem to understand some basic physical principles of the world though they may be too young to act on that knowledge in certain ways. For example, they may know an object still exists though it has been hidden, but they may be unable to reach for it.

Self-produced actions play a central part in the theory of Jean Piaget, a major figure in the area of cognitive development. Piaget has suggested that the growth of the child's ability to think logically occurs in four stages: sensorimotor, preoperational, concrete operational, and formal operational. The movement from one stage to the next involves the emergence of new types of schemes in the child's thinking. Schemes are something like mental blueprints for organized patterns of action. Two complementary processes called assimilation and accommodation advance the child's thinking.

Theorists from the sociocultural perspective emphasize that cognitive development occurs in a particular cultural and social context. Lev Vygotsky, the theorist generally credited with originating this perspective, stressed the importance of the relationship between language and thought in human cognitive development. One of Vygotsky's primary beliefs was that language becomes the means of symbolic thought.

Theorists from the information-processing perspective attempt to understand cognitive development in terms of developmental changes in the components of the mind, such as working memory or episodic long-term memory. They also regard development as more domain-specific and less holistic than Piaget claimed.

Even young infants can distinguish phonemes, the basic units of speech sound. Early in life, infants begin to coo and babble, two forms of vocalization that prepare them for later speech and appear to be types of play. Children move on to acquire words, slowly at first and then at a faster pace. At first they speak one word at a time, but they soon learn to produce progressively longer utterances that are meaningful and indicate some understanding of the rules of grammar. A number of observations suggest that children do not simply mimic the speech around them but infer the underlying rules of language.

The child's acquisition of language is one of the most amazing aspects of cognitive development. In general, developmentalists believe that it depends both on innate mechanisms that predispose the child to learn language and on an environment that supports such learning.

Efforts to teach nonvocal forms of language to chimpanzees and other nonhuman primates have generally shown that, although they can learn to use symbols in a referential way, they cannot acquire more than a slight knowledge of grammar. A chimp named Washoe, for example, learned to use sign language, and a bonobo named Kanzi learned to use geometric shapes called lexigrams to communicate.

LOOK over the table of contents for this chapter in your textbook before you continue with your study.

Notice that there are focus questions in the margins of the text for your use in studying the material. The following chart lists which Study Guide questions relate to which focus questions.

The Integrated Study Workout

COMPLETE one section at a time.

Introduction AND *How Infants Learn About the Physical World*   (pages 383–390)

CONSIDER these questions before you go on. They are designed to help you start thinking about this subject, not to test your knowledge.

How can psychologists learn about an infant's perception or knowledge if the infant can't tell them about what it perceives or knows?

Can an infant who sees an interesting object—say, a bright red ball—continue to think about it once it has disappeared from view?

READ this section of your text lightly. Then go back and read thoroughly, completing the Workout as you proceed.

Developmental psychologists seek to understand the changes in abilities and disposition that come with increasing age. Development is shaped not only by what occurs during an individual's lifetime, but also by evolutionary and cultural forces. Developmental psychologists have most often focused their efforts on infancy and childhood, though adult development has received some attention. Two key interests have been the development of thought and the development of language. The foundations for psychological development are laid in infancy with the exploration of the physical world.

1. *Infancy* is defined as the first _____ to _____ months after birth.

2. Describe the infant's sensory preparedness for being an explorer.

3. What evidence suggests that infants prefer novel stimuli? How is this preference used by psychologists as an assessment tool?

4. Discuss evidence that even young infants are interested in controlling their environment and respond emotionally to gaining or losing control.

5. Briefly note the infant's exploratory behavior at each of the following ages:
   a. 3 to 4 months old

   b. 5 to 6 months old

6. What constitutes examining, and how do we know that it involves active mental processing?

7. Present evidence that infants adjust their examining to fit the object's properties and that they do learn something about them.

8. Do infants need to be taught or encouraged to examine the objects available to them? Support your answer.

Infants, beginning at about 6 to 12 months, use what they see adults do to guide what *they* do.

9. Name and describe three ways that infants use social cues to guide their behavior. Briefly note the period when such behavior begins.
   a.

   b.

   c.

Adults share certain assumptions about the nature of physical reality. We expect these core principles always to be true, are surprised when they appear to be violated, and know that the "violation" is only a matter of appearances.

10. What is the origin of such knowledge? Describe two contrasting views.
    a. empiricist philosophers, such as Locke and Berkeley

    b. nativist philosophers, such as Descartes and Kant

Though psychologists have not resolved the nativist-empiricist debate, they have shown that humans exhibit knowledge of physical reality beginning at a very young age.

11. What is a common method used today to assess early knowledge of physical principles? Be sure to explain the general procedure and the rationale.

12. What are some core principles that even 2½- to 4-month-olds appear to possess based on this method?

According to Jean Piaget, a pioneer in development research, object permanence is lacking in infants younger than 5 months and is still not fully developed by 9 months.

13. The core principle that says objects continue to exist even when out of view is called

_____ .

14. Briefly describe two of Piaget's hidden-object tasks and give the age at which infants typically succeed at each.
    a. simple hiding problem

    b. changed hiding-place problem

15. How do some researchers explain the discrepancy between results from Piaget's studies and those from selective-looking studies?

16. How might the development of self-produced locomotion lead to an improvement in retrieving hidden objects?

Two Classic Theories of Cognitive Development: Piaget's and Vygotsky's (pages 390–398)

CONSIDER these questions before you go on. They are designed to help you start thinking about this subject, not to test your knowledge.

What aspect of the child's experience promotes the development of new capabilities in logical thinking?

What role does language play in the development of thought?

How does a child's social world support cognitive development?

READ this section of your text lightly. Then go back and read thoroughly, completing the Workout as you proceed.

As they grow older, children become increasingly logical in their thinking, and thus more capable of solving problems. Developmental psychologists want to know how to describe these changes in logical capabilities and how to explain their occurrence. Jean Piaget is widely regarded as the most influential theorist in this area of research.

1. What was Piaget's basic approach to research? his most fundamental idea?

2. What is a scheme? How does the nature of schemes change with development?

3. Complete the following sentences.

   a. _____ is the process by which experiences are incorporated into existing schemes.

   b. _____ is the change in an existing scheme or set of schemes that results from the assimilation of an event or object.

4. Identify each of the following descriptions as focusing primarily on assimilation or accommodation. (Note that each example involves both processes.)

   _____ A child sees a woodcarving of a human figure and thinks of it as a doll.

   _____ A child discovers that the pencil scribblings she has produced can be erased.

   _____ A child is surprised to hear a neighbor's cat "meow" given that it looks a lot like a "doggy."

5. What are operations? operational schemes? Why did Piaget consider operations so important?

Piaget developed a four-stage theory of the child's developing understanding. In Piaget's theory, transition to a given stage is gradual and is based on the child's thoughts and activities at the previous stage. Children may move ahead on some categories of problems before they progress to new schemes with other categories. The four stages are loosely associated with ages, but children vary in their rate of progress. According to Piaget, all children must go through the four stages in order, however.

6. Characterize each of the following stages, being careful wherever possible to indicate the kind of scheme associated with each, the kinds of abilities such schemes support, and the way that advancement to the next stage is promoted.

   a. sensorimotor stage (birth to about 2 years old)

   b. preoperational stage (about 2 to 7 years old)

   c. concrete-operational stage (about 7 to 12 years old)

d. formal-operational stage (from onset of adolescence through adulthood)

Piaget's theory is widely admired even today, but, like any scientific theory, it has its limitations. The process whereby theories are developed, criticized, defended or modified, and so on, is part of the nature of the scientific endeavor.

7. Why is Piaget's work so admired?

8. List and explain three types of criticisms of Piaget's theory. Where possible, describe evidence supporting the critics' point of view.
   a.

   b.

   c.

Another view of cognitive development is offered by the sociocultural perspective. Lev Vygotsky is usually regarded as the originator of this perspective.

9. On what points did Vygotsky agree with Piaget? How did they differ on the aspects of the environment most relevant to development?

10. Why is language so important to cognitive development in Vygotsky's view? Contrast his view on this with Piaget's view.

11. How did Vygotsky interpret children's private or noncommunicative speech? Describe some evidence consistent with Vygotsky's view.

Vygotsky proposed that growth occurs first at the social level and only then at the individual level.

12. Vygotsky used the term _____ _____ to refer to the difference between what a child can do alone and what that child can do together with someone more competent.

13. How does critical thinking develop, according to Vygotsky? What are some research results that support his view?

14. In contrast to Piaget's conception of the child as a little _____, Vygotsky saw the child as a(n) _____.

The developing child's thought occurs not in a void but rather in a *particular* social and cultural context. The child's experience is structured by a variety of social routines—making a purchase at a store, hearing a bedtime story, and going to the movies in some cultures; hunting, building shelters, and ceremonial dancing in others.

15. How can cognitive development be characterized in terms of roles?

16. What is the real goal of mental development?

Development of the Mind's Information-Processing Capacities (pages 398–402)

CONSIDER these questions before you go on. They are designed to help you start thinking about this subject, not to test your knowledge.

How are changes in a child's memory and mental speed related to changes in the child's ability to think logically?

Which aspects of memory capability develop sooner and which develop later?

READ this section of your text lightly. Then go back and read thoroughly, completing the Workout as you proceed.

The information-processing perspective approaches cognitive development not in terms of the whole mind, as Piaget did, but rather in terms of interacting mental components. These mental components are organized as a system for handling information, analogous to a computer's operating system. The mind also contains some specific strategies and rules for a variety of circumstances, much like special-purpose computer programs. From this perspective, cognitive development can be explained in terms of changes in the mind's operating system or in specific programs or both.

1. Trace the development of the following:

  a. implicit memories

  b. explicit semantic memories

  c. explicit episodic memories

2. Why do adults typically recall little from early childhood?

3. Why are developmental changes in working memory thought to be particularly important?

4. How does working memory capacity change during childhood?

5. How might working-memory improvements be due to an increase in processing speed? What evidence suggests that the faster processing results from biological maturation?

Developmental changes in working-memory capacity and processing speed are "all-purpose" changes, affecting many intellectual processes. Some researchers have explored the acquisition of more specific capabilities of the mind—rules and strategies that might apply to only a select type of problem.

6. Summarize Robert Siegler's work on the development of the ability to solve balance-beam problems. (See Figure 11.4 on text page 401.)

7. How does Siegler's account illustrate the fundamental difference between the information-processing and Piagetian approaches?

Children's Understanding of Minds
(pages 402–405)

CONSIDER these questions before you go on. They are designed to help you start thinking about this subject, not to test your knowledge.

Do young children have any conception of other people's psychological or subjective reality?

How does pretend play benefit cognitive development?

READ this section of your text lightly. Then go back and read thoroughly, completing the Workout as you proceed.

Another fact of social life is that children learn *about* other people as well as from them.

1. In what sense are we all everyday psychologists?

2. What evidence suggests that children start to interpret the behavior of others in terms of mental constructs beginning quite early in life?

A child's understanding that people's actions are related to their beliefs takes time to develop. For example, 3-year-olds seldom explain someone's behavior in terms of beliefs. It takes even longer for the child to understand that a person's beliefs can be incorrect.

3. How do 3- and 4-year-olds differ in terms of their performance on the test involving the blue and red cupboards? Is the difference in their performance simply a function of memory? Explain.

4. What did 3-year-olds do when confronted with their own false beliefs in a situation involving candles and crayons?

5. Describe evidence that pretend play is a precursor to understanding false belief.

6. Alan Leslie suggests an evolutionary explanation for the occurrence and importance of pretend play. What is his position?

7. What other sorts of logical reasoning might pretend play help to foster?

The Nature of Language and Children's Early Linguistic Abilities   (pages 406–413)

CONSIDER these questions before you go on. They are designed to help you start thinking about this subject, not to test your knowledge.

Can children respond to language even before they are born?

What do the babbling and cooing of young infants have to do with language development?

READ this section of your text lightly. Then go back and read thoroughly, completing the Workout as you proceed.

Perhaps the most incredible feat of the developing human mind is its rapid progress toward the mastery of language. Children typically acquire considerable facility with their native language before they can manage many other, simpler tasks.

1. Most developmentalists agree that language learning requires a combination of
_____ mechanisms that predispose children to it and a(n)
_____ that provides models and opportunities for practice.

Though there are at least 3000 different languages, all have so much in common that we can reasonably speak of human language in a generic sense.

2. Entities that stand for other entities are called
_____. _____, the smallest meaningful units in a language, are symbols that stand for ideas, events, objects, and so on. For example, the word *unhappiness* contains _____ such units (*un-*, *happy,* and *-ness*). The main meaning of a sentence is carried by _____,

which include nouns, verbs, adjectives, and adverbs. In English, conjunctions, prepositions, articles, and some prefixes and suffices are classified as _____; though they primarily serve grammatical functions, they also contribute to _____.

3. What does it mean to say that a morpheme is arbitrary? Why is arbitrariness important?

4. What does it mean to say that a morpheme is discrete?

5. How do arbitrariness and discreteness distinguish linguistic symbols from nonverbal communication signals?

Language can be described in terms of a four-level hierarchy. Units at each level of the hierarchy can be combined to form the units of the next-higher level.

6. From the highest to the lowest level of the hierarchy, the units are _____,
_____, _____ or
_____, and _____,
which are the elementary vowel and consonant sounds of a language. The rules that specify the permissible ways to arrange units at one level of the hierarchy to produce the next-higher level constitute the _____ of the language. These rules, which exist in some form in all languages, include rules of phonology, which pertain to combining _____; rules of morphology, which pertain to combining

_____; and rules of
_____, which pertain to combining words into phrases and sentences.

7. Is grammar something one learns in school? Support your answer.

8. How is implicit knowledge of grammar demonstrated?

Speech sounds appear to have special status in human development.

9. Summarize evidence that infants are sensitive to and interested in speech stimuli as soon as they are born and possibly even while they are still in the womb.

10. Describe one experimental technique used in research on infants' abilities to distinguish phonemes.

11. What do such experiments suggest about the abilities of infants up to 6 months of age? What happens to their abilities after the age of 6 months? Why is this apparent loss actually valuable?

A familiar (sometimes all-too-familiar) form of infant vocalization is crying. Other types of infant vocalization are cooing and babbling.

12. Repeated, drawn-out vowel sounds, such as *oooh-oooh*, are referred to as _____; _____ consists of repeated consonant-vowel sounds, such as *baa-baa*. Cooing begins to appear at about _____ months and gradually changes to babbling at about _____ months. Cooing and babbling occur most often when the infant is happy and seem to be forms of _____ that have evolved to _____ the vocal apparatus.

13. Are cooing and early babbling influenced by the speech sounds infants hear around them? Explain your answer and be sure to compare the development of deaf and hearing children.

A child's first words are generally greeted with great parental excitement and pride. But infants appear to understand some words well before they are able to say them.

14. How has such understanding been demonstrated?

15. Babies generally speak their first recognizable words at about _____ to _____ months of age. These words are often intended to _____ things or to _____.

16. Describe the growth of the child's vocabulary. Do children acquire most of their new words through explicit instruction? Explain.

17. How do children determine what aspect of the environment a new word refers to?

18. A child's application of the term *car* to a truck or bus would be an instance of _____.
In contrast, a child who fails to include a picture of a chicken in a stack of pictures of birds may be _____ the term *bird*, though this can be hard to detect.

19. How does Eve Clark explain overextensions?

A major step in language development is taken when the child begins to put words together to form rudimentary sentences. This usually occurs at about 18 to 24 months.

20. What kinds of words do children tend to include in early sentences? Do they use word order correctly to indicate their meaning?

21. What evidence has shown that young children learn grammatical rules rather than simply imitating what they hear? (See Figure 11.8 on text page 409.)

22. Explain the assertion that children *discover* the rules of their language.

Internal and External Supports for Language Development   (pages 413–420)

CONSIDER these questions before you go on. They are designed to help you start thinking about this subject, not to test your knowledge.

How is it possible that children who have not mastered the simple tasks of dressing themselves or using eating utensils can produce and understand something as complex as language?

Can other species acquire something like human language?

READ this section of your text lightly. Then go back and read thoroughly, completing the Workout as you proceed.

The process of language development occurs early in life and appears to involve little work on the part of the child or anyone else. That is largely because it is promoted by both internal and external supports. Some theorists emphasize the internal support provided by human biology.

1. Identify some ways in which humans are specially equipped for language.

2. In what sense was the approach to grammar developed by Noam Chomsky, a linguist, inherently psychological?

3. Chomsky's concept of the LAD, or

_____, refers

to the entire set of innate mechanisms for the child's quick and efficient language acquisition. It includes the foundations for

_____ as well as

mechanisms that guide learning of the child's own particular native language.

4. What has Derek Bickerton concluded from studying the development of creole languages?

5. How does the development of sign language in Nicaragua support Bickerton's contention that children play a crucial role in imposing grammar in a new language? How might the children's improvements in grammar be more a matter of their perceptions than of their creativity?

6. Describe evidence for the critical-period hypothesis.

Other theorists point out that the social environment is also necessary to the development of language.

7. Define the LASS. How is it demonstrated in our culture? What is some evidence of its effectiveness in promoting language acquisition?

8. How can social-learning theorists make sense of language development in Kalikuli infants?

Language is considered uniquely human. Only humans acquire such a complex communication system, one based on symbols and grammar, as a normal part of development. But many people have wondered whether it is possible for other species to acquire language under special circumstances. Most efforts to answer this question have focused on chimpanzees or other species of apes. Because these animals lack the vocal apparatus for speech, most efforts have used nonvocal language systems.

9. Who was Washoe? What did the Gardners teach her?

10. What LASS did Sue Savage-Rumbaugh provide for the bonobo Kanzi?

11. What kinds of linguistic accomplishments has Kanzi demonstrated? Have any other apes performed at a similar level?

12. Summarize the overall findings from studies of language learning in apes.

Be sure to READ the Concluding Thoughts at the end of the chapter. Note important points in your Workout. Then consolidate your learning by answering the focus questions in the margins of the text.

After you have studied the chapter thoroughly, CHECK your understanding with the Self-Test that follows.

Self-Test 1

Multiple-Choice Questions

1. Infants' use of a caregiver's emotional expressions to gauge the possible safety or danger of their own actions is called _____ and begins _____.
   a. joint visual attention; soon after birth
   b. joint visual attention; by the time they can crawl or walk on their own
   c. social referencing; soon after birth
   d. social referencing; by the time they can crawl or walk on their own

2. _____ originated the term _____ to refer to the difference between what the child can do alone and what the same child can do in collaboration with more competent others.
   a. Piaget; concrete operations
   b. Piaget; reversible operations
   c. Vygotsky; private speech
   d. Vygotsky; zone of proximal development

3. Young infants will generally look longer at _____ than at _____.
   a. homogeneous stimuli; patterned stimuli
   b. novel stimuli; familiar stimuli
   c. dark, rounded shapes; bright, angular shapes
   d. stimuli that are controlled by others; stimuli they control themselves

4. Which of the following types of long-term memory develops first?
   a. explicit episodic memory
   b. explicit semantic memory
   c. implicit memory
   d. working memory

5. Piaget referred to the child's ability to think of an object that is not immediately present as:
   a. object permanence.
   b. displacement.
   c. objectification.
   d. overextension.

6. Which of the following is true of infants tested shortly after birth for their response to speech sounds?
   a. They show a preference for human speech over instrumental music.
   b. They show no preference for the sound of the mother's voice over the voice of another woman.
   c. They show a preference for the voices of children over those of adults.
   d. All of the above are true.

7. A child's application of the term *kitty* to cats, dogs, and stuffed bears is best described as:
   a. overextension.
   b. underextension.
   c. a delay in understanding false beliefs.
   d. an instance of the LASS.

8. With regard to children's language acquisition, Noam Chomsky contends that:
   a. children's general intelligence is enough to help them acquire language.
   b. children have a set of innate learning aids that specifically help them to acquire language.
   c. learning is not involved in the acquisition of language.
   d. children do not acquire language rules but merely learn to repeat what they hear and are reinforced for producing the sounds.

9. The fact that in our culture adults speak much more simply and clearly to young children than they do to other adults supports the idea of:
   a. the LAD.
   b. the LASS.
   c. syntax.
   d. a pidgin language.

10. Studies of language learning by chimpanzees and other species of apes:
   a. have repeatedly shown that they are incapable of using language symbolically and of learning rules of grammar.
   b. have recently led researchers to conclude that they are fully capable of both basic symbolic usage and grammar.
   c. have consistently shown that they are capable of learning grammar but incapable of using language symbolically.
   d. have led to the general conclusion that they can use language symbolically but have only the slightest capacity for grammar.

11. Piaget's theory has been criticized for:
   a. overestimating age differences in ways of thinking.
   b. being too specific about the process of change and ignoring the "big picture."
   c. overestimating the role of the social environment.
   d. all of the above.

12. In Piaget's theory, the capacity for thinking hypothetically comes when children:
   a. reach the formal-operational stage.
   b. develop schemes.
   c. understand reversible actions.
   d. are capable of communicative speech.

13. Which approach attempts to understand specific changes in the child's cognitive abilities in terms of specific changes in the mind's components?
   a. the Piagetian approach
   b. the information-processing approach
   c. Vygotsky's sociocultural approach
   d. all of the above

14. The view that a broad range of problems can be solved through general principles once the appropriate stage of development has been reached is held by _____ and disputed by
   _____.
   a. Piaget; information-processing theorists
   b. Piaget; sociocultural theorists

   c. information-processing theorists; Piaget
   d. information-processing theorists; sociocultural theorists

15. The Soviet psychologist Lev Vygotsky suggested that:
   a. thought involves a hidden form of the muscular movements that are part of speech.
   b. language is separate from thought in very young children but gradually comes to be used for private thought.
   c. language plays little or no role in the development of thought.
   d. thought cannot occur in the absence of some linguistic symbol system.

Essay Questions

16. Describe the development of the young infant's abilities to distinguish and produce phonemes.

17. Discuss Jean Piaget's beliefs about the role of action in cognitive development during the sensorimotor stage. Be sure to include in your discussion the concept of schemes.

After you have assessed your understanding on the basis of Self-Test 1 and have tried to strengthen your preparation in any areas of weakness, GO ON to Self-Test 2.

Self-Test 2

Multiple-Choice Questions

1. The physical structure of morphemes need not be similar to the concept they stand for; in other words, morphemes are:
   a. discrete.
   b. arbitrary.
   c. grammatical.
   d. literal.

2. Lev Vygotsky used the analogy of a(n) _____ to characterize the developing child.
   a. scientist
   b. sponge
   c. apprentice
   d. computer

3. Motherese is:
   a. observed in all languages studied to date.
   b. the best evidence of the LAD.
   c. commonly observed but has not been shown to affect language development.
   d. associated with more rapid language development in children.

4. Piaget used hiding problems to test the development of:
   a. conservation.
   b. object permanence.
   c. reflexive actions.
   d. operations.

5. Which of the following statements is *not* true of babbling?
   a. It consists of consonant-and-vowel sounds such as *baa-baa-baa*.
   b. Deaf infants begin to babble at the same age as infants who can hear.
   c. Infants babble only the sounds heard in their own native language.
   d. Babbling is a form of vocal play.

6. The earliest evidence that children understand what is in another person's mind comes at about age:
   a. one year.
   b. two years.
   c. three years.
   d. four years.

7. The fact that children overgeneralize the past tense *-ed* ending to create such utterances as "He comed over" helps to illustrate the fact that they:
   a. prefer their own individual speech patterns to adult speech patterns.
   b. tend to overextend more than underextend.
   c. must reach the stage of formal operations before they can acquire an understanding of syntax.
   d. learn grammatical rules rather than simply mimic what they hear.

8. The case of the girl known as Genie provides evidence _____ the idea that _____.
   a. for; children acquire language rules
   b. against; children acquire language rules
   c. for; there is a critical period for some aspects of language acquisition
   d. against; there is a critical period for some aspects of language acquisition

9. Which of the following is true of young children's earliest word combinations?
   a. They typically use only content words.
   b. They must be explicitly taught to combine words.
   c. Their word order is essentially random.
   d. They generally use the passive voice before the active voice.

10. In Piaget's theory, as children become mentally free from the strict control of the here and now, they enter which stage of cognitive development?
    a. sensorimotor
    b. formal operational
    c. concrete operational
    d. preoperational

11. According to Piaget, schemes are associated with which state of development?
    a. sensorimotor
    b. concrete operational
    c. formal operational
    d. all of the above

12. Piaget refers to change in an existing scheme that results from incorporating new experiences as:
    a. an operation.
    b. assimilation.
    c. accommodation.
    d. reversibility.

13. The violation-of-expectancy method of studying infant cognitive development is used to reveal the child's:
    a. use of social referencing.
    b. core knowledge of physical principles.
    c. emotional reaction to loss of control.
    d. grasp of the belief-reality distinction.

14. Robert Siegler's research on children's ability to solve balance-beam problems showed that the children could:

a. not profit from feedback regardless of which rule it disconfirmed.

b. profit from feedback regardless of which rule it disconfirmed.

c. profit from feedback that disconfirmed their current rule and confirmed the next rule in the developmental sequence.

d. profit from feedback that disconfirmed their current rule and also disconfirmed the next rule in the developmental sequence.

15. The sociocultural perspective points out that children learn better when they work on problems:

a. alone.

b. with peers at the same level of understanding.

c. with a younger child whom they can teach.

d. with parents or older children who are more competent.

Essay Questions

16. Describe and provide evidence for the difference between 3-year-olds and 4-year-olds in understanding false beliefs. What if anything, can help such an understanding to develop?

17. Discuss Lev Vygotsky's views on the phenomenon of noncommunicative speech.

Answers

Introduction AND *How Infants Learn About the Physical World*

1. 18; 24

13. object permanence

Two Classic Theories of Cognitive Development: Piaget's and Vygotsky's

3. a. Assimilation
   b. Accommodation

4. assimilation; accommodation; accommodation

12. zone of proximal development

14. scientist; apprentice

The Nature of Language and Children's Early Linguistic Abilities

1. innate; environment

2. symbols; Morphemes; three; content morphemes; grammatical morphemes; meaning

6. sentences; phrases; words *or* morphemes; phonemes; grammar; phonemes; morphemes; syntax

12. cooing; babbling; 2; 6; vocal play; exercise

15. 10; 12; name; point things out

18. overextension; underextending

Internal and External Supports for Language Development

3. language-acquisition device; universal grammar

Self-Test 1

1. d. (p. 387)

2. d. (p. 397)

3. b. This fact is interesting in its own right, but it is also important because it provides a methodological tool. The infant's preference for novelty can be used to test the infant's ability to discriminate be-

tween the familiar stimulus and the novel one. If the infant prefers the new stimulus, it must be able to tell that it is different from the previous stimulus or, in other words, novel. (p. 384)

4. **c.** (p. 399)

5. **a.** His tests of this ability, however, may not reveal the infants' knowledge as well as selective-looking studies. (pp. 388–389)

6. **a.** (p. 408)

7. **a.** (pp. 411–412)

8. **b.** Chomsky dubbed this set of special language-learning aids the LAD, or language-acquisition device. (pp. 413–414)

9. **b.** (pp. 416–417)

10. **d.** (p. 419)

11. **a.** (p. 394)

12. **a.** (p. 394)

13. **b.** (pp. 398–399)

14. **a.** Piaget's approach is holistic, referring to global changes in the mind that allow wide-ranging and new problem-solving capabilities. Information-processing theorists, in contrast, are concerned with changes in individual components of the mind and believe that children learn specific rules that better equip them to handle particular classes of problems. (p. 398)

15. **b.** (p. 396)

16. Even very young infants are able to distinguish among phonemes, the elementary vowel and consonant sounds that make up speech. Infants under 6 months of age can detect differences between any pair of speech sounds that are different phonemes in *any* of the world's languages, which includes some very similar sounds. After the age of 6 months, they start to lose the ability to distinguish subtly different sounds that constitute different phonemes in other languages but belong to the same phoneme category in their native language. This loss actually represents an adaptive change.

Infants can also produce a wide variety of phonemes in their cooing and babbling. Cooing, which starts at about 2 months, consists of the rep-

etition of long, drawn-out vowels (such as *ooooh-ooooh*). Babbling involves consonant-and-vowel combinations (such as *gaaa-gaaa* or *noo-noo*) and starts at about 6 months. Both are forms of vocal play that help to exercise the vocal apparatus in preparation for speech. The phonemes that the infant produces initially do not appear to come from experience. Evidence for this comes from the fact that deaf infants coo and babble as many different sounds as hearing babies and from the fact that young infants' sounds are not much influenced by the particular language they hear. A baby who hears English spoken in the home will produce not only the phonemes of English but also the phonemes of other languages. But this changes by 8 months of age, when babbling begins to resemble the language the baby hears both in rhythm and pitch patterns. By about 10 months, the hearing child's babbling increasingly reflects the syllables and words of the child's native language. Deaf infants begin to babble manually if exposed to sign language. (pp. 407–410)

17. In Piaget's view, action is synonymous with knowledge during infancy. The infant is initially incapable of representing objects and events in terms of mental symbols. During the sensorimotor period, he or she internalizes actions as schemes, mental blueprints for action. In other words, the infant can think about objects and events in terms of action schemes, such as schemes for sucking, kicking, grasping, and so on. Objects become assimilated into schemes for the actions that can be performed on them. Sensorimotor schemes only allow the child to think about objects that are present. (pp. 391–392)

Self-Test 2

1. **b.** (p. 406)

2. **c.** Piaget thought of the child as a little scientist. (p. 397)

3. **d.** (p. 417)

4. **b.** (pp. 388–389)

5. **c.** (p. 409)

6. **a.** (p. 403)

7. **d.** (p. 412)

8. **c.** (p. 416)

9. **a.** (p. 412)

10. **d.** (pp. 392–393)

11. **d.** (pp. 392–394)

12. **c.** Assimilation is matching a new experience to an existing scheme. Accommodation occurs when the object assimilated does not quite fit the scheme to which it is matched such that the scheme must be modified accordingly. (p. 391)

13. **b.** (p. 388)

14. **c.** Siegler suggested that children move sequentially through a series of four rules and that they cannot use feedback that would require them to skip over the next rule in the sequence. (p. 401)

15. **d.** (p. 397)

16. Children under the age of four years have some ability to understand and detect other people's perceptions, emotions, and desires. But they do not generally think in terms of other people's beliefs and do not really understand that beliefs (their own, as well as other people's) can be false or mistaken. In a typical test of the ability to understand false beliefs, the children hear a simple story and see it acted out with puppets. For example, they are told and shown that Maxi put his candy bar in a blue cupboard. Then they are told that Maxi leaves and his mother moves the candy bar to a different cupboard—a red one. When asked where Maxi will look for his candy when he returns, 4-year-olds say the blue one, but 3-year-olds say the red one. They can't seem to grasp that someone can believe something that isn't true. Make-believe or pretend play may help children to develop an understanding that belief does not equal reality. (pp. 403–404)

17. Vygotsky observed that 4- to 6-year-old children often produce speech that does not take other people into account. That is, it is noncommunicative. What they say is not tailored for the comprehension of another person but does have value and purpose. The child may say "Oh, there's the pig I need" when playing with toys representing a barnyard scene, for example. Vygotsky felt that language (rather than action, as in Piaget's theory) was the foundation of thought, and thus of cognitive development. In his view, such noncommunicative speech was the child's thinking out loud, using language as a support to thought, helping to guide behavior and aid in planning. Vygotsky explained the decline in this form of speech in terms of the child's progress at internalizing language. By the age of 7, the child could depend on inner speech or verbal thought, rather than audible speech, to aid thinking. (p. 396)

Social Development

Chapter 12

READ the introduction below before you read the chapter in the text.

We are all social beings who must continue to adapt to the social environment throughout our lifetimes. Attachment is a major focus of infant social development. The term *attachment* refers to the emotional bonds that infants develop toward principal caregivers, usually their mothers. Research on humans and other primates indicates that physical contact with the caregiver is an important element of attachment. Human infants first show signs of attachment at about the time they begin to crawl, which makes evolutionary sense. Secure attachment in infancy is associated with greater confidence and sociability and with better emotional health and problem-solving performance later in childhood. The quality of care is a major influence on the quality of attachment. Cross-cultural differences in infant care are considerable. Western cultures are in many ways less indulgent of infants' desires than many other cultures. Hunter-gatherer cultures are, in contrast, especially indulgent toward infants.

Childhood is a time when powerful forms of socialization are at work. Among the earliest influences are interactions with caregivers. Children seem to be predisposed toward prosocial behaviors such as giving and helping but must also learn to restrain themselves and learn compliance. The emergence of empathy-based guilt during the third year of life seems to promote moral growth as well as self-restraint. Theorists have devised ways of categorizing different styles of parental discipline and have argued that some styles are more effective than others. Theorists generally agree that play serves developmental functions but disagree about what they are. Some theorists emphasize its value as a means of learning about social roles and rules and about morality; others, its useful-

ness in skill development and the transmission of culture. Age-mixed play has some powerful benefits, such as a lessening of competitiveness. Gender is also a factor in socialization. Gender enters into treatment of boys and girls by parents, by teachers, and by children themselves.

Adolescence lasts from the first signs of puberty until an individual is accepted as a full member of adult society. During adolescence, individuals typically become more independent of parents and more dependent on peers. Theorists have tried to explain the increased recklessness and violence of this period, particularly notable in boys, in terms ranging from a quest for or reaction against adult roles to a genetically ordained struggle for status. Adolescence is also a time in which individuals may have gained the intellectual capabilities that permit sophisticated moral reasoning, as described in Lawrence Kohlberg's theory of moral reasoning. Problems of emerging sexual relationships are compounded by the continuing sexual double standard and cultural messages glorifying sex. The choice in favor of sexual restraint or promiscuity may reflect adaptive strategies and evolutionary pressures.

Adulthood centers largely around the themes of love and work. In many ways, adult romantic love is similar in form to infant attachment. Research suggests that mutual liking, commitment, good communication, and understanding are among the characteristics of happy marriages. Because work is such a large part of adult life, job satisfaction is very important to life satisfaction and it appears to derive largely from occupational self-direction. Men and women differ in the satisfaction they derive from work at home versus work out of the home. The chapter concludes with a look at old age and points out that life satisfaction in later years is often greater than younger people would predict. Older people are also more focused on the present and less afraid of dying than younger people are.

LOOK over the table of contents for this chapter in your textbook before you continue with your study.

Notice that there are focus questions in the margins of the text for your use in studying the material. The following chart lists which Study Guide questions relate to which focus questions.

The Integrated Study Workout

COMPLETE one section at a time.

Introduction AND Infancy: Using Caregivers as a Base for Growth   (pages 423–431)

CONSIDER these questions before you go on. They are designed to help you start thinking about this subject, not to test your knowledge.

Does a caregiver "spoil" a child by being very responsive?

How do Western cultures compare with other cultures in terms of infant care?

Why do some infants cling to a security blanket?

READ this section of your text lightly. Then go back and read thoroughly, completing the Workout as you proceed.

Humans live their lives not only in a physical environment, but in a social one as well.

1. What does the term *social development* mean?

2. Briefly comment on Erik Erikson's theory as it relates to infancy.

3. How did John Bowlby regard the emotional bond between infant and caregiver? According to this theorist, what promoted the bond?

Human infants are born with a biological preparedness for identifying their caregivers, developing an emotional bond with them, and eliciting their help.

4. Describe the preferences and emotional signals that help infants to build bonds with their caregivers. What term is used to refer to such emotional bonds?

Attachment is not restricted to human infants. Harry Harlow's experimentation on attachment in rhesus monkeys is classic.

5. Discuss the method and results of Harry Harlow's experiment on infant monkeys' attachment to surrogate mothers. (See Figures 12.1 and 12.2 on text pages 424 and 425.)

The concept of attachment is central to John Bowlby's theory of development. Bowlby, like Harlow, developed his theory in the 1950s, but he focused on human infants.

6. What observations did Bowlby make about the behavior of attached children?

Because these attachment behaviors have been noted in a variety of cultures and in other species of mammals, they are thought to have a strong biological basis.

7. Discuss the emergence of such attachment behaviors from an evolutionary perspective.

8. What happens to attachment at about 6–8 months? Why?

Some means of measuring attachment is needed in order to study it objectively. Mary Ainsworth provided one such test.

9. Name and describe the most commonly used method for measuring attachment.

10. How do the responses of securely attached infants differ from those of infants who are not securely attached? (Distinguish between infants with an avoidant attachment and those with an anxious attachment.)

11. How common is each type of attachment in middle-class North American infants?

12. What are some limitations of the strange-situation test?

Psychologists have attempted to learn more about both the causes and the effects of attachment.

13. What early behaviors in the caregiver are correlated with secure attachment?

14. How were these correlations interpreted by Bowlby and Ainsworth? What are some alternative interpretations?

15. How did research by Dymphna van den Boom support Ainsworth's and Bowlby's interpretation?

Many psychologists have suggested that the quality of an infant's early attachment has long-term consequences.

16. What is some evidence that early attachment influences psychological functioning in later childhood and young adulthood? Why must we be cautious about cause-effect conclusions?

17. How does daycare affect development and attachment?

Cross-cultural studies show large differences in the way infants are cared for. In contrast to other cultures, Western culture is notable for its relative lack of physical contact between infant and caregiver. For example, infants and young children in Western society typically sleep alone, whereas infants in a great many other cultures typically sleep with their mothers or other related adults.

18. According to a cross-cultural interview study, how did Mayan and American women differ in beliefs as well as in sleeping practices? What findings suggest that co-sleeping may be beneficial for children? Are there also risks?

19. How might sleeping arrangements be related to attachment to an inanimate object?

20. Why have some psychologists chosen to study hunter-gatherer societies?

21. How are infants cared for in !Kung society? in Efe society? among the Aka?

22. Does indulgent infant care lead to spoiled or overly dependent children? Explain.

23. How does such early indulgence seem to be related to the size of extended families?

Childhood I: Continuing Interactions with Caregivers   (pages 432–437)

CONSIDER these questions before you go on. They are designed to help you start thinking about this subject, not to test your knowledge.

Are children naturally selfish or naturally giving?

Is it better to be a firm, no-nonsense, no-explanations-given type of parent, or are other styles of discipline more effective?

READ this section of your text lightly. Then go back and read thoroughly, completing the Workout as you proceed.

Erik Erikson proposed three stages that occur during the ages 1–12 years.

1. With what issue is each successive stage mainly concerned?

2. What role does child-caregiver interaction play in determining how each stage turns out?

During childhood, powerful forces of socialization are at work. But the child is not a passive object of socialization. Rather, the child actively uses the resources of the social environment, including caregivers, peers, and others, to achieve socialization. One area of interest is the development of behaviors and emotions that support morality.

3. Do very young children enjoy or resist giving? Support your answer with evidence.

4. How does the !Kung culture compare with ours in terms of the attention paid to children's giving?

5. Do children of this young age join in to help with adult tasks?

6. What evidence suggests that empathy begins in infancy? How might empathy be related to children's giving and helping?

Children not only develop prosocial behaviors such as giving but must also learn to deal with situations in which they *cannot* do what they want or must do something they would rather not do.

7. When does the child begin to show a capacity for guilt? Is there a sense in which guilt can be socially and personally constructive?

8. Are all forms of guilt constructive? Explain. Are sensitive parenting and secure attachment related to positive instances of guilt?

One classic topic of research in social development has been parenting styles, particularly styles of parental discipline. Martin Hoffman and Diana Baumrind have each analyzed discipline and found that certain approaches are associated with more positive outcomes.

9. Label the following techniques of discipline identified by Hoffman.

_____ the use or threatened use of punishment or reward to control the child's behavior

_____ a form of verbal reasoning in which the parent leads the child to think about his or her actions and their consequences for others

_____ a style in which parents often unconsciously express disapproval of the child, not just of the undesirable behavior

10. Which technique does Hoffman favor? Why? Is power assertion ever necessary?

11. Complete the following three sentences about the discipline styles identified by Baumrind.

_____ parents are the most tolerant of their children's disruptive behaviors and least likely to discipline them.

_____ parents are more concerned with helping the child to acquire and use principles of right and wrong than they are with pure obedience.

_____ parents want obedience for its own sake and often use power assertion to get it.

12. What was Baumrind's main finding? How do her findings fit with Hoffman's categorization? Is there other research that supports Hoffman's theory?

As you know, we must exercise caution when interpreting correlations between parents' disciplinary styles and children's behavior. No causal relationship is established simply by a correlation. More recent research has helped to reveal more about who is influencing whom.

13. Does children's behavior influence the parents' disciplinary style or does the parents' disciplinary style influence the children's behavior? Explain.

Childhood II: Roles of Play and Gender in Development   (pages 437–444)

CONSIDER *these questions before you go on. They are designed to help you start thinking about this subject, not to test your knowledge.*

What functions are served by children's play?

In what ways do adults treat boys and girls differently? What are some of the consequences of this differential treatment?

READ *this section of your text lightly. Then go back and read thoroughly, completing the Workout as you proceed.*

Children are strongly oriented toward other children, and after the age of 4 or 5 they spend most of their waking hours with peers. Much of that time is spent in play, which serves development in a number of ways. Play occurs in comparable forms in every culture studied.

1. List universal forms of play among children:

Play occurs in a cultural as well as an evolutionary context.

2. Describe evidence that play reflects and helps to transmit the skills and values of the culture in which it occurs. How might it also help to shape that culture?

Play helps the child to better understand rules, social roles, and morality.

3. According to Piaget, how does play with peers allow the child to develop the ability to reason about right and wrong? Is there evidence to support his view?

4. Is play inherently free and spontaneous in Vygotsky's view? Explain. What developmental value does this have?

5. What evidence supports Vygotsky's view?

Play among children of mixed ages appears to be especially valuable for children's development.

6. Describe some of the special qualities and advantages of age-mixed play.

In every culture studied, boys and girls differ, and so do their experiences of life. Different biology can explain some but not all of the disparities.

7. Distinguish between the terms *sex* and *gender*.

8. On average, how do boy and girl infants differ behaviorally?

Differential treatment of boys and girls by adults begins very early indeed. To some extent, this may reflect responsiveness to actual differences in the children, but it also stems in part from adult expectations based on gender.

9. List some examples of how adults respond differentially to boys and girls.

10. What consequences might arise from such differential treatment of boys and girls?

Children play a significant part in shaping their own gender-related behavior.

11. What is gender identity? How do children actively adapt to and assert their own gender identity?

Children reinforce gender distinction through their peer groups. Boys and girls interact more with members of their own gender. A preference for same-sex playmates is present even at age 3 but peaks between ages 8 and 11.

12. What do children do in their gender-segregated play groups?

13. How and why is gender segregation more strongly reinforced for boys than for girls?

Some have suggested that the peer groups of boys and girls are really different subcultures.

14. Compare the world of boys with the world of girls as described by some social scientists. How might this view exaggerate the typical differences? How might it be related to age-segregation vs. age-mixing?

Adolescence: Breaking Out of the Cocoon
(pages 445–455)

CONSIDER these questions before you go on. They are designed to help you start thinking about this subject, not to test your knowledge.

What role do peers play in the lives of adolescents?

Why are some adolescents reckless or even delinquent?

What is the developmental basis of morality and of moral reasoning? What leads some young people to act out of extraordinary idealism?

READ this section of your text lightly. Then go back and read thoroughly, completing the Workout as you proceed.

Adolescence, a bridge between childhood and adulthood, begins at the onset of puberty and ends when a person is considered a full member of adult society. Developmental psychologists generally agree that adolescents actively move away from their childhood identities and toward independent adult identities, though most disavow Erikson's notion of an identity *crisis*.

1. Why is adolescence longer in our culture compared with earlier times and other cultures?

2. Adolescence as a time of rebellion is a popularly accepted notion. In what sense do adolescents "rebel"? In what sense do they not? Is conflict linked more to age or to physical maturation?

As adolescents move toward independence from their parents, they become increasingly dependent upon their peers for emotional support.

3. Present some evidence of this shift from parental dependence to dependence on friendships with peers.

4. How do adolescent peer groups lead to reduced gender barriers and to romantic relationships?

5. Briefly discuss positive and negative effects of peer pressure. Be sure to mention cross-cultural differences between the United States and China.

Though adolescence may be difficult and turbulent, it is not equally so for all individuals. For some, adolescence is marked by increased recklessness and delinquency, especially among young males.

6. What are some characteristics of adolescent cognition and motivation that have been noted as potential explanations for such behavior?

7. How does Terrie Moffitt explain adolescent recklessness and delinquency in terms of segregation from adults? What evidence does she present?

8. What alternative position is taken by Judith Harris, and how does her theory account for such risky behaviors as train surfing that are not adult-like?

9. Following the lead of Wilson and Daly, argue for an evolutionary explanation of the greater increase in risk taking and violence among young males.

10. Are females also more violent on average in adolescence? Explain.

Idealism and increasing moral vision distinguish adolescence as well. The roots of morality lie in the ability to reason logically, according to Lawrence Kohlberg.

11. Briefly describe Kohlberg's research method. What aspect of people's responses was of greatest interest to Kohlberg?

12. In what sense do Kohlberg's five stages represent a true developmental progression, according to Kohlberg? How do the stages reflect a broadening social perspective? (See Table 12.1 on text page 450.)

13. What is the motivating force that pushes a person on to the next stage of moral reasoning? Does everyone eventually reach Stage 5? Explain.

14. Is moral reasoning related to moral behavior? Explain.

15. How did Daniel Hart and his colleagues approach the study of moral development? What has been found to promote exceptional moral commitment?

Sexuality is a topic that must be addressed in any full consideration of adolescence; after all, the beginning of adolescence coincides with the onset of puberty. With the physical changes that permit reproduction come powerful drives and emotions, as well as potentially troublesome behaviors. In modern cultures, a prolonged period of sexual maturity before adulthood is reached may contribute to problems associated with emerging sexual relationships. So may the attitudes that exist within those cultures.

16. Which factors tend to lead to teenage pregnancy and which help to reduce its incidence?

17. Is there really a sexual double standard for girls and boys? Explain.

18. List some factors that may lead to the high frequency of date rape.

19. How would Robert Trivers explain the greater desire for uncommitted sex among males?

Though nature may have created certain tendencies toward sexual behavior that differ between males and females, those tendencies can be moderated by the social environment. For example, the restraint—or lack of it—on the part of one sex may help to determine the sexual strategy of the other sex. Patricia Draper and Henry Harpending suggest that childhood cues, such as the presence or absence of a caring father in the home, may incline individuals toward either restraint or promiscuity.

20. Explain the theory offered by Draper and Harpending, and comment on the evidence available for it.

Adulthood: Finding Satisfaction in Love and Work   (pages 456–462)

CONSIDER these questions before you go on. They are designed to help you start thinking about this subject, not to test your knowledge.

What makes some marriages happy and others unhappy?

What contributes most to satisfaction in work?

How does becoming a parent affect a marriage?

Is old age a sad and fearful time of life?

READ this section of your text lightly. Then go back and read thoroughly, completing the Workout as you proceed.

Love and work are the joint themes of adult development. Romance and marriage are found in all cultures studied, and psychologists have sought to understand the essentials of both.

1. List the characteristics that seem to be common both to romantic love and to infant attachment. Is the quality of attachment in infancy related to the quality of later romantic attachment?

In the study of love relationships, psychologists have asked why some marriages work while others do not.

2. What do studies of happily married couples reveal about them?

3. How does the success of a marriage depend especially on the husband's willingness and ability to be sensitive, caring, and responsive?

Working outside the home is a fact of life for most men and women in the United States, but it is a happier fact for some than for others.

4. What are some factors positively associated with job satisfaction? What term does sociologist Melvin Kohn apply to this set of job characteristics?

5. How does high occupational self-direction affect workers? their children? Were these effects dependent on salary level or job prestige?

Women who work outside the home often have two roles—their outside employment and their work at home. And they often feel torn between the two sets of obligations.

6. Where are husbands and wives happier—working at home or working out of the home? What might explain this?

Given current estimates of life expectancy, today's college student can reasonably hope to live well past retirement age—in fact, past the age of 80.

7. Old age is undeniably a period that involves loss, but is old age as bad as it seems to the young? Explain.

8. Label the theories of aging briefly described below.

_____ Elderly people gradually and voluntarily withdraw from the world around them into a more subjective, inner world.

_____ Elderly people prefer to remain involved in the world and are happier when they can remain so.

_____ Elderly people become more focused on the present than on preparing for the future as the "size" of that future decreases.

9. What observations fit well with Carstensen's socioemotional selectivity theory?

10. How do older people differ from younger people in their emphasis on the positive?

Death awaits everyone eventually, but with advancing age one grows ever closer to that point.

11. Do the elderly fear death more than people in other age groups? Explain.

12. Does everyone approach death in essentially the same way—by going through a sequence of stages, for example, or by reviewing his or her life? Support your answer.

Be sure to READ the Concluding Thoughts at the end of the chapter. Note important points in your Workout. Then consolidate your learning by answering the focus questions in the margins of the text.

After you have studied the chapter thoroughly, CHECK your understanding with the Self-Test that follows.

Self-Test 1

Multiple-Choice Questions

1. Hunter-gatherers such as the !Kung or Efe are much _____ indulgent toward infants, which clearly _____ result in overly demanding and dependent children.
   a. less; does
   b. less; does not
   c. more; does
   d. more; does not

2. Which of the following is a universal form of human play?
   a. chase games
   b. play nurturing
   c. constructive play
   d. all of the above

3. The willfulness of the 2-year-old is moderated in the third year of life by the gradual development of a capacity for:
   a. social referencing.
   b. guilt.
   c. negotiation.
   d. trust.

4. Mary Ainsworth's strange-situation test is used to:
   a. measure the developing child's ability to become involved in various kinds of play.
   b. promote the developing adolescent's resistance to peer pressure.
   c. enhance the developing child's ability to engage in moral reasoning.
   d. measure the developing infant's attachment to a person.

5. Cross-cultural research has shown that Western culture is atypical in that Western parents generally:
   a. require young children to sleep in a different room from adults.
   b. employ an authoritarian style of parenting.
   c. use power assertion to gain behavioral compliance from children.
   d. give in most readily to demands for attention from young children.

6. Martin Hoffman described one type of parental discipline in which parents use verbal reasoning to lead the child to think about his or her actions and their consequences. He called this type of discipline:
   a. authoritarian.
   b. permissive.
   c. induction.
   d. power assertion.

7. In the view of Lev Vygotsky, the most important function of play is that it:
   a. promotes spontaneity and creativity.
   b. provides a time of relaxation and release for children, who outside of play experience considerable pressure to learn and to become socialized.

c. allows children to express deep, unconscious wishes and conflicts and thereby helps to alleviate emotional problems.

d. gives children a context for learning about rules and social roles and learning how to control their own impulses.

8. Which of the following is true of self-imposed gender segregation in children?

a. Boys avoid playing with girls more than the reverse.

b. Girls avoid playing with boys more than the reverse.

c. It peaks at about 6–7 years of age.

d. It declines at the ages of 8–11 years.

9. Studies show that adolescent rebellion is primarily directed against:

a. school authorities rather than parents.

b. peers rather than authority figures.

c. ethical or political injustices in society rather than family matters.

d. parental constraints on personal freedom rather than parental values.

10. Research suggests that there _____ a double standard of sexual behavior for boys and girls and that this may tend to _____ acts of sexual aggression.

a. is still; contribute to

b. is still; prevent

c. is no longer; contribute to

d. is no longer; prevent

11. The fact that newborns cry reflexively in response to other babies' crying has been suggested as evidence of the early roots of:

a. social referencing.

b. empathy.

c. compliance.

d. rebellion.

12. In his studies of moral development, Lawrence Kohlberg was mainly interested in:

a. the decision someone reached about resolving a dilemma.

b. the reasoning involved in reaching a decision about a dilemma.

c. the action someone had taken in a real-life moral dilemma.

d. the empathy people expressed for those involved in the dilemma.

13. Jobs with greater _____ have been found to positively affect personality, parenting style, and even the development of the workers' children.

a. income

b. self-direction

c. prestige

d. structure

14. Interviews with exceptionally morally committed young people show that they are primarily motivated by:

a. a selfless sense of duty.

b. abstract principles of right and wrong.

c. positive aspects of their self-image.

d. the desire for adult approval.

15. Carstensen's socioemotional selectivity theory of aging suggests that as people get older, they become increasingly focused on:

a. their inner, subjective world.

b. connecting in new ways with the world around them.

c. death.

d. the present.

Essay Questions

16. Discuss infant attachment in terms of its nature, causes, prerequisites, and results.

17. What qualities tend to distinguish happy marriage?

After you have assessed your understanding on the basis of Self-Test 1 and have tried to strengthen your preparation in any areas of weakness, GO ON to Self-Test 2.

Self-Test 2

Multiple-Choice Questions

1. Daycare that is of high quality:
   a. nevertheless results in slower, poorer development.
   b. actually interferes with secure attachment to mothers and fathers.
   c. generally yields better intellectual development but poorer social development.
   d. none of the above

2. In Harry Harlow's study of attachment in infant monkeys, attachment:
   a. was based purely on whichever surrogate "mother" provided nutrition.
   b. developed toward the wire "mother" but not the cloth "mother."
   c. developed toward the cloth "mother" but not the wire "mother."
   d. was based on whichever surrogate "mother" the infant was first exposed to.

3. Bowlby claimed that infant attachment is based on:
   a. sociocultural learning.
   b. instinctive tendencies in infant and caregiver.
   c. the earlier phenomenon of social referencing.
   d. a combination of reward and punishment from the mother or other caregiver.

4. Angela promptly comforts her infant son whenever he shows signs of distress. Research suggests that this is likely to:
   a. spoil the child.
   b. develop an unhealthy dependence in the child.
   c. promote secure attachment.
   d. promote anxious attachment.

5. Martin Hoffman uses the term *love withdrawal* to refer to a disciplinary style in which parents:
   a. use their superior strength or control of resources to induce the child to behave in ways they find acceptable.
   b. express disapproval of the child, not just of the child's specific unacceptable actions.
   c. use verbal reasoning to lead the child to think about his or her actions and the consequences of those actions.
   d. ignore or excuse their children's misbehavior without any attempt at correcting it.

6. Diana Baumrind found that nursery school children were most likely to show positive qualities if their parents applied a disciplinary style she called:
   a. authoritative.   c. power assertion.
   b. authoritarian.   d. permissive.

7. The strange-situation test is commonly used to assess:
   a. marital happiness.
   b. infant attachment.
   c. social intelligence.
   d. parental discipline styles.

8. _____ refers to the clear biological basis for differentiating between male and female, while _____ refers to the whole set of differences attributed to males and females.
   a. Gender; gender identity
   b. Gender identity; sex
   c. Sex; gender
   d. Sex; gender identity

9. Which of the following correctly describes a research finding about the ways that adults respond differently to boys and girls?
   a. They play more gently with infant girls than with infant boys.
   b. They talk more to infant girls than to infant boys.
   c. They offer help and comfort more often to girls than to boys.
   d. All of the above.

10. Draper and Harpending propose that the presence of a caring father in the home tends to lead to increased _____ in adolescence.

a. sexual restraint
b. promiscuity
c. parental dependence
d. gender differentiation

11. Romantic love has been likened to:
    a. a form of role play.
    b. a permissive style of parenting.
    c. attachment in infancy.
    d. cooperation in hunter-gatherer societies.

12. Researchers have found that in happy marriages:
    a. husband and wife highly value and assert their independence.
    b. the couples argue much less than couples in unhappy marriages.
    c. husband and wife like each other as friends and confidants.
    d. the couples pull apart during hard times to avoid stressing the marriage.

13. Wives are more likely than husbands to:
    a. prefer their at-home work to their out-of-home work.
    b. consider themselves happily married.
    c. notice their spouse's unspoken needs.
    d. prefer an authoritarian parenting style.

14. Moral development is promoted by _____, according to Hoffman.
    a. social referencing
    b. parental discipline
    c. empathy-based guilt
    d. anxiety-based guilt

15. Research suggests that life satisfaction in old age is _____ younger people would expect it to be.
    a. much lower than
    b. somewhat lower than
    c. about what
    d. higher than

Essay Questions

16. What is the major function of play, according to Lev Vygotsky? Is there evidence to support his view? Explain.

17. Discuss Lawrence Kohlberg's theory of the development of moral reasoning. Be sure to include in your answer the primary goal of the theory, Kohlberg's methodology, and the basic tenets of the theory.

Answers

Childhood I: Continuing Interactions with Caregivers

9. power assertion; induction; love withdrawal

11. Permissive; Authoritative; Authoritarian

Adulthood: Finding Satisfaction in Love and Work

8. disengagement; activity; socioemotional selectivity

Self-Test 1

1. d. (p. 430)

2. d. (p. 438)

3. b. (p. 434)

4. d. (p. 426)

5. a. This may be related to a research finding that blanket attachments are more common in North American infants than in infants of other cultures, who generally sleep in the same room with a mother or other close adult relative. (p. 428)

6. c. Induction is also the style that Hoffman most favors. (p. 435)

7. d. (p. 439)

8. a. (p. 443)

9. d. (p. 446)

10. a. (pp. 452–453)

11. b. (p. 433)

12. b. Kohlberg, whose work was influenced by that of Piaget, was interested in the development of the ability to *think* about moral situations. He was therefore most interested in the thought processes involved in reaching a conclusion, not the conclusion itself. (p. 449)

13. b. (p. 459)

14. c. For example, they may see themselves as individuals who set a good example. (p. 451)

15. d. (p. 461)

16. Attachment is the emotional bond that an infant develops toward a primary caregiver. It is strongest between the ages of about 8 months and 3 years. The infant expresses distress when the object of attachment leaves, especially in an unfamiliar or frightening situation, and pleasure when he or she returns. The infant is more likely to explore an unfamiliar environment with the object of attachment present and looks to that person for reassurance in the presence of a stranger. John Bowlby, whose research in this field is classic, believed infant attachment is based in evolution. Infants who behaved in an attached way were more likely to survive into adulthood and reproduce.

Longitudinal research indicates that infants who consistently receive comfort and prompt responsive reactions to signs of distress are more likely to be securely attached. Early measures of attachment are correlated with positive outcomes later in childhood, such as greater confidence, problem-solving ability, and emotional health. The warmth and security of romantic attachment in adulthood may also be related to early attachment. Such findings do not show a causal role of attachment in producing such outcomes, however. (pp. 425–428, 456–457)

17. Studies show that happily married people genuinely like each other, regarding their spouses as best friends and confidants as well as marriage partners. They also appear to have an extraordinarily high commitment to the marriage, each individual being willing to give more than his or her share during rough periods in the relationship. In terms of communication patterns, happily married people are willing to listen to each other, show respect for the other partner's views, and focus on the present issue under discussion rather than have a hidden agenda of "winning" or bringing up old hurts. Partners in happy marriages also intersperse their communications, even in arguments, with positive comments and humor. (pp. 457–458)

Self-Test 2

1. d. (p. 428)

2. c. Harlow concluded that the contact comfort afforded by the cloth, but not the wire, "mother" was more important to attachment than feeding was. (pp. 424–425)

3. b. (p. 425)

4. c. (p. 427)

5. b. (p. 435)

6. a. Be sure you can distinguish between authoritarian and authoritative parenting styles. Authori-*tarian* parents value control for its own sake and use a high degree of power assertion. Authorita-*tive* parents value good behavior more than control itself and prefer induction but will use power assertion when necessary. (p. 437)

7. b. (p. 426)

8. c. (p. 441)

9. d. (pp. 441–442)

10. a. (p. 454)

11. c. (p. 456)

12. c. (p. 457)

13. c. In fact, husbands who want happy wives and happy marriages need to do the same. (p. 457)

14. c. (p. 435)

15. d. (p. 460)

16. Vygotsky, who generally emphasized the importance of the social world to development, felt that social play is critical to the socialization process. He argued that play is not the context in which children are most free and spontaneous, as popular belief would have it. Rather, play is a context in which children learn to govern their behavior according to rules of social behavior and according to the social roles they act out. A child playing the role of a robber in cops and robbers, for example, would be forced to think about what it means to be a robber—what behavior makes a person a robber, how a robber interacts with other people such as police, and so on. The child would also have to fit his or her behavior to that role as it is understood. This ability to assume roles later spills over into the child's nonplay activities, as the child begins to move into such social roles as student or junior gardener or pet caretaker. Research consistent with Vygotsky's position suggests that children actually do think about and enforce rules in their social play. Further, the amount of sociodramatic play children engage in is correlated with their social competence. (pp. 439–440)

17. Kohlberg recognized that moral development is at least in part the development of the ability to think logically about moral situations. He sought to understand this aspect of moral development by asking people what the protagonists of hypothetical moral dilemmas should do and why. His interest was not so much in the conclusions subjects reached but in the nature of the reasoning they used to reach those conclusions.

On the basis of such research, Kohlberg proposed that there is an invariant sequence of stages through which moral development proceeds. Initially, an individual thinks only of himself or herself. In the fifth and highest stage, which is not attained by everyone, universal moral principles are the basis of judgment. Progression from the first to the fifth stage involves a growing inclusiveness of others in the social world that is, a broadening social perspective. As the limitations of one stage become evident, the individual is drawn toward the next stage. (pp. 449–451)

Social Perception and Attitudes

chapter 13

READ the introduction below before you read the chapter in the text.

A major focus of social psychology is the study of the mental processes and systematic biases underlying perceptions of the social world, including ourselves as well as other people. Many social judgments depend on interpreting the causes of behavior. A decision about the causes of a behavior is called an *attribution*. Harold Kelley developed a model of the logic involved in making attributions. Fritz Heider, a pioneer in this area, claimed that we have a natural tendency to attribute behavior to the characteristics of the person who is behaving, though we sometimes attribute behavior to the situation. Various factors, including culture and the identity of the person carrying out the behavior, affect our tendency to make attributions to the person or to the situation.

Just as we form schemas for trees, modes of transportation, and furniture, we form schemas—organized sets of information or beliefs—for people. The schema you have for an individual helps you to interpret and organize new information about that individual, though it can also distort your perceptions of the person. This distortion often occurs because we are unduly influenced by first impressions, which may be superficial (deriving from physical appearance, for example) or may simply be wrong. Part of the reason we tend to like people more if we first meet on the Internet rather than in person may be that we are not biased by appearances.

Our self-concepts and behavior are affected by other people's expectations of us, such that expectations can become self-fulfilling prophecies. In a variety of ways, we come to view ourselves by looking at what the social world around us seems to reflect back about us. Charles Cooley called this the looking-glass self. Our own active comparisons of ourselves with others also help to determine our self-concepts. The particular reference group with which we compare ourselves may affect how smart, how tall, or how talented we think we are. In Western cultures, people have a tendency to enhance their views of themselves in a number of ways, but people in East Asian cultures are not similarly disposed.

Individuals appear to have both personal identities and social identities that depend on group membership—a certain family, nation, ethnicity, faith, fraternity, and so on. In different cultures, the relative importance of personal and social identities may vary.

Stereotypes, which are schemas about groups of people, can distort our impressions of individual members of those groups even if we consciously combat the influence of stereotypes in our thinking. Psychologists have ways (such as priming) to reveal stereotypes that the individual may not even be aware of. Such implicit stereotypes can still affect judgments of and behavior toward the stereotyped group.

Attitudes are beliefs or opinions that have an evaluative component. The attitudes we have toward objects, events, people, concepts, and so on serve several functions. Our attitudes can be shaped in part by the social groups with which we identify. The drive to reduce cognitive dissonance, the psychological discomfort that exists when there is disagreement among our beliefs, attitudes, and/or behaviors, can also have interesting effects on our attitudes. For example, if we freely perform some behavior contrary to our attitudes with little or no incentive, we may change our attitudes to be more consistent with the behavior. The formation of attitudes may involve virtually no thought (as in classical conditioning), minimal thought (as in the use of decision rules or heuristics), or systematic, logical thought. We are more likely to devote systematic, logical processing to matters that have high personal relevance to us. Implicit attitudes automatically affect behavior, but explicit attitudes must be retrieved from memory to have an effect.

LOOK over the table of contents for this chapter in your textbook before you continue with your study.

Notice that there are focus questions in the margins of the text for your use in studying the material. The following chart lists which Study Guide questions relate to which focus questions.

Focus Questions	Study Guide Questions
Introduction and Forming Impressions of Other People	
1–2	1–9
3	10
4	11–12
5	13–14
6	15
7	16–17
8–9	18–21
10	22–23
Perceiving and Evaluating the Self	
11	1
12	2
13–14	3
15	4–6
16	7–9
17	10
18	11
19	12
Perceiving Ourselves and Others as Members of Groups	
20	1–2
21–22	3–4
23	5–9
24	10
25	11
26	12
Attitudes: Their Origins and Their Effects on Behavior	
27	3–5
28	6
29–30	7–10
31	11
32–33	12–13
34	14
35	15–16

The Integrated Study Workout

COMPLETE one section at a time.

Introduction AND *Forming Impressions of Other People*   (pages 466–474)

CONSIDER these questions before you go on. They are designed to help you start thinking about this subject, not to test your knowledge.

If someone throws a tantrum, gives a lot of money to charity, or trips on the stairs, how do we decide what caused this behavior? Is it the individual's personal characteristics, the situation, or something else?

Are our perceptions of other people unduly influenced by such factors as physical appearance?

READ this section of your text lightly. They go back and read thoroughly, completing the Workout as you proceed.

We are social creatures, dependent upon human community. Our cognitive capabilities are constantly being applied to the social world in which we find ourselves. We strive to understand such things as what other people want, how they're likely to behave, how we should or actually do relate to them, what our culture expects of us, and so on.

1. Define the term *social psychology*.

2. Briefly explain Fritz Heider's term *naïve psychologists*.

3. Are naïve psychologists able to make accurate assessments of other people's personalities? To what extent?

4. When are people most susceptible to the influences of social biases?

5. Why are social psychologists interested in the biases that affect social judgments?

c.

Because behavior is observable and personality is not, we must decide what, if anything, a given behavior indicates about a person. The study of attributions—which in the study of person perception means inferences about the causes of behavior—was pioneered by Fritz Heider.

6. What do we tend to remember later, a person's behavior or our attribution?

7. According to Heider, what is a major problem we face in making attributions?

Heider's work was elaborated upon by Harold Kelley, who produced a model of the logic that might be involved in the attribution process.

8. There are three types of information people would ideally take into account in making an attribution. Write three general questions that you might ask to obtain this information.

a.

b.

9. For each of the examples below, indicate the kind of attribution that would logically be made on the basis of the information provided. (S = situational; P = personality in general; PS = personality in a particular situation)

Attribution

_____ **a.** Ruth is arguing with her mother, something she often does. Ruth rarely argues with other people, and other people rarely argue with Ruth's mother.
_____ **b.** Cally has missed her bus home after stopping to talk a bit too long with a classmate she would really like to know better.
_____ **c.** Gene has criticized his friend for not trying hard enough in his classes, but the friend doesn't hear this from anyone else. Gene regularly criticizes this friend—and his sisters, and the president, and the janitor, and the clerk at the video store, and . . .
_____ **d.** Richard almost always slows down and looks both ways before driving through a particular intersection, even when he has the green light. So do many other drivers.

Heider suggested that people give too much weight to personality factors and too little to the situation in making attributions. This is called the person bias.

10. What is some evidence for the existence of the person bias?

11. Why is this bias sometimes called the fundamental attribution error? Is it really so fundamental?

12. What factors promote a person bias?

13. The _____ bias may disappear or even be reversed when we make attributions about ourselves rather than others. This difference is called the _____.

14. Explain the knowledge-across-situations hypothesis, and describe an observation consistent with it. Now do the same for the visual-orientation hypothesis.

15. Is the tendency toward the person bias equally likely across cultures? Explain.

The organized set of information or beliefs that we have about a person can be thought of as a schema for that person. The schema we already have may influence our interpretation of the person's behavior and of new information we receive about the person.

16. Briefly describe the method and results of an experiment on student perceptions of a guest lecturer at MIT.

17. Why are first impressions often hard to change?

A person's appearance is often the first information we have about him or her. It may influence the construction of our initial schema of the person and thereby have undue influence on our perception of that person.

18. Describe and provide evidence for each of the following.
    a. attractiveness bias

    b. baby-face bias

19. How has Zebrowitz applied the baby-face bias to explain perceived psychological differences between the sexes?

20. What was Konrad Lorenz's thinking on this subject?

READ this section of your text lightly. Then go back and read thoroughly, completing the Workout as your proceed.

Unlike the members of most other species, we humans have a rich conceptual representation of ourselves. The roots of that representation are evident even in infancy.

1. Describe the rouge test and how it has been used to demonstrate species differences in self-recognition. Is social interaction a determining factor in whether chimpanzees develop self-recognition?

21. Briefly put our bias toward infant facial features in an evolutionary perspective.

22. How do initial Internet meetings compare with initial face-to-face meetings in terms of the impressions each person forms of the other?

We are obviously not born with a self-concept, and we do not pluck one out of thin air. Instead, our views of ourselves arise at least in part from the social world around us.

2. Explain Charles Cooley's concept of the looking-glass self.

23. What are some possible explanations of this difference?

Self-fulfilling prophecies or Pygmalion effects demonstrate how powerfully others' appraisals affect us.

3. Summarize evidence suggesting that our self-concepts and behavior can be affected by others' evaluations of us. Discuss some mechanisms and limitations on this type of influence.

Perceiving and Evaluating the Self
(pages 474–482)

CONSIDER these questions before you go on. They are designed to help you start thinking about this subject, not to test your knowledge.

How do we arrive at a sense of who we are as individuals? Are we influenced by the ways others view us?

Do we compare ourselves with others to see how we "measure up"?

Does it matter who we are comparing ourselves with?

Self-esteem is a term commonly used in our culture. It can be defined as one's feelings of approval and acceptance of oneself and is generally measured through questionnaires.

4. What are the essential ideas of the sociometer theory of self-esteem?

5. Present evidence supporting the sociometer theory.

6. Explain the sociometer theory's evolutionary explanation of the function of self-esteem.

Our self-perceptions arise in part from the fact that we actively measure ourselves against others to determine how smart we are, how good-looking, how happy, how resourceful, and so on. This process is called social comparison.

7. Define the term *reference group*. What evidence supports the role of the reference group in forming a self-concept?

8. How can our selection of a reference group affect our self-esteem? Support your answer with research findings on the big-fish-in-little-pond effect. What reference group do you use when thinking of your athletic ability? of your academic ability? of your appearance?

9. Briefly discuss William James's views on reference groups. How did his thinking bear out in Medvec's research on Olympic medalists?

Are you a child of Lake Wobegon? Apparently most of us see ourselves as above-average to such an extent that we create a statistical joke.

10. Present three possible explanations for our inflated opinions of ourselves and provide evidence if available.

    a.

    b.

    c.

11. There we marked cross-cultural differences in self perception. Describe Triandis's distinction between individualist and collectivist cultures. How are the differences reflected in individuals' self perceptions?

12. Do East Asians self-enhance to the extent that Westerners do? Answer carefully.

Perceiving Ourselves and Others as Members of Groups   (pages 482–489)

CONSIDER these questions before you go on. They are designed to help you start thinking about this subject, not to test your knowledge.

How do our culture's stereotypes of certain groups— of women, blacks, students, or southerners, for example—affect the way people perceive individual members of those groups?

How can we combat prejudice?

How do the groups to which we belong affect the ways we feel about ourselves?

READ this section of your text lightly. Then go back and read thoroughly, completing the Workout as you proceed.

Our social nature is reflected not only in the formation of the self-concept but in its content.

1. Distinguish between personal identity and social identity.

2. How flexible are we in thinking of ourselves in terms of both personal and social identities? Why might this be adaptive?

3. How could the success of a group with which we identify either boost or lower our self-esteem?

4. Do people extend to their groups the types of attributional biases that favor themselves as individuals? In other words, is there evidence of group-enhancing biases? Explain.

Preconceptions influence our evaluation not only of an individual person but also of whole groups of people.

5. A schema for a whole group of people is called a(n) _____.

6. Briefly describe the origin, nature, and effects of stereotypes.

7. Distinguish among explicit (public and private) and implicit stereotypes.

8. How is priming used to reveal implicit stereotypes? What have such studies shown?

9. What are implicit association tests and how are they used?

10. Can implicit stereotypes promote prejudiced actions and attributions even in people who appear not to hold conscious prejudices? Support your answer.

11. Present evidence that implicit prejudice can even have deadly results.

12. What can we do to reduce explicit negative stereotypes? implicit negative stereotypes?

Attitudes: Their Origins and Their Effects on Behavior   (pages 490–498)

CONSIDER these questions before you go on. They are designed to help you start thinking about this subject, not to test your knowledge.

Are our attitudes influenced by the attitudes of groups that we want to think well of us, such as fraternity brothers, fellow English majors, or people in the photography club?

If you don't really like someone, but you do him or her a favor anyway, could doing so change your attitude toward that person?

How well can we predict someone's behavior by knowing his or her attitudes?

READ this section of your text lightly. Then go back and read thoroughly, completing the Workout as you proceed.

The study of attitudes is of central importance in social psychology because attitudes tie individuals to the whole social world. One can have attitudes toward birthday parties, police, justice, the man at the corner market, aerobic dance, fruitcake, and so on, ad infinitum.

1. Define the term *attitude*.

2. Define values.

Attitudes are learned. Thought can be an important factor in the formation of attitudes—but not always. Sometimes little or no thought is required.

3. Explain how classical conditioning can be regarded as an automatic attitude-formation system.

4. How do advertisers exploit classical conditioning to shape our attitudes? Does research suggest that such attitude manipulation can be effective?

5. What evidence suggests that no conscious thought is required in forming attitudes through classical conditioning?

In other cases, some thought is involved in forming an attitude.

6. How do heuristics, or decision rules, provide a way to evaluate information and form an attitude with minimal thought? Give three examples of such decision rules.

Systematic, logical thought is used in the development of some attitudes.

7. When are we most likely to engage in such systematic thought in attitude formation, according to the elaboration likelihood model? What evidence supports this view? (See Figure 13.9 on text page 492.)

Social groups play an important part in shaping and maintaining our attitudes.

8. Why might people tend to have attitudes similar to those of the people with whom they live or interact?

We all have attitudes about many, many things. Sometimes our attitudes and beliefs fit harmoniously with one another and with our behavior—but sometimes they do not.

9. Define the term *cognitive dissonance*, and state the fundamental tenet of Leon Festinger's theory of cognitive dissonance. Is dissonance reduction adaptive? Always?

10. Describe research evidence showing that people sometimes avoid dissonant information.

11. Do people usually feel more confident of a decision just before or just after they have made it? Why?

12. What is the insufficient-justification effect? Give an example.

13. Describe two conditions that are essential to the insufficient-justification effect and describe evidence that they are necessary.

When social scientists first began to study attitudes, they assumed that attitudes would predict behavior. Early research profoundly challenged this assumption, but later research has shown that there are many cases in which attitudes *are* related to behavior.

14. Were attitudes toward cheating correlated with cheating behavior in Corey's classic study? Explain.

The question asked by social psychologists these days is not *whether* attitudes and behavior are correlated but *when*—that is, under what conditions. A valuable distinction is the one between explicit and implicit attitudes.

15. What are implicit attitudes? Describe their influence on behavior and give an example.

16. What are explicit attitudes? When do they affect behavior?

Be sure to READ the Concluding Thoughts at the end of the chapter. Note important points in your Workout. Then consolidate your learning by answering the focus questions in the margins of the text.

After you have studied the chapter thoroughly, CHECK your understanding with the Self-Test that follows.

Self-Test 1

Multiple-Choice Questions

1. If we have an organized set of information or beliefs about someone, we have a(n):
   a. stereotype.   c. attribution.
   b. prejudice.   d. schema.

2. According to Harold Kelley, if John regularly feels happy in situation A and if most other people also feel happy in situation A, then John's happiness in situation A should logically be attributed to:
   a. general aspects of John's personality.
   b. situation A.
   c. the combination of John's personality and this particular situation.
   d. chance.

3. Social psychologists have found that first impressions:
   a. are actually easy to change because they are often sketchy.
   b. resist change because subsequent information is interpreted to be consistent with the existing view.
   c. have a lasting effect only if confirmed by later independent judgments.
   d. are easily changed if they are positive but not if they are negative.

4. When we watch someone carry out an action, we are looking more at the person than at the environment; but when we ourselves carry out an action, we see the environment, not ourselves. This point has been used as a possible explanation of:
   a. the self-effacing bias.
   b. the actor-observer discrepancy.
   c. the big-fish-in-little-pond phenomenon.
   d. knowledge across situations.

5. Research has shown that a person bias in making attributions is:
   a. so strong that it is virtually universal.
   b. more likely if the judgment is made very soon after the relevant action is observed.
   c. more likely if subjects are tired or distracted.
   d. both b and c.

6. Priming has been used to reveal the impact of:
   a. public stereotypes.
   b. private stereotypes.
   c. implicit stereotypes.
   d. explicit stereotypes.

7. Self-esteem depends on your estimate of the degree to which other people you care about hold you in esteem. That is the essential idea of:
   a. attribution theory.
   b. elaboration likelihood theory.
   c. sociometer theory.
   d. insufficient justification.

8. The idea that we form the self-concept by considering the ways other people react to us is referred to as:
   a. social identity.   c. social comparison.
   b. social adjustment.   d. the looking-glass self.

9. People in Eastern cultures are more likely than those in Western cultures to:
   a. describe themselves in terms of their social roles and groups.
   b. exhibit a self-serving attributional bias.

c. to behave in accordance with their implicit attitudes.

d. make the fundamental attribution error.

0. Values are a subcategory of:

a. attributions.
b. attitudes.
c. personality traits.
d. none of the above.

11. Compared with people who meet for the first time face-to-face, people who initially meet on the Internet tend to like each other:

a. much less.
b. slightly less.
c. about the same.
d. more.

12. The common desire for cognitive consistency can lead us to:

a. avoid information that would conflict.
b. firm up an attitude.
c. change an attitude.
d. do all of the above.

13. The fundamental attribution error is another name for the:

a. actor-observer discrepancy.
b. person bias.
c. self-enhancing bias.
d. self-effacing bias.

14. People tend to use automatic or superficial approaches to attitude construction *except* when messages have:

a. high personal relevance.
b. high complexity.
c. the voice of authority behind them.
d. vivid arguments.

15. In an early study of the relationship between attitudes and behavior, it was found that college students:

a. with strong anticheating attitudes were just as likely to cheat as those with weak anticheating attitudes.
b. with strong anticheating attitudes were much less likely to cheat than those with weak anticheating attitudes.
c. who cheated were likely to change their attitudes to be less negative toward cheating.
d. who did not cheat tended to believe that other students were also unlikely to cheat.

Essay Questions

16. How is a person's self-concept affected by other people's perceptions and expectations? Cite research evidence to support your answer.

17. Discuss cross-cultural differences in self-enhancing biases.

After you have assessed your understanding on the basis of Self-Test 1 and have tried to strengthen your preparation in any areas of weakness, GO ON to Self-Test 2.

Self-Test 2

Multiple-Choice Questions

1. An inference about the cause of a particular behavior is called a(n):

a. impression.
b. attribution.
c. schema.
d. expectation.

2. Suppose subjects in an experiment are given evidence regarding either a crime of negligence or a crime of deliberate deception. Baby-faced defendants would be more likely than mature-faced defendants to be found:
   a. innocent of either charge.
   b. innocent, but only for a crime of deliberate deception.
   c. innocent, but only for crime of negligence.
   d. guilty of either charge.

3. People are more likely to judge their close friends' behavior as dependent on the situation than they are to judge a stranger's behavior as dependent on the situation. This supports the _____, an explanation of the _____.
   a. visual-orientation hypothesis; fundamental attribution error
   b. visual-orientation hypothesis; situation bias
   c. knowledge-across-situations hypothesis; actor-observer discrepancy
   d. knowledge-across-situations hypothesis; effects of prior information

4. Adults in India and other East Asian countries were _____ likely than American adults to attribute behaviors to personality, a finding that _____ the universality of the person bias.
   a. more; supports
   b. more; challenges
   c. less; supports
   d. less; challenges

5. The big-fish-in-little-pond effect illustrates the importance of _____ to _____.
   a. one's reference group; self-esteem
   b. one's reference group; attitude formation
   c. self-enhancing biases; self-esteem
   d. self-enhancing biases; attitude formation

6. Suppose the other members of a group to which we belong perform exceptionally well. This tends to _____ our self-esteem if our _____ identity is foremost in our minds.
   a. raise; personal
   b. raise; social
   c. lower; social
   d. lower; implicit

7. By placing a dot of rouge on children's or animals' faces before they look in a mirror, researchers have found that:

   a. only humans recognize themselves.
   b. only humans and great apes, such as chimpanzees, recognize themselves.
   c. most vertebrates, including cats and dogs, recognize themselves.
   d. most species that exhibit some type of social organization recognize themselves.

8. Which of the following messages to children has been shown experimentally to produce the greatest improvements in math performance?
   a. telling the children why math is important
   b. telling the children they should try to become good at math
   c. telling the children they are good at math
   d. telling the children they should try to do their best in everything

9. The tendency of people to attribute their successes to their own characteristics and their failures to the situation is known as the:
   a. actor-observer discrepancy.
   b. self-serving attributional bias.
   c. fundamental attribution error.
   d. self-effacing bias.

10. The attractiveness bias has led:
    a. teachers to rate physically attractive students as brighter and more successful.
    b. judges to give longer prison sentences to physically unattractive people.
    c. adults to attribute a physically attractive child's misbehavior to the situation and the same behavior from an unattractive child to personality.
    d. all of the above.

11. Joanna consciously believes that arts majors are brave, independent thinkers, but priming shows that she perhaps unconsciously finds them lazy and frivolous. The former opinion is _____ and the latter _____.
    a. an implicit stereotype; an explicit stereotype
    b. a private stereotype; a public stereotype
    c. an explicit stereotype; an implicit stereotype
    d. a stereotype; an attitude

12. Systematic, logical analysis of the message content occurs in:
    a. classical conditioning.
    b. the application of heuristics.
    c. both **a** and **b**.
    d. neither **a** nor **b**.

3. An awareness of disagreement or lack of harmony among the attitudes or beliefs in one's mind creates psychological discomfort. This condition is called:
   a. the fundamental attribution error.
   b. cognitive distinctiveness.
   c. cognitive dissonance.
   d. cognitive bias.

4. If a person is induced to behave in a way that is contrary to his or her attitude, and lacks any obvious way to justify that behavior, the person's attitude will tend to:
   a. move in a direction consistent with the behavior.
   b. become strengthened in the direction of the original attitude.
   c. remain unchanged because of the conflict between thought and behavior.
   d. become neutralized so that it is neither positive nor negative.

5. Zebrowitz has found evidence that perceived psychological differences between men and women can be partly explained in terms of:
   a. the baby-face bias.
   b. the person bias.
   c. the attractiveness bias.
   d. none of the above.

Essay Questions

16. How can we decrease explicit and implicit stereotypes in ourselves?

17. Create an everyday scenario in which a person bias in attribution is extremely likely. Be certain to point out three factors in your scenario that would tend to produce this bias.

Answers

Introduction AND *Forming Impressions of Other People*

9. a. PS, b. PS, c. P, d. S

13. person; actor-observer discrepancy

Perceiving Ourselves and Others as Members of Groups

5. stereotype

Self-Test 1

1. d. (p. 470)

2. b. (p. 467)

3. b. (p. 471)

4. b. (p. 468)

5. d. (pp. 467–468)

6. c. Implicit stereotypes can affect judgments and behaviors even in people who consciously reject those stereotypes. Both private and public stereotypes are explicit. (p. 486)

7. c. (p. 477)

8. d. In this case, the "mirror" is the social world and we come to see ourselves in the image that it seems to reflect back to us. (p. 475)

9. **a.** (p. 481)

10. **b.** (p. 490)

11. **d.** (p. 473)

12. **d.** (p. 493–495)

13. **b.** (p. 468)

14. **a.** (p. 491)

15. **a.** (pp. 496–497)

16. One way in which the social world influences the self-concept is through the expectations other people have of us. Someone's beliefs about us can affect his or her behavior toward us, which can affect how we see ourselves and how we behave in such a way that it leads to a self-fulfilling prophecy. This is one example of the "looking-glass self" (seeing ourselves in the "social mirror") in operation, but taken a step further.

   In Rosenthal and Jacobson's study, elementary school teachers were told that a group of students were about to undergo an intellectual growth spurt when in reality these children were just randomly selected. Several months later, these children showed superior gains in academic performance and IQ. Further research showed that the teachers' expectations caused them to act differently toward the children, by praising their work more often or giving them more challenging assignments, for example. This different treatment may well have caused the children to regard themselves more positively and to act in ways consistent with their improved self-concept.

   The ways that other people describe us are also a means by which the social world reflects to us who we are. Children told that they are neat or that they are good at math appear to modify their self-concepts accordingly and then behave in ways that fit those beliefs about themselves. (pp. 475–476)

17. In the West, we tend to inflate ourselves, to see ourselves as better than we are. A simple and comical example is Garrison Keillor's Lake Wobegon where "all the children are above average." But it's not just an amusing idea from a humorist. Many surveys show that we rate ourselves as better than average on a variety of dimensions. We manage to hold these overly positive views of ourselves through a variety of means, such as accepting praise at face value, attributing our success to ourselves and our failures to other causes, and using our own criteria to define success. In East Asian countries, there tends to be little or no such effect. In Japan, there may even be a reversal. When administered the Twenty Statements Test, for example, U.S. students gave 2 to 1 positive to negative self-statements. In Hong Kong, the balance was to 1, and in Japan negative self-statements outweighed positive ones 2 to 1. This may be due to the high value placed on modesty in the East. In fact, some studies show that Japanese will show self-enhancement if patience or another quality valued in their culture is the one on which they rate themselves. (pp. 480–482)

Self-Test 2

1. **b.** (p. 466)

2. **b.** Because people tend to perceive baby-faced individuals as more naive, honest, helpless, kind and warm than mature-faced individuals of the same age, it is harder to believe them guilty of crime of deliberate deception. (pp. 471–472)

3. **c.** (pp. 468–469)

4. **d.** (p. 469)

5. **a.** (p. 478)

6. **b.** (p. 483)

7. **b.** (pp. 474–475)

8. **c.** When children are led to believe that they are good at math, they apparently incorporate that belief into their self-concept. They expect more of themselves and try to live up to those expectations. (p. 476)

9. **b.** (p. 479)

10. **d.** (p. 471)

11. **c.** (pp. 485–486)

12. **d.** (pp. 490–491)

13. **c.** (p. 493)

14. **a.** This is termed the insufficient-justification effect. (pp. 494–495)

15. **a.** (p. 472)

6. Because implicit and explicit stereotypes are quite different from one another, they can most effectively be dealt with in different ways. Explicit stereotypes are products of conscious thought and can be modified through logic and deliberate learning. Implicit stereotypes, on the other hand, came about through more primitive, emotional mechanisms. They can be fought by the same means that brought them into existence-classical conditioning. Associating positive feelings with members of the stereotyped group—by making friends or exposing oneself to admirable characters in literature or the media—can reduce implicit prejudice. (pp. 488–489)

7. In her hometown of Pittsburgh, Pennsylvania, Sandra is looking for someone from whom she might borrow some change for bus fare. She is feeling tired and stressed after being in an unfamiliar part of town and having her ride home fail to show up. She can see the bus at a red light two blocks away. While looking for someone on the street who seems approachable, she sees a woman grab a shopping bag from an old man's hand and rush off. Sandra later tells her sister that she saw a thief steal a shopping bag from an old man. What Sandra didn't see was that the bag was originally in the woman's possession and the man had quietly taken it when she set it down to rummage for her car keys in her purse. Sandra has incorrectly attributed the bag-grabbing incident to the woman's dishonesty when in fact it was due to the situation she was in.

The tendency to make a person attribution in this scenario was increased by (a) the fact that Sandra is an American and the person bias is stronger in her culture than in some other cultures; (b) the fact that the woman was a stranger to her rather than a friend whom she had observed in a number of situations; and (c) the fact that Sandra made a quick and automatic judgment about the situation given her fatigue, the time pressure she was under, and the incident's relative unimportance to her. (A fourth factor would be that her task—finding someone who looked as if he or she might help her out—already had her oriented to assessing people.) (pp. 467–469)

Social Influences on Behavior

READ the introduction below before you read the chapter in the text.

As participants in a social world, we are all influenced by a host of social pressures that may take a variety of forms—such as direct or indirect requests, commands, expectations, and so on. Our behavior can be affected by the mere presence of other people. In social facilitation, performance with onlookers present is superior to performance when alone. In social interference, performance suffers when others are present. Robert Zajonc has explained both phenomena in terms of the effects of arousal on the performance of different kinds of tasks. Social interference is an example of the more general phenomenon of choking under pressure, which appears to occur because extraneous thoughts compete with the task itself for limited-capacity working memory. Our interest in the judgments people make about us affects us in other ways as well. For example, we try to project a certain view of ourselves to others, a tendency psychologists call impression management.

Why do people conform? Solomon Asch asked whether people would conform to the judgment of a majority when a simple perceptual task was involved. He found that people often *did* conform to the opinion expressed by the majority—even if they knew it was wrong. Conformity can also help to explain a commonly observed phenomenon in which people fail to help someone in apparent trouble if there are multiple witnesses. Many decisions are the product not of individuals but of groups working together. Group discussion can sometimes polarize attitudes; if people who agree on some matter get together to discuss it, they will generally emerge with a more extreme version of their original opinion. Groupthink is a faulty mode of thinking that may result when members of a cohesive group place unanimity above the realistic appraisal of alternatives. This type of group decision-making has led to calamitous actions in the real world—including some that affected the course of history.

Some psychologists have found that people have a general tendency to comply with requests, although they can be more or less compliant depending on a number of factors. Certain techniques can induce greater compliance and are sometimes exploited by people whose job it is to persuade us to behave in certain ways, such as to buy a given product. Two of these are the low-ball technique and the foot-in-the door technique, which take advantage of the human desire to reduce cognitive dissonance. People may be particularly likely to comply when the request is perceived as an order from an authority. A classic series of experiments by Stanley Milgram revealed that ordinary people will under some circumstances obey orders that they consider wrong, even if they believe another person will be seriously harmed as a result. Some theorists have applied these experimental results to situations such as the Nazi Holocaust. The ethics of the experiments themselves have been questioned.

Social dilemmas pit self-interest against the good of the group. Cooperation to promote the good of the group is more likely in some conditions than in others. For example, cooperation is more likely if there is an opportunity to establish reciprocity or if people share a group identity. A computer program called TFT successfully elicits cooperation from other players (computer or human) in social dilemma games by way of a simple strategy. Setting up superordinate goals that unite groups in a common pursuit can reduce conflict and increase cooperation as illustrated in the classic Robbers Cave experiment.

Emotions play a fundamental role in social life. Social pain, for example—which is importantly related to physical pain—motivates us to maintain social ties. Emotional contagion, such as the spread of laughter or fear from person to person, may promote group cohesion. And self-conscious emotions, such as guilt or embarrassment, can motivate a variety of useful social behaviors.

LOOK over the table of contents for this chapter in your textbook before you continue with your study.

Notice that there are focus questions in the margins of the text for your use in studying the material. The following chart lists which Study Guide questions relate to which focus questions.

Focus Questions	Study Guide Questions
Effects of Being Observed and Evaluated	
1	1–5
2	6
3	7
4	8–10
Effects of Other's Examples and Opinions	
5	1
6–8	2–5
9	6
10	7
11	8
12–13	9–10
14	11–12
Effects of Other's Requests	
15–16	1
17	2
18	3
19	4
20	5
21	6
22	7
23	8–9
To Cooperate or Not: The Dilemma of Social Life	
24	1
25	2
26	3
27	4
28	5
29	6
30	7–8
31	9
32–33	10–13
Emotional Foundations of Our Social Nature	
34	1
35	2
36	3–4
37	5–6

The Integrated Study Workout

COMPLETE one section at a time.

Introduction AND *Effects of Being Observed and Evaluated*   (pages 501–506)

CONSIDER these questions before you go on. They are designed to help you start thinking about this subject, not to test your knowledge.

Why do people sometimes choke on a test, in a big game, or on stage?

Do you behave differently with your friends than with your professors? with your parents than with your boss? If so, why?

READ this section of your text lightly. Then go back and read thoroughly, completing the Workout as you proceed.

The individual living in the midst of the social world is subject to a multitude of pressures from that world, some real and others imagined. We may feel pressure to be polite, to marry, to go into the family business, or to wear a certain style of clothing. And pressure can come from the mere presence of others who are in a position to observe our performance.

1. Complete the following statements.

    a. _____ is the tendency to perform a task better in front of others than when alone.

    b. _____ is a decline in performance when others are present as compared with performance when alone.

2. How did Robert Zajonc relate the occurrence of social facilitation at some times and social interference at other times to the nature of the task? to arousal?

3. Present some evidence in support of Zajonc's view.

8. Define *impression management*.

4. Explain how the presence of others might lead to increased arousal in humans. Provide supporting evidence.

9. What metaphor did Erving Goffman use to characterize impression management? What alternative metaphor is offered in the text and why is it a valuable addition?

5. How is social interference related to choking under pressure?

Our concern for impression management varies depending on the audience.

10. Which types of "audiences" lead us to engage in more impression management? Why?

6. What is the working-memory explanation for choking? Present some evidence from research on academic tests.

Effects of Others' Examples and Opinions (pages 506–514)

CONSIDER these questions before you go on. They are designed to help you start thinking about this subject, not to test your knowledge.

---

7. What is stereotype threat? Describe evidence of such an effect. Does awareness of the phenomenon help or harm the performance of affected people?

How can people stand by and watch someone in trouble—someone apparently having a heart attack or being robbed, for example—without doing anything to help?

Can the opinions expressed by a majority cause people to say things that are contrary to their beliefs just so they will fit in? Can the majority cause them to change their minds about what is true?

For a variety of reasons, we are interested in others' impressions of us, and we do not generally leave those impressions to chance. In fact, behavior can to some extent be regarded as performance.

What kinds of conditions can lead to poor group decision making? What can promote good group decision making?

READ this section of your text lightly. Then go back and read thoroughly, completing the Workout as you proceed.

How are people who are asked to express a view influenced by the views expressed by others around them? Does the majority opinion alter what people believe? Or does it change only what they say? These are some of the questions addressed in research on social conformity.

1. Distinguish between informational and normative influences on conformity.

2. Briefly describe the basic procedure and results of Solomon Asch's conformity studies.

3. How did Asch test the relative importance of informational and normative influences in his studies, and what did he find? Be sure to mention the variable of task difficulty considered in later studies by other researchers.

In Asch's basic research, the confederates were unanimous in giving the wrong answer. Other experiments have examined the influence of a minority opinion—that is, of a nonconformist.

4. What happens to conformity if one of the confederates disagrees with the rest? Does this also occur if the dissenting confederate simply gives a different wrong answer?

5. Is the impact of a minority opinion due to its effect on normative or informational influences? Explain.

In everyday life, the social context is much broader than what we see or hear from people in a room in a university building.

6. What argument does the "broken windows theory of crime" make about normative influences on the crime rate?

7. How does Cialdini suggest we should construct a public service message for maximum effectiveness? Does he appear to be right? Explain.

The phenomenon of conformity can also help us to understand why people sometimes fail to help others in emergencies.

8. If you were the victim of an accident, would you be more likely to receive help if there was one witness or more than one? Why? Support your answer.

Group discussions, such as those that take place in creating a new product's marketing plan, in a school committee on campus safety, or in a congressional task force, also involve the influence of social pressure. A well-documented phenomenon in group discussion is the polarization of attitudes.

9. Define *group polarization*. Give an example of group polarization from research. Can it have important consequences in everyday life? Support your answer.

10. How is group polarization explained in terms of informational and normative influences? (Be sure to name and describe two specific hypotheses that concern normative influences.)

Depending on a number of factors, groups can produce decisions that are better or worse than those made by individuals. Irving Janis explored causes of bad group decisions by studying some notorious government decisions, such as those involved in the Bay of Pigs invasion and the Watergate burglary and cover-up.

11. Explain Janis's concept of groupthink, and present evidence supporting his view.

12. List some factors that tend to promote better group decisions.

Effects of Others' Requests   (pages 514–522)

CONSIDER these questions before you go on. They are designed to help you start thinking about this subject, not to test your knowledge.

How can salespeople sometimes manipulate us into buying things that we don't want or need?

Why do people still obey the orders of authorities when they believe those orders to be wrong, even unethical? What factors help people to resist obeying such orders?

READ this section of your text lightly. Then go back and read thoroughly, completing the Workout as you proceed.

Both research and everyday experience reveal that most people have a tendency to comply with direct requests. In fact, they seem to need a good excuse before they feel free to refuse. As you know, people are motivated to reduce cognitive dissonance, the discomfort experienced when one's beliefs clash with one another or with one's behavior. Robert Cialdini has shown that cognitive dissonance is the basis for some techniques that people use to increase other people's compliance to their requests.

1. For each of the following, give a general description, an example, and an explanation for its effectiveness.

   a. low-ball technique

   b. foot-in-the-door technique

Another basis for gaining compliance is the reciprocity norm.

2. Describe the reciprocity norm and give an example of how it can be exploited to gain compliance.

3. What happens if the foot-in-the-door technique and pregiving are combined? What does this tell us about the means by which each technique works?

4. Can even very slight, superficial connections increase compliance? Explain.

Obedience is defined as compliance with a request that is perceived as an order from an authority figure or leader. Though obedience is often positively valued as necessary to social order, it can in some cases lead to crimes of obedience, such as those of the Nazi Holocaust. Stanley Milgram carried out a classic study of obedience—one that had disturbing results.

5. Describe the basic method and results of Milgram's study.

6. How consistent is this finding? Is it dependent on using a particular type of person as a subject? Explain.

7. State five factors that are important in explaining the obedience found in experiments such as Milgram's. Where possible, indicate evidence that supports these explanations.

a.

b.

c.

d.

e.

8. Summarize the *ethical* criticisms of Milgram's obedience studies. Are these criticisms valid? Support your answer.

9. Summarize criticisms of Milgram's obedience studies that are based on their dissimilarity to real-world situations. Do you think these criticisms are valid?

2. Explain the basic prisoner's dilemma game as played in a psychology laboratory. How do players in a one-trial game tend to play if they are anonymous, unable to converse, and motivated to maximize their personal gain? Does this serve them well? Explain.

To Cooperate or Not: The Dilemma of Social Life   (pages 522–529)

CONSIDER these questions before you go on. They are designed to help you start thinking about this subject, not to test your knowledge.

What causes conflict between groups of people and how can such conflict be reduced?
What makes people work together cooperatively?

3. Why are players more likely to cooperate in an iterative (repeated) prisoner's dilemma game?

4. Why was Rapoport's TFT program so successful?

READ this section of your text lightly. Then go back and read thoroughly, completing the Workout as you proceed.

People have a variety of needs and goals in life. Sometimes those needs and goals are shared and other times they conflict.

1. What are social dilemmas? How might such dilemmas be a matter of human survival? Give three examples of social dilemmas.

Public-goods games are social-dilemma games that permit any number of players, unlike the two-person prisoner's dilemma games.

5. Describe a typical public-goods game. Which is more likely to cooperate—a small group or a large one? Why?

Scientists have often studied people's choices in social dilemmas through games.

Often, the choices people make indicate that they are not motivated purely by immediate self-interest. Through evolution, cultural history, and personal experience, we come to take into account longer-term interests that frequently rely on good social relations. Many aspects of human social nature can be thought of as adaptations for cooperating in social dilemmas.

6. How and why does the TFT strategy use accountability, reputation, and reciprocity?

7. How do real-life social dilemmas compare with laboratory games with regard to accountability, reputation, and reciprocity? How do such factors explain the general tendency to help others if the cost to ourselves is small and inhibiting factors are absent?

8. Discuss some ways in which a sense of justice and a willingness to punish promote cooperation.

Recall the distinction between personal identity and social identity presented in Chapter 13. A person's social identity is related to the tendency to cooperate or compete.

9. Define social identity and describe research showing its impact on cooperation in social-dilemma games.

Group identification can unfortunately lead to conflict between different groups. Muzafer Sherif and colleagues conducted the Robbers Cave experiment to study conflict and ways of resolving that conflict.

10. How did the experimenters establish groups?

11. What resulted from the series of competitions between the groups?

12. List some methods tried in this and similar experiments that did *not* work as a means of reducing intergroup hostility.

13. What strategy for reducing intergroup hostility at Robbers Cave was successful? Explain.

Emotional Foundations of Our Social Nature
(pages 530–534)

CONSIDER these questions before you go on. They are designed to help you start thinking about this subject, not to test your knowledge.

Can emotion be contagious? Does laughter or anger really tend to spread among people in a group?

Do unpleasant emotions such as guilt or embarrassment nevertheless have social value?

Is the pain of social loss at all related to physical pain?

READ this section of your text lightly. Then go back and read thoroughly, completing the Workout as you proceed.

A social species such as ours has a number of re-quirements. We need to stay connected with one an-other, coordinate our behavior, acquire and keep the acceptance of others, all the while managing not to let others take advantage of us. Emotions play a major part in all of these situations.

1. What is social pain? How is it related to physical pain? What is its purpose?

2. What is emotional contagion, and why is it valu-able socially? How might it be related to the abil-ity to lead others? Can it occur unconsciously?

Some emotions arise from self-consciousness—that is, from thoughts of ourselves or our behavior. Though such emotions may sometimes create discomfort, they can also help us to get along with others by making us more socially acceptable.

3. What are two primary means by which self-conscious emotions have been studied?

4. Explain the causes and social functions of the fol-lowing self-conscious emotions, providing evi-dence for your statements.
   a. guilt

   b. shame

   c. embarrassment

5. When do we experience the self-conscious emo-tion of pride? When and how are we served by the *expression* of pride? By the *feeling* of pride?

6. Pride can be considered the opposite of
   _____; while pride increases
   _____, its opposition emotion
   diminishes it.

Be sure to READ the Concluding Thoughts at the end of the chapter. Note important points in your Workout. Then consolidate your learning by answering the focus questions in the margins of the text.

After you have studied the chapter thoroughly, CHECK your understanding with the Self-Test that follows.

Self-Test 1

Multiple-Choice Questions

1. Social _____ tends to occur when an audience is present and the task is _____
   a. facilitation; dominant.
   b. facilitation; nondominant.
   c. interference; dominant.
   d. interference; instinctive.

2. A friend tells you about a terrible accident he wit-nessed, where none of the six people watching came forward to help. You can best explain this well-known phenomenon in terms of:
   a. compliance.
   b. the tragedy of the commons.
   c. personal identity.
   d. conformity.

3. Social identity promotes _____ within groups and _____ between groups.
   a. cooperation; cooperation
   b. cooperation; competition
   c. competition; competition
   d. competition; cooperation

4. A salesperson who gets customers to agree to a very good price and then "discovers" that the price is really higher is using the _____ technique to try to gain compliance.
   a. reciprocity-norm
   b. broken windows
   c. foot-in-the-door
   d. low-ball

5. In Milgram's classic study _____ percent of subjects went all the way to the most severe level of punishment.
   a. 5   c. 35
   b. 15   d. 65

6. Which of the following self-conscious emotions is thought to motivate the repair of relationships?
   a. pride   c. guilt
   b. shame   d. embarrassment

7. Strong ethical objections have been raised to:
   a. Cialdini's work on principles of compliance.
   b. Zajonc's work on social interference and facilitation.
   c. Asch's work on conformity.
   d. Milgram's work on obedience.

8. Which of the following has *not* been supported as a partial explanation of the obedience shown in experiments such as those conducted by Stanley Milgram?
   a. the proximity of the experimenter
   b. the incremental nature of the requests
   c. the experimenter's acceptance of responsibility
   d. the sadistic tendencies of the subjects

9. Stereotype threat is a powerful cause of _____ and works through interfering effects on _____.
   a. conformity; social identity
   b. conformity; motivation
   c. choking; working memory
   d. choking; motivation

10. The metaphor of an intuitive politician was used to convey the nature of _____ in the text.
    a. impression management
    b. public-goods games

c. obedience
d. social facilitation

11. People seem to have a greater desire to impress:
    a. close friends.
    b. family members.
    c. acquaintances.
    d. both **a** and **b**.

12. Reciprocity can help to explain:
    a. the foot-in-the-door technique.
    b. the low-ball technique.
    c. cooperation in an iterative prisoner's dilemma game.
    d. all of the above.

13. People who share the same view initially will tend to hold a more extreme version of that view after discussing the subject with one another. This phenomenon is called:
    a. social facilitation.
    b. normative influence.
    c. group polarization.
    d. groupthink.

14. In social dilemmas, cooperation is promoted by:
    a. anonymity.   c. norms of fairness.
    b. high payoffs.   d. all of the above.

15. TFT offers:
    a. a strategy for eliciting cooperation in social-dilemma games.
    b. a way of measuring self-monitoring.
    c. a means of reducing conformity behavior in groups.
    d. a foolproof means of gaining compliance in a sales situation.

Essay Questions

16. How did Solomon Asch study conformity in the laboratory, and what was his basic finding? Why did subjects behave this way? What factor was found to help subjects resist conformity?

7. What are two possible explanations of group polarization? Choose one explanation that is normative and one that is informational. Be sure to state which is which.

After you have assessed your understanding on the basis of Self-Test 1 and have tried to strengthen your preparation in any areas of weakness, GO ON to Self-Test 2.

Self-Test 2

Multiple-Choice Question

1. Which can be thought of as the emotion opposite to pride?
   a. guilt
   b. shame
   c. embarrassment
   d. a or b

2. Social psychology suggests that emotional contagion is:
   a. a myth and not an actual psychological phenomenon.
   b. possible for negative but not positive emotions.
   c. of value in promoting group cohesion.
   d. a type of self-conscious emotion.

3. An interviewer conducting a survey asks Max for a few seconds of his time and Max consents. Then Max is asked to respond to 10 yes-or-no questions and he agrees. Finally, the interviewer works up to the primary aim, asking for a half-hour interview in Max's home. The interviewer is using the _____ to gain compliance.

   a. low-ball technique
   b. reciprocity norm
   c. foot-in-the-door technique
   d. impression-management technique

4. Which of the following sales techniques is believed to work on the principle of cognitive dissonance?
   a. foot-in-the-door
   b. low-ball
   c. pregiving
   d. both a and b

5. Students who were asked to produce philosophical counterarguments did worse when in the presence of other people than when alone. This experimental result illustrates:
   a. social comparison
   b. the occurrence of cognitive dissonance.
   c. social interference.
   d. the phenomenon of groupthink.

6. Public-goods games are used to study:
   a. social facilitation.
   b. social interference.
   c. compliance.
   d. cooperation.

7. Researchers have found that the relative amount of informational as compared to normative influence on conformity varies depending on the:
   a. personal persuasiveness of individuals in the majority.
   b. difficulty of the task.
   c. gender of confederates and subjects.
   d. amount that subjects are being paid.

8. Jim, Anne, and Karen believe that the workers in their factory should unionize. They believe this even more firmly after talking together about the issue. This could be explained in terms of:
   a. groupthink.
   b. group polarization.
   c. social facilitation.
   d. none of the above.

9. Group polarization results because people tend to hear a limited range of arguments strongly favoring their group's existing opinion, according to the _____ type of explanation.
   a. one-upmanship
   b. group-differentiation
   c. informational
   d. reciprocity

10. The kind of thinking that arises when people immersed in a cohesive ingroup strive for unanimity more than for realistic appraisal of alternatives for action is called:
    a. groupthink.
    b. a prisoner's dilemma.
    c. superordinate goal construction.
    d. obedience.

11. Garrett Hardin's allegory—*the tragedy of the commons*—illustrates the dynamics of:
    a. obedience to authority.
    b. stereotyping.
    c. social dilemmas.
    d. compliance.

12. Players are most likely to cooperate in a(n):
    a. one-shot prisoner's dilemma game.
    b. iterative prisoner's dilemma game.
    c. brief, anonymous interaction with a stranger.
    d. social-dilemma game in which players see themselves as individuals rather than groupmates.

13. What led to intergroup hostility in Sherif's Robbers Cave experiment?
    a. competitive games between groups
    b. group solidarity
    c. the fairness norm
    d. the reciprocity norm

14. In his Robbers Cave experiment, Sherif successfully ended intergroup hostilities between the boys by:
    a. arranging for joint participation in pleasant activities.
    b. setting up individual rather than group competitions.
    c. establishing superordinate goals.
    d. arranging peace meetings between group leaders.

15. Which of the following is an accurate statement about the relationship between social pain and physical pain?
    a. Social pain increases suffering from physical pain.
    b. Drugs that reduce physical pain also reduce social pain.
    c. Social pain involves some of the same brain areas involved in physical pain.
    d. All of the above are accurate statements.

Essay Questions

16. Summarize the method and results of Stanley Milgram's classic study of obedience. Give two explanations that have been offered for these results.

17. Define the terms *social facilitation* and *social interference*. How did Zajonc explain these phenomena and thereby predict when each would occur?

Answers

Effects of Being Observed and Evaluated

1. a. Social facilitation
   b. Social interference

Emotional Foundations of Our Social Nature

6. shame; self-esteem

Self-Test 1

1. a. (p. 502)

2. d. (p. 510)

3. b. (p. 527)

4. d. (p. 514)

5. d. (p. 518)

6. c. (p. 532)

7. d. (pp. 520–521)

8. d. The subjects did not comply because they enjoyed harming the "learner"; they clearly showed evidence of distress as they carried out the experimenter's orders. The impact of Milgram's finding stems from the fact that these *were* normal subjects. Their behavior is something that normal people are capable of. (pp. 519–520)

9. c. (pp. 503–504)

10. a. (pp. 504–505)

11. c. (p. 505)

12. c. Both **a** and **b** are produced by cognitive dissonance. (p. 524)

13. c. (p. 511)

14. c. (p. 526)

15. a. (p. 524)

16. Solomon Asch started out by testing whether people will conform when objective conflicting evidence is clear-cut. He arranged for each subject to join a group of people who appeared to be fellow subjects but who were in reality confederates of the experimenter. On each trial, subjects (real and fake alike) were to compare a standard line to a set of three comparison lines and to indicate the one line that was the same length as the standard. The task was extremely simple. The real subjects were seated so that they were the next to last to give their answers. The confederates had been instructed beforehand to give the same wrong answer on certain trials.

Most subjects were influenced by the clearly wrong answers of the confederates, at least sometimes. Some conformed to the unanimous wrong answer on every one of these trials. Subjects apparently conformed primarily because of the normative influence of the group. When subjects were led to believe that they were late and should therefore give their answers in writing rather than aloud, the level of conformity dropped dramatically. Research suggests that conformity is due mostly to normative influence on easy tasks but mostly to informational influence when the task is difficult. Having another person disagree with the majority opinion apparently helps subjects to resist compliance. (pp. 507–508)

17. Group polarization may be due to the tendency of like-minded people to present arguments favoring their own position but not the opposite view. As a result, each member will only be persuaded to hold his or her original position more firmly. This is an informational effect. The one-upmanship hypothesis, a normative hypothesis, suggests that people may try to outdo one another in the extremity of their support for the common view. (pp. 511–512)

Self-Test 2

1. b. (p. 533)

2. c. (p. 530)

3. c. (p. 515)

4. d. (pp. 514–515)

5. c. (p. 502)

6. d. (pp. 524–525)

7. b. (p. 508)

8. b. (p. 511)

9. c. Both **a** and **b** are normative hypotheses about the causes of group polarization. (p. 512)

10. a. (p. 513)

11. c. (p. 522)

12. b. Here, reciprocity has a chance to develop cooperation. (p. 524)

13. a. (p. 528)

14. c. (pp. 528–529)

15. d. (p. 530)

16. Stanley Milgram had subjects take the role of teacher, while the role of learner—supposedly played by another subject—was actually played by a confederate of the experimenter. The learner was placed in a separate room and the real subject stayed with the experimenter. The subject's job was to read questions on a verbal-memory test and to shock the learner when he made an error. (The shocks were, of course, not real.) As the experimental session progressed with the learner making many mistakes, the shock level was increased and the learner began to show signs of distress, then to scream for the shocks to stop, and finally to fall silent. If the subject hesitated to continue the shocks at any point, the experimenter responded with firm prompts demanding cooperation.

Sixty-five percent of the subjects continued to the highest level of shock, despite apparent reluctance to do so. This result has been partially explained in terms of subjects' preexisting beliefs about the appropriateness of obeying authorities, especially if they represent a legitimate endeavor such as social science research at a prestigious university. Another factor that seems to be important is the degree to which the experimenter appears to accept responsibility. In a similar experiment in which subjects were told they should accept responsibility for the learner's welfare, obedience was sharply reduced. (pp. 517–520)

17. In a variety of tasks, the presence of others has been found to improve performance relative to performance when subjects are alone. This well established effect is known as social facilitation. However, another well-established effect appears to contradict social facilitation. Social interference is a frequently replicated phenomenon in which the presence of others causes performance to worsen relative to performance when subjects are alone.

Robert Zajonc suggested that the task determines which phenomenon will result. Social facilitation will occur when tasks are dominant (for example, well learned or simple), whereas social interference will occur when tasks are nondominant (for example, unfamiliar or complex). The underlying explanatory concept is arousal. The presence of other people increases physiological arousal. High arousal is known to affect simple or well-learned tasks positively and complex or unfamiliar tasks adversely. Psychologists believe the increased arousal in the presence of other humans is due to evaluation anxiety. (pp. 502–503)

Personality

READ the introduction below before you read the chapter in the text.

Psychologists use the term *personality* to mean an individual's general style of interacting with the world, especially with other people. Theories of personality are efforts to systematically describe and explain variations among people in this general style of behaving.

Trait theories focus on describing individual differences by attempting to specify the most fundamental dimensions underlying personality. A trait is a relatively stable predisposition to behave in a certain manner. Trait theorists typically collect data using paper-and-pencil questionnaires and subject the results to factor analysis to identify a manageable number of independent personality traits. Pioneering this general approach, Raymond Cattell described personality in terms of sixteen trait dimensions. Many trait researchers today, however, believe that there are only five basic traits, which they call the Big Five. Each of the five global traits has six subordinate trait dimensions called facets. Some major issues for trait theorists are the stability of traits over time, their relationship to behavior, and their genetic basis.

Another useful approach to the issue of personality variation is to consider it from the evolutionary perspective, which requires us to ask how personality differences are adaptive and what might lead to particular adaptations. Personality variation, like all other forms of diversity produced by genetic mechanisms of sexual reproduction, allows the investment in offspring to be protected, essentially by hedging one's bets in an uncertain and ever-changing world. Both genetic diversity and developmental flexibility allow individuals to develop strategies that promote their survival and reproduction within various niches. Nonhuman animals have personality-like variation and the bold-cautious dimension in fish has been a fruitful area of study for researchers taking an evolutionary perspective. People may carve out a unique niche for themselves in their families, by contrasting themselves with siblings, for example. Biological sex and culturally defined gender may also lead us to become different based on the different niches they cause us to occupy.

Freud's personality theory and his approach to psychotherapy are both called psychoanalysis, which is classified as a psychodynamic theory—that is, one that focuses on mental forces. In this theory, unconscious motivation is the main cause of behavior; people are often unaware of or wrong about their true motivations because sex and aggression—the chief forces motivating us, according to Freud—involve wishes and desires unacceptable to the conscious mind. However, mental association, dreams, and mistakes such as speech errors (Freudian slips) can give clues to the contents of the unconscious. To reduce the anxiety produced by unacceptable aspects of our own minds, we use self-deceptive defense mechanisms. Karen Horney and Alfred Adler also developed psychodynamic theories, retaining Freud's core idea of unconscious mental forces but differing in their emphasis on social rather than sexual/aggressive drives.

Humanistic theories of personality were born partly out of a conviction that psychodynamic theories dehumanized people. Humanistic theories emphasize those characteristics of people that are uniquely human. They typically have a phenomenological orientation, which means that they emphasize subjective mental experience; they are generally holistic, looking at the whole person rather than analyzing the person into components; and they are concerned with people's tendency to actualize themselves, that is, to grow and to realize their individual potential. Carl Rogers and Abraham Maslow are pioneers of this approach. Based on the life stories people tell, Dan McAdams has proposed that personal myth is an important construct for understanding personality.

Social-cognitive theories of personality are distinguished by using traditional areas of laboratory research, such as learning, cognition, and social influence, as well as clinical data. They emphasize beliefs and habits of thought. Julian Rotter's concept of locus of control, the tendency to believe that rewards are or are not usually controllable by one's own efforts, is an example of a cognitive construct used as a personality variable. A related idea is Albert Bandura's concept of self-efficacy, the belief in one's own ability to perform specific tasks. Social-cognition research suggests that a positive, optimistic outlook is associated with various benefits. Walter Mischel suggests, with good evidence, that traits must be considered with respect to specific situations. This section concludes with a brief discussion of cross-cultural personality differences.

LOOK over the table of contents for this chapter in your textbook before you continue with your study.

Notice that there are focus questions in the margins of the text for your use in studying the material. The following chart lists which Study Guide questions relate to which focus questions.

Focus Questions	Study Guide Questions
Personality as Behavioral Dispositions, or Traits	
1–2	1–3
3	4
4	5–7
5–6	8–11
7–8	12–14
9	15
10	16
11–12	17–19
13	20
Personality as Adaptation to Life Conditions	
14–16	1–5
17	6–7
18–19	8–10
20–21	11–12
22–25	13–15
Personality as Mental Processes I: Psychodynamic and Humanistic Views	
29	1–6
30	7
31	8–11
32–33	12–13
34	14–16
35–37	17–21
38	22–24
39	25
40	26–28

Personality as Mental Processes II: Social-Cognitive Views	
41	1–2
42–43	3–6
44–45	7–8
46–47	9–11
48	12–14
49	15
50–51	16

The Integrated Study Workout

COMPLETE one section at a time.

Introduction AND *Personality as Behavioral Dispositions, or Traits* (pages 537–548)

CONSIDER these questions before you go on. They are designed to help you start thinking about this subject, not to test your knowledge.

Can the fundamental ways in which personalities differ be efficiently summarized in terms of two dimensions? in terms of five? Or does it take many more dimensions to do the job?

Will a person who is suspicious today tend to be suspicious 20 years from now?

How much of a role does heredity play in determining the personality differences among individuals?

READ this section of your text lightly. Then go back and read thoroughly, completing the Workout as you proceed.

George is shy, Susan reckless, and Sam friendly. As social beings, we are constantly making judgments about people's personalities—that is, about their style of interacting with the world in general and other people in particular. Psychologists seek to understand personality in a more formal, systematic way. Trait theories have the description and measurement of individual differences in personality as their main purpose.

1. Define the term *trait*, and distinguish traits from states.

2. Are traits all-or-none characteristics—that is, does a person either have a trait or not have a trait? Do traits *explain* individual differences?

3. What is the primary goal of trait theories?

Factor analysis has been an essential statistical tool in the development of trait theories of personality.

4. Factor analysis is designed to help researchers make sense of patterns of _____ by revealing _____ that underlie those patterns. The process begins with the collection of data—specifically, personality measures—from a large _____ of people. Correlations between each pair of measures (e.g., honest and patient) are computed. Then mathematical _____ are _____ and finally meaningful _____ are associated with each factor. We gain some sense of which traits are related and which are _____ of each other.

Raymond Cattell, a pioneer of the trait approach to personality, describes personality in terms of sixteen dimensions. His was the first prominent trait theory. (See Table 15.2 on text page 541.)

5. How did Cattell's background in chemistry influence his thinking?

6. How did Cattell develop his theory?

7. Describe the results of Cattell's research.

Some trait theorists consider Cattell's theory too complex. A contemporary of Cattell's, D. W. Fiske, reanalyzed Cattell's data and found evidence for only five different factors. In fact, many factor-analytic studies over the past several decades have produced results that are remarkably consistent, even though testing was conducted in different countries, with different languages, different subjects, and different personality measures. The five traits revealed in these studies are called the Big Five. (See Table 15.3 on text page 541.)

8. What are the five global traits of the Big-Five theory?

9. What are facets of a trait?

10. Which questionnaire is most commonly used to measure individuals on the Big Five traits and their facets?

11. What is a general weakness of almost all personality questionnaires?

Suppose we can describe a person in terms of personality traits today. Will that description still apply in the future?

12. How is the stability of traits over time studied? What are the general findings?

13. Are there general trends in personality change with age? Explain.

14. Describe some influences on individual personality change, which can move in any direction at any age.

Do scores on personality tests actually predict behavior? That is a matter of validity—the extent to which a measure actually reflects what it is purported to reflect.

15. Discuss the ability of personality tests to predict behavior, giving one specific example of evidence for each Big Five trait.

   a.

   b.

   c.

   d.

   e.

16. Are personality differences *more* or *less* apparent in novel situations or life transitions? Explain.

Many trait theorists believe that stable behavioral dispositions such as the Big Five arise at least in part from inherited physiological characteristics of the nervous system. How heritable are personality traits? As with the heritability of other characteristics, such as intelligence, twin and adoption studies have been key to answering the question.

17. Describe the most common approach to studying the heritability of personality traits. What is the usual finding? What possible flaw in methodology calls into question the results of such studies?

18. How did David Lykken and his colleagues get around the methodological pitfalls of other twin studies? Were their results consistent with other studies?

19. Discuss the relative lack of effect on personality of sharing the same family environment. Give a well-rounded answer.

Researchers are now only beginning to link behavior genetics and physiological approaches, searching for the actual genes that are responsible for the heritable portion of a given trait and examining its physiological influences.

20. Comment on attempts to find the genetic underpinnings of particular personality traits.

Personality as Adaptation to Life Conditions
(pages 548–557)

CONSIDER these questions before you go on. They are designed to help you start thinking about this subject, not to test your knowledge.

Why do people differ so widely in personality? What purpose does such variety serve?

Can knowing whether a person is the first-born or the youngest child in the family help to predict anything about personality?

Do men's and women's personalities really differ on average, or are such ideas simply cultural myths?

READ this section of your text lightly. Then go back and read thoroughly, completing the Workout as you proceed.

Personality can also be thought of in terms of adaptation to life conditions. Both proximate and ultimate explanations for personality are sought by theorists. Proximate explanations, as you may recall from Chapter 3, are concerned with the causal mechanisms that operate within the individual's lifetime. Ultimate explanations, in contrast, are concerned with the evolutionary survival value—with the very function—of variation in personality. The fact that sexual reproduction exists, given that there are easier biological means of reproduction, suggests that the diversity it produces confers evolutionary advantages. By extension, it seems unlikely that the particular mechanisms leading to personality differences would have evolved if they produced no survival advantage. (Note that this is true not only for humans but for animal life in general—many nonhuman species have been shown to have variation in behavioral styles.)

1. How is diversification among offspring like owning a diversified investment portfolio?

2. Describe two types of pumpkinseed sunfish.

3. What are some advantages and disadvantages of being a bold or a cautious fish?

4. How does having both types of offspring serve the parents?

5. Is "personality" change possible in fish? Explain.

Personality traits in humans can be thought of as different problem-solving strategies.

6. Choose two of the Big-Five personality dimensions. Then speculate about how extremes on these dimensions might relate to different life strategies and thus to survival and reproductive chances. What evidence did David Buss find to suggest that such correlations exist?

7. How can an evolutionary perspective help to explain both heritable and nonheritable variation in personality dimensions?

Many theorists have assumed a special importance of the early family environment in shaping personality. However, some psychologists now say that the family influence has been overemphasized. They point out that individuals raised in the same home are about as different from one another in personality as people raised in different homes (if we keep the degree of genetic relatedness constant).

8. Explain how children in the same home could have quite different personality-forming experiences.

9. Define the following terms:
   a. sibling contrast

   b. split-parent identification

10. How might sibling contrast and split-parent identification be valuable in reducing sibling rivalry and increasing the diversification of the parental investment in offspring? Provide evidence to support your answer.

Except in cases of multiple births (such as twins or triplets), the children in a family each occupy a different position in terms of birth order.

11. Describe the consistent birth-order differences found by Frank Sulloway. What types of data did he use to reach his conclusions?

12. Has subsequent research by others supported Sulloway's theory of birth order? Explain and point out any contradictions or limitations of the theory.

The psychological differences between men and women—whatever they may be and whatever their extent—may be due to the fact that men and women adapt to different niches. Those niches may stem in part from biological sex, but they are also due to socioculturally defined gender categories.

13. What personality differences have been found between men and women?

14. How might gender influence the relationship between personality and life satisfaction?

15. Discuss the possible evolutionary and cultural contributions to gender differences in personality. Include evidence in your discussion.

Personality as Mental Processes I: Psychodynamic and Humanistic Views (pages 538–567)

CONSIDER these questions before you go on. They are designed to help you start thinking about this subject, not to test your knowledge.

Are we generally aware of why we do what we do?

Can our dreams tell us anything about ourselves that we don't already know?

What do people mean when they say such things as "I just want to know who the real me is"?

READ this section of your text lightly. Then go back and read thoroughly, completing the Workout as you proceed.

Unlike trait theories, some theories focus on the processes and contents of the mind to understand personality and the behaviors that it gives rise to. One such theory is Sigmund Freud's. His theory of personality and his approach to psychotherapy are both referred to as psychoanalysis. It would be difficult to exaggerate the impact of Freud's thought on modern psychology. Freud's psychoanalysis is the prime example of a psychodynamic theory.

1. Comment briefly on Freud's professional life and the origins of his theory.

2. What does the term *psychodynamic* mean? What are the guiding principles of psychodynamic theories?

3. What role does the unconscious mind play, according to Freud's theory?

4. Relate the concept of unconscious motivation to posthypnotic suggestion as Freud did.

5. Characterize Freud's general approach for revealing the unconscious. What aspects of thought and behavior did he consider to be the best clues?

6. Which two drives are central to personality differences in Freud's view? Explain. Be sure to mention the broader sense in which Freud used these terms as his thinking evolved.

Freud believed that people are essentially asocial, being held together in society only because of their needs. Most post-Freudian psychodynamic theorists have instead regarded people as fundamentally social and as motivated by needs that go beyond the sexual and aggressive drives that Freud emphasized.

7. Describe the drives or needs considered essential to personality differences in the psychodynamic theories of each of the following:
   a. Karen Horney (pronounced **horn**-eye)

   b. Alfred Adler

Anna Freud, Sigmund Freud's daughter, was also a psychoanalyst. She was most responsible for developing the theory of defense mechanisms.

8. What is a defense mechanism?

9. Define each of the following defense mechanisms, explaining how each defends against anxiety.
   a. repression

   b. displacement and sublimation

   c. reaction formation

   d. projection

   e. rationalization

10. Indicate which defense mechanism each of the following individual's is using.

   _____ a.   Garth is partying too much to get his studying done. He tells himself that he needs a lot of relaxation to handle the pressure of school.
   _____ b.   Yolanda is a sculptor who loves to take a piece of stone and carefully chisel it into a smooth curving form.
   _____ c.   Eric unconsciously harbors great hostility but instead perceives that his brother Joe is hostile.

11. At present, how well accepted is the concept of defense mechanisms? Is there any research evidence to support Sigmund and Anna Freud's views about them?

15. What was Vaillant's basis for deciding to which category a defense mechanisms belonged?

16. How is defensive style related to a successful, happy life, according to Vaillant's research?

Repression is one of the defense mechanisms on which contemporary research has focused.

12. What are some of the issues that make repression of traumatic memories a controversial topic?

The founders of humanistic psychology objected to what they saw in psychodynamic theories. Theorists from this alternative perspective proposed a different way of viewing personality.

17. Explain each of these aspects of humanistic psychology.
   a. humanistic approach

13. What characterizes repressors? How do they differ from nonrepressors?

   b. phenomenological reality

A major avenue of personality research inspired by the psychodynamic approach involves the exploration of people's defensive styles.

14. According to George Vaillant, some defenses are more mature than others. Comment on each of the following and list specific examples.
   a. immature defenses

The personality theory of Carl Rogers, one of the most influential representatives of humanistic psychology, often is called *self theory* because of its focus on the individual's sense of self.

18. In Rogers's view, one of the most common goals that people have when they enter therapy is to become _____.

   b. intermediate defenses

19. According to Rogers, what does it mean to be oneself?

   c. mature defenses

20. Describe research findings on the response to medical advice that is supportive of Rogers's view.

21. Define *self-actualization*. What metaphor did Rogers use to convey his view of self-actualization?

Abraham Maslow proposed a set of five types of needs, all of which must be met to achieve self-actualization.

22. Complete the five levels of Maslow's hierarchy of needs.

    Highest level _____

    _____

    _____

    _____

    Lowest level _____

23. With regard to the hierarchy of needs, what must one do to become a self-actualizing person?

24. Discuss Maslow's hierarchy from an evolutionary perspective.

An increasingly accepted means of learning about individuals is to ask them to tell their life stories.

25. How is the life-story approach consistent with humanistic psychology?

26. What common factors has Dan McAdams found in the many life stories he has studied?

27. Why does McAdams refer to the self-told life story as a personal myth? Is the myth generally static? Explain.

28. What does the study of personal transformation conducted by Miller and C'deBaca suggest about the modifiability of personality in adulthood?

Personality as Mental Processes II: Social-Cognitive Views (pages 567–574)

READ this section of your text lightly. Then go back and read thoroughly, completing the Workout as you proceed.

Is positive thinking really beneficial? Can we predict that a person who is polite in dealing with employer will be polite with store clerks? with children? with coworkers?

CONSIDER these questions before you go on. They are designed to help you start thinking about this subject, not to test your knowledge.

cial-cognitive theories (also called social-learning or cial-cognitive-learning theories) are tied to laboratory research on learning, cognition, and social influence, as well as to the perspective of a clinician.

. Instead of instinctive, unconscious motives, seen as prime determinants of personality by psychodynamic theorists,

_____ and

_____ stemming from one's

_____ are the focus of social-cognitive theorists. Social-cognitive theorists use the term "unconscious" to mean

_____ .

. How are social-cognitive and humanistic approaches similar? different?

he cognitive constructs most often studied in the cial-cognitive approach to personality involve beefs or habits of thought that affect a person's ability take control of his or her own life.

. What led Rotter, the primary founder of this approach, to conclude that people's beliefs about their ability to control rewards affect their behavior?

. Explain locus of control as a personality trait. In what kinds of situations does this generalized disposition govern behavior?

5. Describe some correlational data consistent with the concept of locus of control.

6. Why is the trend toward studying domain-specific control valuable? Provide an example in your explanation.

Another major construct in social-cognitive theory is Albert Bandura's concept of self-efficacy.

7. Define the term *self-efficacy*, and distinguish it from locus of control. Do the two usually go hand in hand (for example, internal locus of control and high self-efficacy)? Give an example of a case in which they don't.

8. Is self-efficacy positively correlated with performance on tasks? Does it play a causal role? Support your answer.

Many people believe that positive thinking has numerous benefits.

9. Does psychological research support this notion? Be specific.

10. How might optimism produce its positive effects?

11. Can optimism be maladaptive? Can pessimism be adaptive? Explain.

If you are honest when you detect a bank error in your favor, does that necessarily mean that you will be honest on tests or with your doctor? Social-cognitive theorist have pointed out that it is not enough to know global traits. One must also consider context.

12. Summarize Walter Mischel's position on situation specificity.

13. How did Mischel and Peake study the trait of conscientiousness? What did they conclude?

14. What were the conclusions of Mischel's study at a summer camp?

Social-cognitive theorists, because of their perspective on the nature of personality, suggest that there must be cross-cultural differences in personality.

15. Distinguish between allocentrism and ideoce trism. Which type of culture is associated wi each? How strong is the association?

The very concept of personality is given more impo tance in the West and different traits are emphasize

16. Compare Chinese and Western conceptions of pe sonality. What does this suggest about personali measurement in other cultures?

Be sure to READ the Concluding Thoughts at the end of t chapter. Note important points in your Workout. Then consolidate your learning by answering the focus question in the margins of the text.

After you have studied the chapter thoroughly, CHECK yo understanding with the Self-Test that follows.

Self-Test 1

Multiple-Choice Questions

1. A Big-Five personality dimension that does n show a significant overall gender difference is th of:
   a. neuroticism.
   b. conscientiousness.
   c. agreeableness.
   d. openness to experience.

2. Research has shown that male and female mai mals _____ humans differ in sponse to _____, with males b coming more aggressive and females mo nurturant and motivated to strengthen social ti
   a. other than; stress
   b. other than; success
   c. including; stress
   d. including; success

3. Freud believed that the best clues to the contents of a person's unconscious are those elements of thought and behavior:
   a. that are least logical.
   b. that are most logical.
   c. for which the person can offer no explanation.
   d. that most clearly signal a lack of self-esteem.

4. Two brothers, Roberto and Silvio, have sought consciously or unconsciously to make themselves different from each other. Whereas Roberto is seem by himself and others as the athletic and friendly one, Silvio projects his personality as being intellectual and artistic but a little withdrawn. This "strategy" most clearly represents the idea of:
   a. birth order.
   b. sibling contrast.
   c. split-parent identification.
   d. self-actualization.

5. According to Alfred Adler, an inferiority complex represents:
   a. an inability to overcome or cope with the normal feeling of inferiority that accompanies the dependence of early childhood.
   b. a mask for unacceptable feelings of superiority that arise from sexual and aggressive drives.
   c. a failure to recognize the difference between one's real self and one's ideal self.
   d. an exaggerated tendency to compare ourselves with others and an overreliance on other people's judgments of our worth.

6. Post-Freudian psychodynamic theories differ significantly from Freudian psychoanalysis in their greater emphasis on:
   a. early childhood experiences.
   b. social drives.
   c. the role of the unconscious.
   d. sex and aggression.

7. An emphasis on phenomenology is especially characteristic of _____ theories of personality.
   a. psychoanalytic   c. trait
   b. social-cognitive   d. humanistic

8. According to humanistic psychology, people are powerfully motivated toward:
   a. self-actualization, the direction for which must be environmentally determined.
   b. self-actualization, the direction for which must be determined from within the individual.
   c. self-esteem, which is defended with such mechanisms as rationalization and projection.

   d. self-esteem, which comes from adapting oneself to the norms and judgments of the larger human community.

9. Locus of control and self-efficacy are major constructs in _____ approaches to personality.
   a. social-cognitive   c. evolutionary
   b. psychodynamic   d. trait

10. Studies show consistent trends in personality changes as people grow older. A trend that holds up even across cultures is an increase in:
    a. agreeableness and conscientiousness.
    b. agreeableness and neuroticism.
    c. neuroticism and conscientiousness.
    d. neuroticism and openness to experience.

11. Louise believes that whether she gets into graduate school depends primarily on her own efforts; she also believes that she can succeed in this endeavor. Louise appears to have an _____ locus of control and to be _____ in self-efficacy.
    a. external; high   c. external; low
    b. internal; low   d. internal; high

12. The theorist who has most emphasized the situational specificity of personality variables is:
    a. Cattell.   c. Mischel.
    b. Rotter.   d. Rogers.

13. Which of the following is true of traits as they are seen from the perspective of trait theory?
    a. A trait is a characteristic that a person either has or doesn't have in all-or-none fashion.
    b. *Trait* and *state* are equivalent terms, but the former is applied to cognitive characteristics, whereas the latter is applied to motivational and emotional characteristics.
    c. Traits are characteristics of the person rather than of the environment.
    d. Traits are temporary, changeable characteristics that can be inferred from current behavior patterns.

14. Which of the following correctly reflects the order of needs (from *bottom* to *top*) according to Abraham Maslow's hierarchy?
    a. physiological needs, esteem needs, safety needs, self-actualization needs, attachment needs
    b. safety needs, physiological needs, esteem needs, attachment needs, self-actualization needs
    c. self-actualization needs, esteem needs, physiological needs, safety needs, attachment needs

d. physiological needs, safety needs, attachment needs, esteem needs, self-actualization needs

15. Research from the trait theory approach generally shows that personality is:
    a. fairly stable over the course of adult life for about 60% of people and extremely stable for the other 40%.
    b. not at all stable over the course of adult life.
    c. stable prior to age 50 but relatively unstable thereafter.
    d. increasingly stable up to about age 50 when stability levels off.

Essay Questions

16. Define the term *defense mechanism*, and describe two specific defense mechanisms, providing examples for each.

17. Describe the aims of trait theorists. How do the "Big Five" fit in with these aims?

After you have assessed your understanding on the basis of Self-Test 1 and have tried to strengthen your preparation in any areas of weakness, GO ON to Self-Test 2.

Self-Test 2

Multiple-Choice Questions

1. A personality theory that emphasizes the importance of mental forces in shaping personality and determining thought and behavior would, by definition, by a _____ theory.
   a. social-cognitive   c. trait
   b. psychodynamic   d. psychoanalytic

2. To gain information about the contents of a patient's unconscious mind, Freud used all of the following as sources of data *except*:
   a. dreams.
   b. questionnaires.
   c. patients' uncensored reporting of their thoughts.
   d. slips of the tongue.

3. A psychoanalyst would be most likely to describe working with a patient in terms of:
   a. an advertising campaign in which the patient is the product being endorsed as well as the consumer being targeted by the campaign.
   b. law enforcement, with the patient being warned about various ways in which laws of psychological good health are being violated.
   c. serving as a mirror for the patient's thoughts and feelings.
   d. a search for clues about the patient's unconscious mind that must then be fitted together.

4. Which of the following is *not* one of the Big-Five personality dimensions?
   a. conscientiousness   c. agreeableness
   b. optimism   d. neuroticism

5. Brian believes that he intensely dislikes Alicia. The truth is that his real love for her is unacceptable to him. Brian is using a defense mechanism called:
   a. sublimation.   c. reaction formation.
   b. projection.   d. fixation.

6. Dan McAdams's concept of personal myth fits best with:
   a. the Big-Five theory.
   b. Freud's psychoanalytic theory.
   c. humanistic theories.
   d. social-cognitive theories.

7. Carl Rogers emphasized the human drive toward:
   a. being one's real self.   c.   security.
   b. achievement.   d.   safety.

8. The generally easygoing Joel is feeling angry about his roommate's loud music on the night before a final exam. Joel's anger is an example of:
   a. a trait.
   b. a state.
   c. a behavioral disposition.
   d. all of the above.

9. The theoretical approach to personality that most emphasizes learned beliefs and habits of thinking is _____ theory.
   a. psychoanalytic   c.   social-cognitive
   b. trait   d.   humanistic

10. Suppose experimenters give subjects a series of problems that are, unbeknownst to the subjects, unsolvable. Some subjects are led to believe that they are able to solve the problems, but others are not manipulated in this way. The results show that those who are led to believe that they can succeed work longer on the problems. This experiment illustrates the effects of:
    a. locus of control.   c.   self-actualization.
    b. self-efficacy.   d.   self-esteem.

11. Cattell was a pioneer in the development of _____theories of personality.
    a. humanistic   c.   social-cognitive
    b. psychodynamic   d.   trait

12. Personality traits are most apparent in:
    a. routine situations.
    b. novel situations.
    c. group discussions.
    d. familiar roles and settings.

13. Allocentrism is higher in _____ cultures, but about _____ percent of people tested in such cultures score on the other side of this personality dimension.
    a. individualist; 5
    b. individualist; 40
    c. collectivist; 5
    d. collectivist; 50

14. Repressors are a category of people who:
    a. regularly repress anxious feelings.
    b. experience less physiological stress than nonrepressors.
    c. experience better health and less chronic pain than nonrepressors.
    d. all of the above.

15. David Lykken and his colleagues have studied _____ and found evidence of heritability scores averaging about .50 for_____.
    a. twins raised apart, as well as twins raised together; both groups on virtually every personality trait assessed
    b. twins raised apart, as well as twins raised together; very few of the personality traits assessed in the former but for most traits in the latter group
    c. families that have adopted two children, some twin and some nontwin biological siblings; virtually every personality trait assessed
    d. families that have adopted two children, some twin and some nontwin biological siblings; very few personality traits assessed

Essay Questions

16. Discuss Abraham Maslow's hierarchy of needs.

17. Describe two general characteristics shared by Freudian and post-Freudian psychodynamic theories and one general characteristic that differentiates post-Freudian psychodynamic theories from Freud's psychoanalysis.

Answers

Introduction AND *Personality as Behavioral Dispositions, or Traits*

4. correlation; factors; sampling (or sample); factors; extracted; labels; independent

Personality as Mental Processes I: Psychodynamic and Humanistic Views

10. **a.** rationalization
    b. sublimation
    c. projection

18. their real selves

22. highest to lowest: self-actualization needs; esteem needs; attachment (belongingness and love) needs; safety needs; physiological needs

Personality as Mental Processes II: Social-Cognitive Views

1. beliefs; habits of thought; one's unique experiences

Self-Test 1

1. **d.** (p. 555)

2. **c.** (p. 556)

3. **a.** Freud wanted to learn what lay behind the consistent, rational explanations so readily offered by the conscious mind. He assumed that what was *least* logical in a person's speech or behavior was most likely to represent the irrational, sometimes troubling contents of that person's unconscious (p. 559)

4. **b.** (p. 552)

5. **a.** Adler suggested that the failure to overcome the sense of inferiority can in some cases lead to a superiority complex. (p. 560)

6. **b.** (pp. 559–560)

7. **d.** (p. 564)

8. **b.** (p. 565)

9. **a.** (pp. 568–569)

10. **a.** (p. 544)

11. **d.** Louise believes that her success in graduate school admission will be determined by her own efforts; that means she has an internal locus of control. She also believes that those efforts will be enough to gain her admission; that means she has high self-efficacy. (pp. 568–569)

12. **c.** (p. 572)

13. **c.** (p. 538)

14. **d.** (pp. 565–566)

15. **d.** (p. 544)

16. Defense mechanisms are mental processes that provide ways to reduce anxiety. They accomplish this by keeping disturbing or unacceptable wishes, memories, and other thoughts out of consciousness. A focus on defense mechanisms is a hallmark of psychodynamic theories. All defense mechanisms involve some form of self-deception. The most basic defense mechanism is repression, in which the mind exerts pressure to push anxiety-provoking material out of consciousness. Reaction formation is a defense mechanism in which we perceive our true feelings as their opposite. For example, if someone is jealous of his brother's accomplishments, he may feel and behave as if he were excessively proud of or happy about those accomplishments. (pp. 560–563)

17. Many personality theorists wish to describe human personality in terms of the inner drives, beliefs, and goals that shape it. For them, explaining individual differences is secondary. Trait theorists, in contrast, are primarily interested in individual differences. Their aim is to discover the most basic dimensions along which personality varies, to efficiently describe individual differences in terms of a limited set of characteristics or traits. Traits are assumed to be relatively stable predispositions to behave in a particular way.

    The usual method for revealing these traits involves the factor analysis of questionnaire data. Different researchers have collected data using different measures and different types of subjects in a variety of cultures and have produced consistent results suggesting that there are five dimensions. They are known as the Big Five personality traits. Introversion–extroversion is one of the Big Five, conscientiousness another. There is fairly good consensus among trait theorists that individual differences in personality can be efficiently described in terms of differences along these five global traits or dimensions and six subordinate traits (facets) associated with each of the Big Five. (pp. 539–542)

Self-Test 2

1. **b.** Freud's psychoanalytic theory is just one example of a psychodynamic theory. (p. 558)

2. **b.** Questionnaires are often used by trait theorists however. (p. 558)

3. **d.** (pp. 558–559)

4. **b.** (p. 541)

5. **c.** In reaction formation, an individual perceives his or her true feelings as their opposites—experiencing hate where there is love or love where there is hate, for example. In projection, the feeling is perceived accurately but is attributed to someone else. Sublimation is a redirection of unacceptable urges into culturally valued channels. (p. 561)

6. **c.** (p. 566)

7. **a.** (p. 564)

8. **b.** (p. 538)

9. **c.** (p. 567)

10. **b.** Studies like this suggest that self-efficacy may have some causal effect on performance. (p. 569)

11. **d.** (pp. 540–541)

12. **b.** (p. 546)

13. **d.** (p. 573)

14. **a.** (p. 560)

15. **a.** By including identical twins reared apart, Lykken and his colleagues avoided the methodological pitfall of some other studies of identical twins. If identical twins are reared together, they not only are genetically identical but may also be treated more alike than fraternal twins are; thus, it would be hard to separate genetic and environmental contributions to their similarities in personality. (p. 546)

16. Maslow's hierarchy of needs ranks different categories of needs from the lowest to the highest: physiological needs, such as the need for food; needs for safety, such as the need for shelter from rain or snow; attachment (belongingness and love) needs, such as the need for family or friendship; esteem needs, such as the need for respect from self and others; and needs for self-actualization, such as the needs for self-expression and creativity. Maslow felt that people must essentially meet these needs in order, seeing that lower needs are at least relatively satisfied before moving on to other needs. If we examine the rank ordering from an evolutionary perspective, it makes sense in terms of the survival value of meeting each type of need; for example, food is more directly essential than friends, and so on. (pp. 565–566)

17. The personality theorists who developed post-Freudian psychodynamic theories generally retained some essential elements of Freud's psychoanalysis. One such element was an emphasis on the unconscious. Both Freud and those followers who broke away from his theory held that a person's conscious thought and behavior are determined by unconscious mental forces. These later psychodynamic theorists also shared with Freud the view that defense mechanisms are designed to keep anxiety-producing thoughts and motives out of awareness.

    Post-Freudian psychodynamic theorists differ from Freud in their emphasis on social needs. Whereas Freud believed that the drives of sex and aggression were at the root of virtually all human thought and behavior, the post-Freudians believed that this emphasis neglected important aspects of personality. They viewed people as inherently social beings and attempted to explain personality in terms of specifically social drives. For example, Karen Horney discussed the need for security, which is fulfilled socially, usually through the influence of the child's parents. (pp. 558–560)

Mental Disorders

*READ the introduction below before you read
the chapter in the text.*

The concept of a mental disorder is not sharply or clearly defined. Practical guidelines introduced by the American Psychiatric Association help clinicians to decide when a given set of symptoms represents a mental disorder, but they leave "gray" areas. *DSM-III* and now *DSM-IV*, the standard diagnostic guides prepared by the American Psychiatric Association, divide disorders into different classes according to their objective symptoms. Though diagnosis is essential for both scientific and clinical purposes, the labeling involved in receiving a diagnosis can affect a person's self-concept, the way others view him or her, and even the person's chances of recovery. It is also important to understand that mental disorders occur within a cultural context. Anorexia nervosa, for example, is a culture-bound syndrome—one limited to specific culture groups, in this case, to Western cultures. Mental disorders have multiple causes, which can be divided into three categories—predisposing, precipitating, and perpetuating. The first type increases susceptibility to a disorder, the second type brings the disorder on in susceptible people, and the third type causes the disorder to persist.

Researchers have investigated the fact that the prevalence of particular mental disorders appears to differ between men and women, identifying several possible reasons. Men are more likely than women to be diagnosed with intermittent explosive disorder and antisocial personality disorder, whereas women are more likely than men to receive a diagnosis of anxiety or mood disorders. The reasons for these sex differences may include clinicians' expectations, different social roles, different responses to stress, and other factors.

Anxiety disorders have anxiety or fear as their most prominent symptom. They include generalized anxiety disorder, which involves a high degree of relatively unfocused anxiety and worry; phobias, which are intense, irrational fears of objects or events; obsessive-compulsive disorder, which involves repetitive thoughts and actions; panic disorder, in which people have unpredictable attacks of overwhelming terror; and posttraumatic stress disorder, which may strike the survivors of extremely traumatic experiences such as plane crashes, wars, or childhood abuse.

Mood disorders fall into two general categories—depressive disorders (major depression and dysthymia), in which the problem is downward mood swings, and bipolar disorders, in which mood swings are both downward and upward. One major biological theory about the cause of depressive disorders implicates underactivity at synapses where the neurotransmitters are norepinephrine or serotonin, but conflicting evidence makes this theory questionable. An alternative biological theory is that depression is associated with a temporary loss of neurons or neural connections in the brain. Other perspectives suggest that depression involves a particular style of interpreting negative experiences. There is evidence for some genetic basis for depression. Research on bipolar disorder indicates that it is strongly influenced by genes and that stressful life events can bring on either depressive or manic episodes in predisposed individuals.

People with somatoform disorders experience some type of bodily ailment that is not due to a physical disease. Somatization disorder involves a long history of dramatic but often vague medical complaints. In conversion disorders, a person loses some bodily function, such as sight or sensation in the hand. Behavior and emotions not only can cause physical symptoms with no physical basis, they can also affect the onset or course of a real physical malady. Research has shown that psychological factors may affect the cardiovascular and immune systems, for example.

Schizophrenia is a serious mental disorder, the symptoms of which include delusions, hallucinations, disorganized speech and behavior, and the absence of some normal emotion and behavior. Schizophrenia is essentially a cognitive disorder—one in which the primary psychological deficits involve information processing functions, such as directing attention, encoding information, or recalling the source of information. Schizophrenia is associated with an unusual pattern of activity at synapses where dopamine is the neurotransmitter. A deficit in glutamate neurotransmission may also be involved. A person's predisposition to schizophrenia may be increased by prenatal stress, birth traumas, and genes. Sociocultural factors may also play a role in the onset or progression of the disorder as well as the chance for recovery.

LOOK over the table of contents for this chapter in your textbook before you continue with your study.

Notice that there are focus questions in the margins of the text for your use in studying the material. The following chart lists which Study Guide questions relate to which focus questions.

The Integrated Study Workout

COMPLETE one section at a time.

Introduction AND *The Concept of Mental Disorder and Its Relation to Culture* (pages 578–584)

CONSIDER these questions before you go on. They are designed to help you start thinking about this subject, not to test your knowledge.

What are mental disorders? Are they illnesses with biological causes, learned patterns of maladaptive thought and behavior, or something else altogether?

Is the prevalence of particular mental disorders the same from one culture to another?

How might labeling a person with a mental disorder affect other people's treatment of him or her? Can it affect the judgment of trained clinical observers?

READ this section of your text lightly. Then go back and read thoroughly, completing the Workout as you proceed.

Everyone's psychological processes are subject to disturbances of one kind or another in the normal course of living. We may experience a temporary lack of motivation that makes it difficult to keep up with our work or relationships. Anxiety may seem to tie us in knots, keeping us from sleeping, concentrating, or even enjoying our favorite activities. Confusion may overtake us, making clear, orderly thought seem beyond our grasp. But the disturbances that are a normal part of life differ from those that characterize mental disorders in intensity, duration, and frequency and in the extent to which they disrupt the individual's life

1. Is *mental disorder* a precisely and unambiguously defined concept? Explain.

2. Complete the following statements.

    a. A(n) _____ is any characteristic of a person's actions, thoughts, or feelings that could potentially indicate a mental disorder.

    b. A(n) _____ is a constellation of interrelated symptoms manifested by a given individual.

3. What three criteria must a syndrome satisfy in order to be classified as a mental disorder, according to the American Psychiatric Association's *DSM-IV*? For each, indicate a question that might arise in its practical application.

    a.

    b.

    c.

The scientific study of mental disorders demands that we have some system for assigning them to specific categories. Categorization is important for learning about causes, treatments, and outcomes. The assignment of labels to a person's mental disorders is called *diagnosis*.

4. The _____ of a diagnostic system is the extent to which different diagnosticians, all trained in the system, reach the same conclusions when independently diagnosing the same individuals.

5. What inadequacy in diagnosis led the American Psychiatric Association to develop the original *DSM*?

6. Specify the overriding goal of the group that developed *DSM-III*. Describe how the creators attempted to reach that goal in *DSM-III* (and *DSM-IV*). Was the goal achieved? Explain.

7. The _____ of a diagnostic system reflects the extent to which the categories it identifies are clinically meaningful.

8. What are some questions that would help us evaluate the validity of a diagnostic system?

Labeling has important clinical and scientific uses, but it also has certain drawbacks.

9. Describe some ways in which labels can have harmful effects.

10. What partial solution to the problem of labeling has been suggested by the American Psychiatric Association?

11. What is medical students' disease? How can you protect yourself against developing a case of it?

Mental disorder—including the nature of the distress, the way it is expressed, and the way others respond to the person suffering from it—differs with the cultural context.

12. What are culture-bound syndromes? Give two examples (one from Asia, one from Western cultures).

13. How does homosexuality illustrate the role of culture in deciding what constitutes a disorder?

14. What is ADHD? How common is it?

15. What biological explanation of ADHD is prominent today? What is the usual treatment for ADHD?

16. How do critics explain the high rate of ADHD diagnosis?

Causes of Mental Disorders   (pages 585–589)

CONSIDER these questions before you go on. They are designed to help you start thinking about this subject, not to test your knowledge.

Why are men diagnosed more often with some mental disorders, and women more often with others?

Are mental disorders permanent?

Is someone with a genetic predisposition necessarily going to get the actual disorder?

READ this section of your text lightly. Then go back and read thoroughly, completing the Workout as you proceed.

Given that all thoughts, emotions, and behaviors are products of the brain, mental disorders are also products of the brain. Some mental disorders are irreversible and stem from brain damage that is irreversible.

1. What are the causes and characteristics of each of the following common irreversible disorders?
   a. Down syndrome

   b. autism

   c. Alzheimer's disease

2. What are episodic mental disorders, and what is the brain's role in these?

Mental disorders have multiple causes which can be divided into three interacting categories.

3. Define each of the following types of causes.
   a. predisposing causes

   b. precipitating causes

   c. perpetuating causes

4. Classify each of the following examples as a predisposing, precipitating, or perpetuating cause.

   _____ a. Lin has more freedom to behave in socially unacceptable ways because many people think such behavior is due to her disorder and beyond her control.

   _____ b. Winona's best friend has committed suicide, which has caused Winona to fall into a deep and long-lasting depression.

   _____ c. Because of his bizarre behavior, Jeremy has been treated unkindly by strangers and rejected by friends, which makes his recovery more difficult.

   _____ d. Ted has a genetically inherited susceptibility to schizophrenia.

   _____ e. From early childhood on, Emma has learned to believe that life is hard and that there is little she can do to affect whatever happens to her.

5. How is the degree of predisposition to a mental disorder related to the amount of stress that will bring on the disorder?

Though men and women suffer mental illness at a similar rates overall, large sex differences exist for specific disorders.

6. What are some disorders more often diagnosed in men? more often diagnosed in women?

7. Briefly discuss four hypotheses offered to explain such sex differences. For each hypothesis, present supporting evidence.
   a. differences in the tendency to report or suppress psychological distress

   b. clinician's expectations

   c. differences in social roles and experiences

d. differences in ways of responding to stressful situations

Anxiety Disorders   (pages 589–595)

CONSIDER these questions before you go on. They are designed to help you start thinking about this subject, not to test your knowledge.

Do people with irrational fears realize that their fears are irrational?

Are men and women equally likely to be diagnosed with phobias about spiders or snakes? about public speaking or meeting new people?

What is it like to experience a panic attack?

What kinds of obsessions and compulsions do people with obsessive-compulsive disorder experience? Are they fundamentally different from those that most people experience at times?

READ this section of your text lightly. Then go back and read thoroughly, completing the Workout as you proceed.

Evolution has equipped us to experience fear, an emotion with adaptive value. But because we are complex, thinking creatures living in cultural environments that present a variety of real and imagined threats, our fear can be triggered in circumstances in which it is not adaptive. In anxiety disorders, fear or anxiety is the most prominent symptom.

1. Are the terms *fear* and *anxiety* used interchangeably? Is worry a major feature? Explain.

2. Do genetic differences play a role in predisposition for anxiety disorders?

DSM-IV recognizes several classes of anxiety disorders. In generalized anxiety disorder, the anxiety is attached to a variety of threats, real and imagined, rather than to one specific threat.

3. What are the symptoms of generalized anxiety disorder?

4. How prevalent is generalized anxiety disorder in North America?

5. Describe the predisposing and precipitating causes of generalized anxiety disorder, along with the role of hypervigilance.

6. From a cultural perspective, briefly discuss the high incidence of generalized anxiety?

A phobia is a type of anxiety disorder in which an intense, irrational fear is clearly associated with a particular category of object or event.

7. Distinguish between *specific* and *social* phobias, and give examples of each.

8. Do people who have phobias fail to realize that their fears are irrational? Explain.

9. Explain the idea that phobias lie on a continuum with normal fears. Which type of phobia is much more common in one gender than the other? Why might this be so?

We do not really know what causes phobias; however, several hypotheses have been offered.

10. Answer the following questions about these hypotheses.
   a. How have behaviorists generally explained the development of phobias? Why is this explanation problematic?

   b. What is Martin Seligman's position on this issue, and what observation does his theory help to explain?

   c. How might hypervigilance play a role in phobias?

Another class of anxiety disorder is obsessive-compulsive disorder.

11. Distinguish between obsessions and compulsions by filling in the blanks below.
   a. A(n) _____ is a disturbing thought that intrudes repeatedly on a person's consciousness even though the person recognizes it as irrational.
   b. A(n) _____ is a repetitive action usually performed in response to an obsession.

12. What is necessary for someone to meet the *DSM-IV* criteria for obsessive-compulsive disorder? How is this disorder both like and unlike phobia?

13. Are the obsessions of people with the disorder similar to those experienced by people who do not have the disorder? Do compulsions always bear a logical relation to the obsessions that trigger them? Explain.

14. How is brain damage apparently involved in obsessive-compulsive disorder?

People with panic disorder are subject to feelings of helpless terror that strike unpredictably and without any connection to specific environmental threats—which means there is no way to avoid the panic by avoiding the threat.

15. Describe a typical panic attack. What type of phobia do most panic-attack victims develop?

16. What learned tendency is thought to be a perpetuating (and possibly predisposing) cause of panic disorder? What is some evidence for this?

Posttraumatic stress disorder differs from other anxiety disorders in that it is clearly connected to one or more traumatic experiences in the affected person's life.

17. Describe the kinds of traumas that most commonly lead to posttraumatic stress disorder.

18. What are the typical symptoms of the disorder? How can some attempts to alleviate symptoms actually compound the problem?

19. Why does the prevalence of the disorder depend greatly on the population sampled?

20. Who is more likely to develop posttraumatic stress disorder—victims of repeated, long-term trauma or victims of a single short-term trauma?

21. Do genes play a predisposing role in posttraumatic stress disorder? What can help to reduce the likelihood of the disorder?

Mood Disorders   (pages 596–603)

CONSIDER these questions before you go on. They are designed to help you start thinking about this subject, not to test your knowledge.

Are biological factors important in determining who suffers from depressive disorders and who doesn't?

Can certain patterns of thinking make people more prone to depression?

Is there any truth to the popular notion that moodiness and creativity are associated?

READ this section of your text lightly. Then go back and read thoroughly, completing the Workout as you proceed.

Some days we seem to experience life through a haze of sadness that affects our view of everything and everyone; at other times, we are full of laughter, warmth, and great expectations, impervious to the frustrations and worries that normally beset us. Moods are a part of normal psychological experience, but if they are too intense or prolonged, as in mood disorders, they can be harmful.

1. The term _____ refers to a prolonged emotional state that colors many, if not all, aspects of a person's behavior.

2. Identify and briefly describe the two main categories of mood disorders.

   a.

   b.

Depression can powerfully affect a person's feelings, thoughts, and actions.

3. What are the symptoms of depression? When is a diagnosis of a depressive disorder warranted, according to *DSM-IV*?

4. Distinguish between major depression and dysthymia. What is double depression?

5. How is depression related to generalized anxiety?

Depression may be causally related to heredity and to stressful experiences.

6. What evidence suggests that genetic predisposition plays a role in depression? What did a twin study suggest about the way genes predispose someone?

7. Why is it risky to accept cause-effect interpretations of correlations between stressful life events and depression? What is the best evidence in *favor* of a cause-effect relationship?

Cognitive theorists suggest that it is not so much what happens to us as how we think about what happens to us that matters in depression.

8. What kind of observation provided a starting point for cognitive theories of depression? Illustrate the cognitive perspective by noting Aaron Beck's conclusions regarding depressed clients.

9. Answer the following questions about Lyn Abramson and Martin Seligman's hopelessness theory of depression.

   a. Describe the attributional style associated with depression in this theory.

   b. Is there evidence to show that this attributional style is *correlated* with depression? that it *causes* depression? Explain.

Much research has been undertaken to discover more about the brain mechanisms related to depression.

10. Why did an early theory focus on the activity of serotonin and norepinephrine? What was the basic contention of the theory and how is it regarded today?

11. What alternative theory are neuroscientists considering now?

12. Is it possible that moderate depression after a loss is adaptive? Explain.

13. What have Keller and Nesse suggested about different types of depression?

In addition to the unipolar disorders of major depression and dysthymia, *DSM-IV* identifies bipolar disorders (commonly called manic-depression), which involve both upward and downward mood swings.

14. Distinguish between bipolar I disorder and bipolar II disorder.

15. Comment on the heritability of bipolar disorders.

16. Name the drug that can help to control bipolar disorder.

17. Characterize manic and hypomanic episodes.

18. Discuss the observed relationship between creativity and hypomania, indicating possible interpretations of it.

Psychological Influences on Physical Symptoms and Diseases   (pages 603–608)

CONSIDER these questions before you go on. They are designed to help you start thinking about this subject, not to test your knowledge.

Can a person experience a problem as severe as blindness or paralysis for psychological reasons?

Can our minds really affect our vulnerability to physical ailments?

READ this section of your text lightly. Then go back and read thoroughly, completing the Workout as you proceed.

People with somatoform disorders experience physical ailments—even ailments as extreme as blindness or paralysis—that are not due to physical causes.

1. Identify two types of somatoform disorders described in *DSM-IV* by correctly labeling the following descriptions.

   _____ a. A person with this disorder has a long history of dramatic complaints about many different medical conditions, most of which are vague and unverifiable, such as dizziness or nausea.

   _____ b. In this disorder, a person temporarily loses some bodily function—even vision, hearing, or motor functions in more dramatic cases.

2. Why are diagnosing and estimating the prevalence of somatization disorder both problematic undertakings?

3. Comment on cultural differences in the prevalence of somatoform disorders.

4. What characteristic has been found to be common in people diagnosable with somatoform disorders?

5. How did Freud interpret conversion disorders? How does the prevalence of conversion disorders in Western cultures today compare with the prevalence in Freud's day?

6. Where are dramatic cases of conversion disorder most likely to be found now? How is this related to trauma? (Use the example of Cambodian survivors of the Khmer Rouge to illustrate.)

7. In what segment of the population might conversion disorder be more common than expected in Western societies? Explain.

8. What does neuroimaging suggest about whether people with conversion disorders are "just pretending"?

DSM-IV notes that the mind can influence the onset or progress of a disease that has a physical basis. Psychological factors affecting medical condition are not mental disorders but have been the focus of research because of their potentially important health consequences.

9. What relationship has been found between being widowed and developing physical diseases? What are some possible mechanisms for this effect?

10. What was the original hypothesis about the relationship between Type-A personality and heart disease?

11. How has the theory been modified after further research?

12. Describe some evidence that emotional distress can increase our chances of getting a cold or flu.

13. Describe evidence that this effect could be mediated by suppression of the immune system.

14. Give an evolutionary explanation of immune suppression during psychological distress.

Schizophrenia   (pages 608–618)

CONSIDER these questions before you go on. They are designed to help you start thinking about this subject, not to test your knowledge.

Are the hallucinations experienced by some people with schizophrenia related to normal mental imagery in people without the disorder?

How might people with schizophrenia differ biologically from people who do not have schizophrenia?

Can people recover from this disorder?

READ this section of your text lightly. Then go back and read thoroughly, completing the Workout as you proceed.

The term *schizophrenia* comes from the Greek words for "split mind." Schizophrenia involves a split in the mental processes, such that attention, perception, emotion, motivation, and thought become disorganized and fail to work together. Bizarre thoughts and behaviors can result. The disorder is both serious and relatively common, occurring in about 1 percent of people at some time during their lives. Recovery, partial or full, is sometimes possible.

1. Though schizophrenia is equally prevalent in males and females, it generally strikes earlier and is more severe in _____. The first symptoms tend to appear in _____ or _____ and the average age of diagnosis is about ____ years later for women than for men.

2. Specify the criteria necessary for a diagnosis of schizophrenia, according to *DSM-IV*.

Symptoms are not constant but rather come and go, with active phases alternating with times of relative normalcy.

3. Describe each of the following types of symptoms, and identify specific forms that each may take in schizophrenia.

   a. disorganized thought and speech

   b. delusions

   c. hallucinations

d. grossly disorganized behavior and catatonic behavior

e. negative symptoms

Individuals with schizophrenia manifest a wide variety of specific symptoms. There is no single profile that fits all cases. Theorists have attempted to subclassify schizophrenia into different types based on the ways symptoms tend to cluster together, but no system of subcategorization has really been satisfactory.

4. Briefly describe three clusters of symptoms that emerge from factor-analytic studies. Indicate each type of symptom's tendency to go into remission and to respond to antipsychotic drugs.

5. Describe the three subcategories of schizophrenia included in *DSM-IV*.

a. paranoid type

b. catatonic type

c. disorganized type

Schizophrenia is essentially a cognitive disorder, which means there are deficits in the processing of information. These deficits are due to adverse changes in the brain.

6. What types of cognitive deficits have laboratory studies shown in people with schizophrenia? Are they present only in active phases of the disorder?

7. What evidence led to the dopamine theory of schizophrenia? What major flaw suggests it is not entirely correct?

8. How have theories of schizophrenia that involve neurotransmitters changed? Why is glutamate a current focus?

9. What are some common structural differences associated with schizophrenia? How might a normal developmental change in adolescence go awry and help bring on schizophrenia?

Because the disorder is both common and very debilitating, the question of causation in schizophrenia has provoked particular interest. Research has not led to definitive answers, however. Biological causes are one area of active investigation. The predisposing role of genes has been very clearly established.

10. In some studies, a group of individuals diagnosed as having schizophrenia is identified. These individuals are called _____ cases. Relatives of these individuals are then examined. The percentage of relatives of a particular class (for example, identical twin, nontwin sibling, and so on) who develop the disorder is called the _____.

11. Look at Table 16.3. It shows that, over many studies, the average concordance for schizophrenia for identical twins is _____ percent, while that for fraternal twins is _____ percent, only a little higher than the concordance for nontwin siblings. Since the concordance for identical twins is not _____ percent, these results suggest that there is a strong _____ component as well as a strong genetic component.

12. What do adoption studies suggest about the heritability of schizophrenia?

13. Do we know anything about the specific genes that predispose people to schizophrenia or contribute to a given symptom?

14. How might prenatal factors and birth traumas be implicated in schizophrenia?

Both familial and cultural environments may play a part in the development of or recovery from schizophrenia.

15. Describe evidence from a long-term study in Finland that factors in the home may promote symptoms in genetically predisposed individuals.

16. What does the concept of expressed emotion refer to? How has it been linked to the prognosis for the diagnosed individual?

17. What have cross-cultural studies of schizophrenia revealed? Be sure to comment on consistencies as well as on a striking difference between developed and developing countries.

18. What are some possible explanations for the difference in recovery found between developed and developing countries?

Be sure to READ the Concluding Thoughts at the end of the chapter. Note important points in your Workout. Then consolidate your learning by answering the focus questions in the margins of the text.

After you have studied the chapter thoroughly, CHECK your understanding with the Self-Test that follows.

Self-Test 1

Multiple-Choice Questions

1. Which of the following statements is true?
   a. The terms *syndrome* and *symptom* are synonymous.
   b. A syndrome is the same thing as a mental disorder.
   c. A syndrome is the constellation of symptoms associated with a disorder.
   d. Syndromes are collections of related mental disorders, such as the various anxiety disorders.

2. Research indicates that the susceptibility for schizophrenia involves a strong genetic contribution. Heredity would thus be considered _____ cause of schizophrenia.
   a. a predisposing
   b. a precipitating
   c. a perpetuating
   d. both a predisposing and a perpetuating

3. Studies show that the diagnostic categories established in *DSM-III* and *DSM-IV* have been shown to have:
   a. both high reliability and high validity.
   b. low reliability but high validity.
   c. high validity, but the question of reliability is harder to answer and will take more research.
   d. high reliability, but the question of validity is harder to answer and will take more research.

4. Labeling people as having a mental disorder:
   a. is essential to our ability to study disorders scientifically.
   b. can affect their self-esteem as well as the way others treat them.
   c. is sufficient to establish the validity of diagnostic categories, provided the scientific community generally agrees with these labels.
   d. involves both **a** and **b**.

5. A person with no other mental disorders experiences anxiety that is not attached to any particular threat. The anxiety persists for a prolonged period, causing excessive tension and worry about a wide range of matters, and disrupts the person's daily functioning. This person appears to be suffering from:
   a. a specific phobia.
   b. obsessive-compulsive disorder.
   c. panic disorder.
   d. generalized anxiety disorder.

6. Behaviorists have suggested that phobias are acquired through:
   a. classical conditioning, which is consistent with the fact that most people with phobias can recall a specific experience that initiated their intense fear.
   b. classical conditioning, which is questioned on the grounds that most people with phobias cannot recall a specific experience that initiated their intense fear.
   c. operant conditioning, which is consistent with the fact that most people with phobias can recall a specific experience that initiated their intense fear.
   d. operant conditioning, which is questioned on the grounds that most people with phobias cannot recall a specific experience that initiated their intense fear.

7. Feelings of worthlessness, sadness, and lack of pleasure in life are particularly characteristic of a person with:
   a. anxiety.   c. hypomania.
   b. depression.   d. somatization disorder.

8. Though this theory is now in doubt, biological explanations of depression have centered on the idea that depression involves:
   a. reduced activity at synapses where serotonin and norepinephrine are the neurotransmitters.
   b. overactivity at synapses where serotonin and norepinephrine are the neurotransmitters.
   c. abnormally small cerebral ventricles.
   d. abnormally large cerebral ventricles.

9. The hopelessness theory of depression most clearly reflects _____ factors.
   a. cultural   c. biological
   b. cognitive   d. psychodynamic

10. A disorder in which the person temporarily and for purely psychological reasons, loses some bodily function—becoming blind, deaf, or paralyzed in the most dramatic cases—is:
    a. schizophrenia.
    b. dysthymia.
    c. somatization disorder.
    d. conversion disorder.

11. A cross-cultural study by the World Health Organization found that schizophrenia was _____ prevalent in developed countries compared to developing countries and that people in developed countries were _____ likely to recover from it.

a. equally; more   c. more; more
b. equally; less   d. more; less

12. The neurotransmitter _____ is now a major focus of research on the causes of schizophrenia.

    a. serotonin   c. norepinephrine
    b. glutamate   d. methylphenidate

13. Katrina, who has been diagnosed with schizophrenia, reports that she has been sent from a parallel universe to study the people of Earth. Her statement clearly reflects:

    a. a catatonic state.
    b. a delusion.
    c. a hallucination.
    d. negative symptoms.

14. Evidence suggests that the hallucinations associated with schizophrenia are.

    a. not related to the mechanisms of normal verbal thought.
    b. experienced as coming from inside the person's own head but controlled by someone else.
    c. much more likely to be visual than auditory.
    d. due to the enhancement of creative ability that occurs during active phases of the disorder.

15. Schizophrenia is found in about _____ percent of people overall.

    a. .025   c. 3
    b. 1   d. 6

Essay Questions

16. Describe the symptoms of bipolar disorders and distinguish two forms. Is there any truth to the notion that some people with bipolar disorders experience heightened creativity? Explain.

17. Discuss hypotheses concerning the biologica causes of schizophrenia that focus on problems o neurotransmission.

After you have assessed your understanding on the basis of Self-Test 1 and have tried to strengthen your preparation in any areas of weakness, GO ON to Self-Test 2.

Self-Test 2

Multiple-Choice Questions

1. Anorexia nervosa is an example of a(n):
    a. anxiety disorder.
    b. culture-bound syndrome.
    c. somatoform disorder.
    d. bipolar disorder.

2. Which of the following does *not* describe a perpetuating cause of a mental disorder?
    a. Norman's anxiety has made him unable to work effectively, which has caused him to lose his job.
    b. Camilla's depression came on as she faced the unexpected demands of caring for her husband during his six-month recovery from an accident.
    c. Bradley's family and friends openly believe it will be impossible for him to recover from schizophrenia.
    d. Burton's phobia has won him a great deal of attention and sympathy from his wife.

3. The major goal of the people who developed *DSM-III* and *DSM-IV* was to:
   a. more clearly distinguish neuroses from psychoses.
   b. define disorders in terms of their causes.
   c. increase the reliability of diagnostic categories.
   d. organize diagnostic categories in terms of the amount of anxiety they involve.

4. According to research evidence, sex differences in the prevalence of anxiety disorders and depression may be due to:
   a. the greater tendency of men to express their anxiety and distress.
   b. gender bias in the expectations of clinicians.
   c. the greater likelihood that males in our society will experience the kinds of stress that contribute to these disorders.
   d. all of the above.

5. The type of anxiety disorder known as a specific phobia:
   a. is more common in males than in females.
   b. is also called a social phobia.
   c. usually involves a fear of something that is also feared to some extent by people who do not have a phobia.
   d. tends to disappear once an individual recognizes the irrational nature of the fear.

6. The majority of panic-attack victims develop _____ at some point after their first panic attack.
   a. bipolar disorder
   b. agoraphobia
   c. obsessive-compulsive disorder
   d. hypomania

7. Posttraumatic stress disorder is an example of a(n) _____ disorder.
   a. irreversible   c. mood
   b. anxiety   d. schizophrenic

8. Research following up on early investigations of Type A personality and heart disease shows:
   a. no relationship between psychological traits and susceptibility to heart disease.
   b. that is it frequent negative emotions such as anger or sadness that promote heart disease.
   c. that it is a rushed, overworked lifestyle that promotes heart disease.
   d. that original interpretations were correct though they fell into temporary disfavor.

9. According to the hopelessness theory of depression, the people most prone to depression are those who attribute their negative experiences to causes that are:
   a. stable and global.
   b. unstable and specific.
   c. unstable and global.
   d. stable and specific.

10. Research has shown that emotional distress:
    a. tends to decrease susceptibility to colds and flu.
    b. can suppress the production of T-cells.
    c. directly enhances immune function, which is an adaptive consequence.
    d. has no measurable effect on immune response.

11. Depression and _____ seem to be predisposed by the same genes and often occur in the same individuals.
    a. obsessive-compulsive disorder
    b. bipolar disorder
    c. social phobias
    d. generalized anxiety disorder

12. Which of the following is *not* an irreversible mental disorder caused by permanent damage to the brain?
    a. autism   c. Down syndrome
    b. schizophrenia   d. Alzheimer's disease

13. Lithium is used to treat:
    a. major depression. c. schizophrenia.
    b. panic attacks.   d. bipolar disorder.

14. An exaggeration of normal changes in the brain during adolescence (specifically pruning) is thought to contribute to the onset of:
    a. schizophrenia.
    b. somatization disorder.
    c. depression.
    d. bipolar disorder.

15. In schizophrenia, the term *negative symptoms* refers to:
    a. those symptoms most distressing to the patient.
    b. those symptoms most distressing to other people who come in contact with the patient.
    c. the absence of, or reduction in, expected thoughts, behaviors, feelings, and drives.
    d. the remission of classic symptoms such as delusions or hallucinations.

Essay Questions

16. Discuss the relationship between mental disorders and normal psychological experiences. What are the American Psychiatric Association's criteria for determining that a particular syndrome represents a mental disorder?

17. Mental disorders, their diagnosis, and their treatments occur in a particular social and cultural context. Make clear the importance of this fact by discussing two topics from the chapter.

Answers

The Concept of Mental Disorder and Its Cultural Relativity

2. a. symptom **b.** syndrome

4. reliability

7. validity

Causes of Mental Disorders

4. a. perpetuating, **b.** precipitating, **c.** perpetuating, **d.** predisposing, **e.** predisposing

Anxiety Disorders

11. a. obsession **b.** compulsion

Mood Disorders

1. mood

Psychological Influences on Physical Symptoms and Diseases

1. a. somatization disorder **b.** conversion disorder

Schizophrenia

1. males; late adolescence; early adulthood; 4

10. index; concordance

11. 48; 17; nontwin siblings; 100; environmental; mis diagnosis

Self-Test 1

1. c. A syndrome is considered evidence of a mental disorder by *DSM-IV* standards only if it meets certain criteria. (p. 577)

2. a. Although one's genetic endowment remains the same after one has developed a disorder, it is not considered a perpetuating cause because the genes are not a *consequence* of the disorder. (p. 586)

3. d. (pp. 579–580)

4. d. Evidence suggests that labeling can change a person's self-esteem and the judgments of clinically trained observers. However, diagnosis is necessary to better understand and more effectively treat mental disorders. (p. 580)

5. d. (p. 590)

6. b. (pp. 591–592)

7. b. (p. 596)

8. a. (p. 599)

9. b. (pp. 598–599)

10. d. Conversion disorder is a somatoform disorder. Somatization disorder is a less dramatic type of somatoform disorder. (p. 604)

11. b. (p. 616)

12. b. (p. 612)

13. b. Katrina is showing evidence of a delusion, which is a false belief maintained despite compelling evidence against it. She would be reporting a hallucination if she said she heard voices telling her to learn more about Earth people or to come back to her home universe. (p. 609)

14. b. (p. 610)

15. b. (p. 608)

16. Bipolar disorders are mood disorders in which the individual has both downward mood swings, called depressive episodes, and upward mood swings, called manic episodes. The depressive and manic episodes vary in duration, and the individual may experience relatively normal mood between episodes. Bipolar II disorder is the less severe form of the disorder, and bipolar I disorder is the more severe type. In bipolar disorder II, the manic phrase is less extreme (hypomania).

Depressive episodes involve the same symptoms found in major depression such as sadness, a sense of worthlessness, a reduced ability to experience pleasure, as well as effects on eating and sleeping. Manic episodes are typically characterized by feelings of confidence, energy, enthusiasm, euphoria, and power. Extreme mania may involve bizarre thoughts and potentially dangerous behaviors, while less severe manias may involve spending sprees, sexual adventures, or other behaviors that the person would not normally engage in and may later regret. In some people, the manic state is experienced as irritability, suspiciousness, and even distinctive rage, however.

Hypomania appears to be associated with enhanced creativity, though the direction of causality is not clear. People with moods alternating between moderate depression and hypomania were found in one study to be more creative than people with more stable moods, for example. (pp. 601–602)

17. A major focus of biological interpretations of the cause of schizophrenia has been dopamine, a neurotransmitter in the brain. The dopamine theory of schizophrenia holds that the symptoms of schizophrenia result from overactivity at synapses where dopamine is the neurotransmitter. Supporting evidence comes from drug effects. The antipsychotic drugs that most reduce this neurotransmitter's activity are most effective in controlling the positive symptoms of schizophrenia. Drugs that increase activity at synapses involving dopamine can exaggerate existing schizophrenic symptoms or even bring them on.

However, not all research findings are clearly supportive of the dopamine hypothesis and few researchers hold to its original, simple form. One reason is that antipsychotic drugs that only block dopamine are not effective for the negative symptoms of schizophrenia. A modified version of the dopamine hypothesis is that schizophrenia involves an unusual form of dopamine activity, one that might include underactivity in some areas and overactivity in others. Another neurotransmitter called glutamate is being studied now. It is possible that people with schizophrenia have defective receptors for glutamate, which is the primary excitatory neurotransmitter at fast synapses in the brain. (pp. 611–612)

Self-Test 2

1. b. (p. 582)

2. b. The unexpected demands of caring for her husband were a precipitating cause of Camilla's disorder. (pp. 586–587)

3. c. To accomplish this end, they attempted to define disorders in terms of objective symptoms that could be reported by the client or observed by the clinician. The reliability of most diagnostic categories in *DSM-III* and *DSM-IV* is reasonably high, provided that the diagnostic criteria are carefully followed. (p. 579)

4. b. (p. 588)

5. c. This illustrates the fact that many symptoms of mental disorders lie on a continuum with psychological experiences that are considered normal. Fears of such things as spiders, blood, or high places are commonplace, but people who have phobias about such things experience more intense fears that may cause them exceptional distress or may interfere with their lives. (p. 591)

6. b. (p. 594)

7. b. (p. 594)

8. b. (p. 606)

9. a. (p. 599)

10. b. (p. 607)

11. d. (p. 596)

12. b. (pp. 585–586)

13. d. (p. 601)

14. a. (p. 613)

15. c. (p. 610)

16. The difference between "normal" and "disordered" is largely arbitrary. This is due in part to the fact that many symptoms associated with mental disorders differ from common psychological experiences not in kind but only in degree. For example, most of us feel unattractive, dejected, or unworthy at times. Such feelings are common in depressive disorders but are generally more severe, long-lasting, and disruptive to the affected person's life. As another example, the delusions that distinguish schizophrenia from other mental disorders are false beliefs that persist despite compelling evidence to the contrary. Who among us is not to some degree holding on to a few beliefs that are irrational, that run counter to apparent fact? Our fears, erroneous perceptions, moods, and worries are similar in many cases to the symptoms of mental disorders.

The American Psychiatric Association has established certain criteria to help clinicians determine when that arbitrary line between the normal and the disordered has been crossed. These criteria are (1) that the syndrome (that is, the person's pattern of symptoms) must involve distress and/or impaired functioning serious enough to warrant professional treatment; (2) that the source of the distress lies within the person, not the environment (such as prejudice, poverty, or other social forces that may lead a person to behave contrary to social norms); and (3) that the syndrome does not represent a deliberate, voluntary decision to behave in a certain way. Even with these guidelines, there is still considerable room for interpretation. We are probably all distressed by our feelings of depression, and we may find it harder than usual to function in our work or relationships, so it is not entirely clear when the distress or impaired functioning is serious enough to justify the label of mental disorder? (pp. 577–578)

17. The social and cultural context in which people develop may exert a variety of influences—affecting people's values, their conception of what is normal and expected in society, their experience of pressures to act in certain ways or to avoid acting in other ways, even their opinions about what it means to have a mental disorder and whether recovery from that disorder is possible.

Labeling is one example of the role that social and cultural factors can play. There is power in labeling someone as abnormal and as suffering from a given disorder. To label a person as having schizophrenia, for example, is to do more than indicate a diagnostic category for other clinicians to use in treating the individual. Labels can stigmatize. They can make an individual see himself or herself in a negative light, have less hope of recovering, and perhaps make less effort at recovery. They can also affect the way others deal with that person. Even clinicians may fall prey to the power of labels. Cross-cultural studies show that the chances of recovering from schizophrenia are better in societies that do not tend to label sufferers in ways that stigmatize them and foist negative expectations on them.

Another type of evidence for the significance of social and cultural factors comes from the existence of culture-bound syndromes. These syndromes occur almost exclusively in particular cultural contexts. Koro and anorexia nervosa are examples of culture-bound syndromes found in Southeast Asia and Western cultures, respectively. Cultural values can also play a large part in what kinds of behavior are labeled as disordered. Homosexuality was once listed as a psychiatric disorder, but no longer is. Currently there is controversy about whether the behaviors that gain a child a diagnosis of ADHD are to some extent normal behaviors that are not accepted or tolerated by present cultural norms. (pp. 581–584)

READ the introduction below before you read the chapter in the text.

For most of human history, people with serious mental disturbances have not received the care they needed; they have often been the victims of other people's ignorance and fear, as well as of their own disorders. Because of nineteenth-century reformers such as Philippe Pinel and Dorothea Dix, as well as modern views on the needs and rights of people with mental disturbances, the treatment of the mentally ill is much better, but certainly not ideal today. A move to deinstitutionalize people and return them to the community that began in the 1950s has only partially succeeded and has also created new problems. The quality of care that people with mental disorders receive depends not only on compassionate public policy but on financial support.

Mental health professionals vary in their training and in the kinds of work they do; they include psychiatrists, clinical psychologists, counseling psychologists, counselors, psychiatric social workers, and psychiatric nurses. Research has shown that most people in the United States who have a mental disorder by *DSM* standards do not obtain care from a mental health professional. Moreover, the chances of obtaining such care differ as a function of education and income. Also, not everyone seeing a mental health professional has a diagnosable mental disorder; many are simply seeking help to deal with a life problem.

Biological treatments for mental disorders include drugs, electroconvulsive shock therapy (ECT), and psychosurgery. Drugs are the most common type of biological treatment. Classes of drugs that are beneficial for schizophrenia, depression, and anxiety, for example, are widely used. These drugs can, however, present problems in the form of harmful side effects and sometimes addiction. ECT is an effective treatment for severe depression; although it can cause some memory loss, a newer form of the technique which treats only the right hemisphere minimizes this problem. Psychosurgery is the most controversial and least often used of the biological treatments. It is a treatment of last resort for certain cases of obsessive-compulsive disorder. Deep brain stimulation may prove to offer a better alternative for such cases.

Psychotherapy refers to any formal, systematic, theory-based approach in which a trained therapist uses psychological means to treat people with mental problems or disorders. Because there are so many varieties of psychotherapy, the chapter focuses on the most common forms.

Psychoanalysts and other psychodynamically oriented therapists try to help people recall emotionally charged memories and mental conflicts buried in the unconscious mind, on the assumption that relief of symptoms will follow. Some major tools used by such therapists are free association, dream analysis, and the phenomena of resistance and transference.

Humanistic therapists emphasize the person's need to grow toward his or her potential—in other words, to self-actualize. Therapy is intended to help the person gain control of his or her life by becoming aware of inner feelings and desires, undistorted by external influences such as the perceived disapproval of parents or other important persons in the individual's life. Carl Rogers's client-centered therapy is the most common humanistic therapy.

Whereas psychodynamic and humanistic therapies are oriented toward the whole person, cognitive and behavioral therapies are more problem-centered. Cognitive therapists assume that much of the mental distress people suffer is due to maladaptive thinking patterns. The cognitive therapist's goal is to help the client replace such thinking patterns with more adaptive ones. Albert Ellis's rational-emotive therapy (RET) and Aaron Beck's cognitive therapy are well-established forms of the cognitive therapeutic approach.

Behavior therapy, rooted in the behaviorist principles of operant and classical conditioning, has close ties to cognitive therapy. In fact, to a considerable degree they have merged to form what is called cognitive-behavior therapy. Behavior therapy in the form of exposure treatment has been especially successful in the treatment of specific phobias. Another important behavioral technique is contingency management.

Does psychotherapy really work? By combining the results of many experiments, researchers have concluded that (1) psychotherapy does work; (2) no one kind of psychotherapy is better overall; and (3) some kinds of psychotherapy may work better than others for specific types of problems. Common factors, such as support, hope, and motivation, which are not unique to any particular psychotherapeutic approach, are important contributors to the effectiveness of therapy.

LOOK over the table of contents for this chapter in your textbook before you continue with your study.

Notice that there are focus questions in the margins of the text for your use in studying the material. The following chart lists which Study Guide questions relate to which focus questions.

Focus Questions	Study Guide Questions
Care as a Social Issue	
1–2	1–3
3	4–5
4	6
Biological Treatments	
5–6	1–10
7	11–15
8–9	16–18
Psychotherapy I: Psychodynamic and Humanistic Therapies	
10–15	1–9
16	10–12
17	13
18	14
Psychotherapy II: Cognitive and Behavioral Therapies	
19	1
20	2
21–22	3–5
23	6
24	7–8
25–26	9–10
27–28	11–12
29	13

Evaluating Psychotherapies	
31	1–2
32	3
33	4–6
34	7–9

The Integrated Study Workout

COMPLETE one section at a time.

Introduction AND *Care as a Social Issue* (pages 622–625)

CONSIDER these questions before you go on. They are designed to help you start thinking about this subject, not to test your knowledge.

How were people with mental disorders "treated" in earlier times?

Where do people obtain treatment for mental problems?

What kinds of professionals offer mental health care?

READ this section of your text lightly. Then go back and read thoroughly, completing the Workout as you proceed.

The history of Western society's response to people with mental disorders is largely one of ignorance, prejudice, absence of compassion, and even cruelty. Throughout the Middle Ages and into the seventeenth century, such people were thought to be in league with the devil, and so were tortured and often killed. According to the more secular views of the eighteenth century, mental disorders were due to the unworthiness and degeneracy of those who suffered from them. The places in which these people were shut away were scenes of misery and horror. Only in the nineteenth century did significant reforms begin.

1. Briefly describe the work of Philippe Pinel in Europe and Dorothea Dix in the United States.

2. What inspired the movement toward deinstitutionalization that began in the 1950s in the United States? What alternative approach to care was envisioned by supporters of this movement? Was the dream realized? Explain.

3. Describe assertive community treatment programs for the severely mentally disordered. Does this approach work? Do most people who need such services in the United States receive them?

The people who provide mental health treatment vary considerably in the nature and extent of their training, in certification, and in the kinds of people they tend to treat.

4. List three types of mental health professionals who hold a doctoral-level degree, and indicate the characteristics that differentiate them from one another.

   a.

   b.

   c.

5. List three types of mental health professionals who have bachelor's or master's degrees, and indicate the characteristics that differentiate them from one another.

   a.

   b.

   c.

6. The chapter describes a large survey on mental health care. What was revealed about the likelihood that a study participant with a mental disorder would receive professional mental health care? no care? other care? Describe the types of care provided.

Biological Treatments   (pages 625–631)

CONSIDER these questions before you go on. They are designed to help you start thinking about this subject, not to test your knowledge.

Can drugs calm anxiety, lift someone out of depression, or stop hallucinations?

What kinds of harmful side effects are caused by drugs used to treat mental disorders?

In what circumstances are people treated with electroconvulsive shock therapy or surgery? Is it safe? Does it work?

READ this section of your text lightly. Then go back and read thoroughly, completing the Workout as you proceed.

Biological treatments are designed to relieve mental disorders by directly affecting bodily processes. Contemporary biological approaches to mental disorders fall primarily into three categories—drugs, electroconvulsive shock therapy, and psychosurgery. Drugs are the most commonly used biological treatment. Although they may have desirable effects, drugs also commonly involve undesirable side effects and some are also addictive. Antipsychotic drugs are drugs used to treat schizophrenia and other disorders in which psychotic symptoms are primary.

1. Answer the following questions about the *typical antipsychotic drugs.*
   a. Comment on the beneficial effects of antipsychotic drugs such as chlorpromazine and haloperidol.

   b. How do they work?

   c. Do these drugs effectively treat the negative symptoms of schizophrenia?

2. Answer the following questions about the newer *atypical antipsychotic drugs.*
   a. What are some atypical antipsychotic drugs?

b. What are the advantages of these drugs?

c. How commonly are they used?

d. How do they work?

3. Discuss the side affects caused by antipsychotic drugs, pointing out those particularly associated with typical and atypical antipsychotics.

4. Answer the following questions about *antianxiety drugs* (tranquilizers).
   a. How effective are benzodiazepines for the various anxiety disorders? What alternative drugs are used for some anxiety disorders?

b. How do benzodiazepines produce their tranquilizing effects?

c. What are some risks of taking these drugs?

5. Answer the following questions about *antidepressant drugs.*

   a. Two categories of antidepressant drugs are _____, such as Tofranil and Elavil, and _____, such as Prozac.

   b. How are these drugs thought to act at the synapse? (Look at Figure 17.1 on text page 628.) Do we know how they reduce depression? Explain.

   c. Cite evidence suggesting that these drugs help people suffering from depression.

   d. Comment on the side effects of the two classes of antidepressant drugs.

When a drug is developed, we cannot, of course, assume that it will work simply because it is biologically plausible. We subject it to direct testing.

6. How is such testing typically done?

7. What are the overall results of such testing for antianxiety and antidepressant drugs?

8. Why do mere placebos work as well as they do?

9. What is spontaneous remission, and how common is it?

10. Explain the term *active placebo.* Why have some researchers favored their use in studies of drug effectiveness?

Public perceptions of electroconvulsive therapy (ECT) often involve images of brutality, even horror, inflicted under the guise of treatment. Such images are no longer consistent with reality. ECT as it is used today is both painless and safe.

11. Describe what happens in ECT today.

12. What disorder is most effectively treated by ECT, and how effective is such treatment?

13. How might ECT produce its antidepressant effect? Do we know for sure what makes it effective?

14. Does ECT treatment cause brain damage? To what extent does bilateral ECT affect memory?

15. Does unilateral ECT to the right hemisphere have adverse effects on memory? Is it as effective as bilateral ECT?

Psychosurgery, still a controversial approach, is by far the least common of the biological treatments for mental disorders. It involves surgically cutting or producing lesions in parts of the brain to alleviate symptoms.

16. Describe the operation called *prefrontal lobotomy*. For which types of disorders was it used and when? Why did this treatment, once held in high regard, become virtually obsolete?

17. Describe the newer, less drastic psychosurgical procedures still in occasional use today? What are these procedures useful for? Are they safe? When are they considered appropriate?

18. Briefly discuss deep brain stimulation, a possible alternative to psychosurgery.

Psychotherapy I: Psychodynamic and Humanistic Therapies   (pages 632–641)

CONSIDER these questions before you go on. They are designed to help you start thinking about this subject, not to test your knowledge.

How might remembering an emotionally charged experience help to alleviate someone's current psychological symptoms?

What causes the problems that bring people into therapy?

How do therapists regard the person being treated? What do they see as their own role?

READ this section of your text lightly. Then go back and read thoroughly, completing the Workout as you proceed.

Psychotherapy refers to any formal, theory-based, systematic approach to treating mental problems or disorders through psychological rather than directly physiological means. It is carried out by a trained therapist working with individuals, couples, families, or groups of unrelated people. Through talking with the client or clients, the therapist attempts to alter ways of feeling, thinking, or behaving.

1. Are there only a few forms of psychotherapy? Are they kept strictly separate in clinical practice? Explain.

2. Define the terms *psychoanalysis* and *psychodynamic therapy*.

3. According to psychodynamic therapists, what gives rise to mental disorders?

4. Why did Freud include the word *analysis* in the name he gave to his approach? What were his principal clues to the unconscious?

5. Briefly elaborate on these sources of clues to the unconscious used by psychodynamic therapists:

    a. free association

    b. dreams

    c. mistakes and slips of the tongue

6. Define the term *resistance*, and give an example of how it might be manifested. How is resistance interpreted by the therapist?

7. What is transference, and why did Freud consider it an important part of psychoanalysis?

8. How are insight and cure thought to be related in psychodynamic therapy?

9. Briefly summarize the case of the Rat Man as Freud interpreted it.

Like psychodynamic therapies, humanistic therapies are designed to help people become aware of their true feelings and desires; but unlike psychodynamic therapies, humanistic therapies expect those feelings and desired to be positive and life promoting. Carl Rogers's client-centered therapy is the most common humanistic therapy.

10. What are the joint aims of humanistic therapy? What are the barriers to attaining them that have led to a need for therapy?

11. How is the humanistic approach related to existential philosophy?

12. Why did Rogers call his approach *client-centered* therapy? What is it called today? Why?

13. In countering the client's maladaptive learning, the Rogerian therapist aims to provide three key elements. Identify each of the following.

a. A _____ is taken, which means allowing the client rather than the therapist to take the lead.

b. _____ refers to the therapist's attempt to comprehend what the client is saying or feeling at any given moment from the client's point of view rather than as an outside observer.

c. _____ implies a belief on the therapist's part that the client is worthy and capable even when the client may not feel or act that way.

14. Briefly summarize Rogers' therapy with Jim.

Psychotherapy II: Cognitive and Behavioral Therapies   (pages 641–649)

CONSIDER these questions before you go on. They are designed to help you start thinking about this subject, not to test your knowledge.

In what ways might a person's beliefs contribute to psychological problems such as anxiety or depression? How can a therapist help a person change maladaptive patterns of thinking?

How can therapy help someone eliminate a fear—say, a fear of dogs or of driving a car?

READ this section of your text lightly. Then go back and read thoroughly, completing the Workout as you proceed.

Cognitive and behavioral therapies are similar and are often combined.

1. What characteristics do cognitive and behavioral therapies share?

Cognitive therapies are based on the notion that people's maladaptive thoughts cause them unnecessary distress, leading to anxiety or depression. These types of therapies focus on conscious thoughts, attempting to replace maladaptive ways of thinking with more productive ones. Albert Ellis and Aaron Beck are pioneers of this approach.

2. What are three general principles of cognitive therapy?

3. What is the name of Ellis's theory? What general style does he have? Illustrate by defining "musturbation" and "awfulizing."

4. Explain Ellis's ABC theory of emotions. (See Figure 17.3 on text page 642.)

5. Do irrational beliefs disappear once they are seen to be irrational? Explain. What technique is used to aid change?

6. Explain how the cognitive therapist moves from a teaching role to a consulting role.

7. Aaron Beck's cognitive therapy was originally designed to treat _____; it was later expanded to include clients with _____ and, most recently, _____.

8. Use the case example of Irene to discuss Beck's way of identifying and correcting maladaptive, automatic thoughts.

Underlying behavior therapy are the behaviorist principles of classical and operant conditioning. Behavior therapy focuses directly on maladaptive behaviors rather than thinking.

9. What, broadly speaking, is contingency management? Describe the general approach taken to change behavior.

10. Briefly describe some contexts in which contingency management is used.

Behavior therapy is especially effective in treating specific phobias, such as a fear of flying or a fear of spiders.

11. Explain how a behaviorist would interpret a phobia in terms of classical conditioning. Why would habituation and extinction be important phenomena from the point of view of a behavior therapist?

In exposure treatments, the patient experiences the feared stimulus in a safe context—that is, in a manner that leads to habituation or extinction of the fear response.

12. Describe the following forms of exposure treatment.
   a. imaginative exposure

   b. in vivo exposure

   c. virtual reality exposure

13. Briefly summarize Miss Moffet's therapy for spider phobia.

Evaluating Psychotherapies   (pages 649–653)

Does psychotherapy really work?

Are some forms of psychotherapy more effective than
others? Are particular therapies better for certain
problems?

How important to the success of therapy are such
factors as a supportive therapeutic atmosphere or
hope?

Just as potential drug therapies must be tested, so must
psychotherapies be put to the test. To evaluate their
effectiveness, we must carry out controlled experiments.

1. Why are case studies not sufficient evidence of the
    value of psychotherapy?

2. The classic Philadelphia experiment assessed the
    effectiveness of two forms of psychotherapy for
    psychiatric outpatients suffering primarily from
    anxiety. Describe the study and its results. (See
    Figure 17.6 on text page 650.)

3. Does psychotherapy work? What is the evidence?
    Is it as helpful as drug therapy?

4. Is one form of psychotherapy generally more ef-
    fective than the others? Support your answer.

5. Are some types of therapy more effective for par-
    ticular problems? Be specific.

6. How might we account for the similar overall ef-
    fectiveness of different types of psychotherapy?

The fact that therapeutic effectiveness depends in part on
qualities of the therapist has led to further study of how
common factors may play a role in therapy outcomes.

7. Describe the factor called *support* and cite research ev-
    idence demonstrating the importance of this factor.

8. Describe the factor called *hope*. What evidence suggests that hope contributes to the effectiveness of psychotherapy?

9. How is motivation thought to be a valuable common factor in psychotherapy?

Be sure to READ the Concluding Thoughts at the end of the chapter. Note important points in your Workout. Then consolidate your learning by answering the focus questions in the margins of the text.

After you have studied the chapter thoroughly, CHECK your understanding with the Self-Test that follows.

Self-Test 1

Multiple-Choice Questions

1. Nineteenth-century reformers such as Philippe Pinel in Europe and Dorothea Dix in the United States sought to:
   a. release people from mental institutions so that they could be returned to the community.
   b. provide humane care in large institutions for those with mental disorders.
   c. replace psychotherapy with the biological treatments that they considered more effective.
   d. promote scientific research to determine the most effective forms of psychotherapy.

2. Therapy outcome experiments such as the classic Philadelphia experiment discussed in the text typically show that _____ therapeutic approach is superior overall to others.
   a. the psychodynamic
   b. the cognitive/behavioral
   c. the humanistic
   d. no

3. Benzodiazepines are the most commonly used class of drugs for the treatment of:
   a. schizophrenia.
   b. depression.
   c. conversion disorders.
   d. anxiety.

4. Tardive dyskinesia is a serious and irreversible motor disturbance caused by:
   a. schizophrenia.
   b. antipsychotic drugs, especially those in the typical category.
   c. antipsychotic drugs, especially those in the atypical category.
   d. none of the above.

5. A psychodynamic therapist would most likely be characterized as a(n):
   a. teacher showing a student how to think in new ways.
   b. detective piecing together clues.
   c. gardener helping plants to grow in their own way.
   d. friend providing an atmosphere of warmth and concern.

6. Margaret keeps "forgetting" to go to her therapy sessions; when she does go, she refuses to talk about certain issues. Her behavior is characterized as _____, an important concept in _____ therapy.
   a. transference; psychodynamic
   b. resistance; psychodynamic
   c. transference; humanistic
   d. resistance; humanistic

7. The only mental health specialists who can regularly prescribe drugs are:
   a. clinical psychologists.
   b. psychiatrists.
   c. counseling psychologists.
   d. both a. and c.

8. Albert Ellis's rational-emotive therapy focuses most directly on the replacement of:
   a. maladaptive thought patterns with more effective ones.
   b. feelings of guilt with feelings of self-acceptance.
   c. rational, thought-based responses with emotional, feeling-based responses.
   d. fear-induced muscle tension with muscle relaxation.

9. Beck's cognitive therapy has been used to treat:
   a. anxiety disorders.
   b. schizophrenia.
   c. depression.
   d. all of the above.

10. Deep brain stimulation is a new procedure used to treat intractable cases of:
    a. bipolar disorder.
    b. posttraumatic stress disorder.
    c. major depression.
    d. obsessive-compulsive disorder.

11. ECT today:
    a. has been banned.
    b. is a safe and effective treatment for obsessive-compulsive disorder.
    c. is often applied unilaterally to the right hemisphere to protect conscious verbal memories.
    d. is known to cause the same devastating brain damage as a prefrontal lobotomy.

12. The most often used antidepressant drugs are:
    a. tricyclics.
    b. SSRIs.
    c. benzodiazepines.
    d. a typical antipsychotics.

13. Imagine that you have just read a study testing the effectiveness of a new antidepressant drug. If these results are consistent with previous studies of this type, you might find _____% improvement in the placebo condition and ___% in the drug condition.
    a. 5; 80   c. 35; 90
    b. 30; 50   d. 50; 50

14. Posttraumatic stress disorder is categorized as a(n) _____ disorder.
    a. anxiety   c. mood
    b. panic   d. schizophrenic

15. Prefrontal lobotomies, used to treat people with severe cases of schizophrenia and other mental disorders:
    a. have been a common and effective treatment since the 1930s for those who do not respond to drug treatment.
    b. are no longer performed, in part because they permanently damage the patients' ability to make and follow plans.
    c. are a new, more refined form of psychosurgery that is nevertheless rarely used.
    d. have not been performed since the 1970s because they were shown to have no real effect on the patients' incapacitating emotions.

Essay Questions

16. Why is Carl Rogers's client-centered therapy named as it is? From the perspective of this therapeutic approach, describe the causes of mental problems, the aims of therapy, and one critical element that must be manifested by the therapist.

17. What are exposure treatments used for? Explain the principles of learning on which they are based, and illustrate by describing one type of exposure treatment.

After you have assessed your understanding on the basis of Self-Test 1 and have tried to strengthen your preparation in any areas of weakness, GO ON to Self-Test 2.

Self-Test 2

Multiple-Choice Questions

1. In the United States, from the 1950s to the 1970s, reform was aimed at deinstitutionalizing mental patients and returning them to the community. This movement:
   a. failed to achieve either goal.
   b. succeeded in achieving both goals.
   c. succeeded in deinstitutionalizing many patients but largely failed to reintegrate them into the community.
   d. succeeded in deinstitutionalizing only a small percentage of patients but successfully reintegrated them into the community.

2. A large-scale survey conducted from 2001–2003 identified thousands of people with clinically significant mental disorders. Of these, _____% had received treatment from a mental health professional in the previous year.
   a. 2   c. 42
   b. 22   d. 72

3. Therapists generally agree that _____ is the most effective treatment for specific phobias.
   a. behavioral exposure treatment
   b. deep brain stimulation
   c. psychoanalysis
   d. drug therapy with antianxiety medication

4. Which of the following was *not* a technique utilized by Freud in psychoanalysis?
   a. dream analysis
   b. interpretation of patient errors
   c. contingency management
   d. free association

5. In _____ therapy, the person seeking help figures out what is wrong, makes plans for improvement, and decides when improvement has taken place.
   a. psychoanalytic
   b. humanistic
   c. rational-emotive
   d. behavior

6. Carl Rogers believed that the therapist should reflect back the ideas and feelings that the client expresses as a way of achieving and demonstrating:
   a. genuineness.
   b. transference.
   c. unconditional positive regard.
   d. empathy.

7. Humanistic therapy resembles psychodynamic therapy in that it:
   a. is problem-centered.
   b. focuses on inner feelings and wishes.
   c. casts the therapist as the expert on the client's problems.
   d. treats self-actualization as a central concept in therapy.

8. According to Albert Ellis's ABC theory of emotions, the therapist should help the client to directly alter _____ in order to change _____.
   a. activating events (A); beliefs (B)
   b. beliefs (B); activating events (A)
   c. emotional consequences (C); beliefs (B)
   d. beliefs (B); emotional consequences (C)

9. Albert Ellis observed a style of irrational thinking in which people tend to _____, a pattern he labeled _____.
   a. minimize positive experiences; awfulizing
   b. maximize negative experiences; awfulizing
   c. misattribute negative experiences to their own deficiencies; musturbation
   d. see their lives as the product of an unalterable fate; musturbation

10. The type of therapist most likely to employ homework assignments as a means of helping clients is a _____ therapist.
   a. psychodynamic
   b. client-centered
   c. cognitive
   d. biologically oriented

11. Agnes is being treated for fear of flying by learning to relax physically while picturing increasingly fearful scenes related to flying. Her therapist is using a technique called:
   a. contingency management.
   b. in vivo exposure treatment.
   c. imaginative exposure treatment.
   d. virtual reality exposure treatment.

12. Acceptance, empathy, and encouragement are aspects of an important common factor in therapy called:
   a. support.
   b. warmth.
   c. hope.
   d. eclecticism.

13. Antipsychotic drugs, such as chlorpromazine, are thought to work by:
    a. increasing dopamine activity at certain synapses.
    b. decreasing dopamine activity at certain synapses.
    c. increasing hormone concentrations in the bloodstream.
    d. decreasing hormone concentrations in the bloodstream.

14. Tardive dyskinesia, a serious and often irreversible motor disturbance, occurs in many patients who receive long-term treatment with:
    a. antidepressant drugs.
    b. antipsychotic drugs.
    c. placebos.
    d. tranquilizers.

15. The form of biological treatment for mental disorders that is least often used is:
    a. drug therapy.
    b. electroconvulsive shock therapy.
    c. psychosurgery.
    d. exposure therapy.

Essay Questions

16. Explain the roots of mental problems from the Freudian perspective. What, then, is the job of the psychoanalyst, and what are some means available for carrying out that job?

17. Why is it necessary to perform experiments in order to determine whether therapy is effective? What has analysis of such studies generally shown? Are different therapies equally effective or ineffective? Explain.

Answers

Biological Treatments

5. **a.** tricyclics; selective serotonin reuptake inhibitors (SSRIs)

Psychotherapy I: Psychodynamic and Humanistic Therapies

13. **a.** non-directive approach, **b.** Empathy, **c.** Unconditional positive regard

Psychotherapy II: Cognitive and Behavioral Therapies

7. depression; anxiety; schizophrenia

Self-Test 1

1. **b.** Although such asylums were built, they did not receive sufficient amounts of continuing financial support and so reverted to the conditions that had originally horrified reformers. (p. 622)

2. **d.** (p. 650)

3. **d.** (p. 627)

4. **b.** This is one reason that drugs in the atypical class are more often prescribed. (p. 626)

5. b. The therapist described in **a** sounds most like a cognitive therapist, while the one described in **c** sounds like a humanistic therapist. The description in **d** is nonspecific. (p. 633)

6. b. (p. 635)

7. b. (p. 623)

8. a. By altering beliefs, one can also alter emotions, according to cognitive therapists such as Ellis. (p. 642)

9. d. (p. 644)

10. d. Though an extreme treatment, it is less so than psychosurgery. (p. 631)

11. c. (p. 630)

12. b. (p. 627)

13. b. (p. 627)

14. a. (p. 627)

15. b. (p. 630)

16. Carl Rogers used the term *client-centered therapy* because the approach focuses on what the *client* knows and what the *client* can do rather than on the therapist's knowledge and abilities. The job of directing therapy, choosing which path to take, deciding how to handle particular issues, assessing progress, and so on, is in the hands of the client. This therapeutic approach is especially consistent with humanistic psychology's respect for the capability and growth potential that lies within each person.

Rogers believed that mental problems stem from people's denial or distortion of the desires and feelings that lie within them. The denial and distortion are thought to result when people learn from parents or other important people that others disapprove of them. Therapy is intended to help clients become aware of and accept their own feelings and desires and to learn to trust their ability to make decisions so they can take control of their own lives. Letting the client take the lead in directing therapy is fully consistent with this goal and powerfully communicates the message that what is inside the client can be trusted.

Rogers believed that empathy was an important element that the therapist must provide to create a climate conducive to the client's learning and growth process. Empathy is the therapist's attempt to understand the client's thoughts and feelings from the client's own viewpoint. (pp. 637–638)

17. Exposure treatments are used by behavior therapists to treat specific phobias. From the behavioral perspective, fears are considered to be learned responses. A stimulus that can elicit an unconditioned fear response may be paired with another stimulus, which thereby becomes a conditioned stimulus capable of eliciting a conditioned fear response. Of course, the fear reflex that is learned can also be made to diminish, according to the behaviorist. If the conditioned stimulus is repeatedly presented without the unconditioned stimulus, extinction will occur. For example, if an intersection with a four-way stop sign was paired with the frightening and painful experience of a car crash in a person's experience, that person might come to fear such intersections. On the other hand, if the person is repeatedly exposed to such intersections without further harm, then the fear should be extinguished. (Even if a particular fear, say a fear of snakes, were unconditioned, it could be made to decline through habituation.) Imaginative exposure is a type of exposure treatment in which a person imagines increasingly frightening forms of the feared stimulus until each is no longer frightening. (pp. 646–648)

Self-Test 2

1. c. (pp. 622–623)

2. b. (p. 624)

3. a. (p. 651)

4. c. (pp. 634–635)

5. b. (pp. 637–638)

6. d. (p. 638)

7. b. (p. 638)

8. d. (p. 643)

9. b. (pp. 642–643)

10. c. (p. 643)

11. c. (p. 647)

12. a. (p. 651)

13. b. (p. 626)

14. **b.** (p. 626)

15. **c.** (p. 630)

16. Freud believed that mental problems stem from unresolved mental conflicts that are fully or at least largely unconscious. Though unconscious, they can affect conscious thoughts, feelings, and behaviors, thus leading to symptoms that cause the sufferer to seek help. Freud believed these conflicts originate in the first five or six years of life and relate to infantile sexual and aggressive wishes.

The psychoanalyst's job is to help the individual become aware of the conflict-laden material buried in the unconscious. According to the theory, when the person faces and deals with such information consciously, symptoms will go away. The psychoanalyst must essentially prospect for and piece together clues about the nature of the underlying memories and conflicts to figure out how the memories and feelings of childhood are meaningfully related to present circumstances and symptoms.

Two means of gaining such clues are dream analysis and free association, in which an individual talks freely about whatever comes to mind in response to specific cue words or in the natural flow of consciousness. The assumption is that what appear to be illogical and unrelated ideas actually reflect symbolically the unconscious memories and wishes that are at the heart of the problem. (Another means is to analyze transference, ways in which the patient relates to the therapist as a symbolic substitute for a significant person in his or her life. The therapist can also gain information by analyzing signs of resistance, which could include canceling appointments, silence, or efforts to redirect the discussion.) (pp. 632–636)

17. Life is full of ups and downs, and it is generally at the low points rather than the high points that people enter therapy. Therefore, the fact that a person feels better and functions more effectively following therapy is not a clear indication that psychotherapy was responsible for the improvement. After all, the person might have improved anyway, perhaps because of changing social circumstances, an alteration in body chemistry, or any number of other factors. Only with the control possible through experiments can we tell whether therapy produces some improvement over and above what would have occurred otherwise.

In general, analysis of many such studies has shown that psychotherapy is effective overall and that no one form of therapy emerges as clearly superior to others. However, some studies indicate that specific types of problems may be more effectively handled with certain types of therapy. For example, specific phobias are especially well treated through exposure treatment, while multiple or diffuse problems may be most successfully treated through psychodynamic or humanistic therapies. (pp. 649–651)

Statistical Appendix

READ the introduction below before you read the Appendix in the text.

This appendix supplements the coverage of statistics in Chapter 2. Psychologists use statistical procedures to help them analyze and understand the data they collect. Simple techniques allow us to organize and describe important characteristics of a set of scores. Scores are often organized into a frequency distribution, which shows the number of times scores in particular intervals occurred. For example, a frequency distribution could tell us how many people in a sample earn between $10,000 and $15,000, between $15,000 and $20,000, between $20,000 and $25,000 and so on.

When a frequency distribution is depicted as a graph, the shape of the curve formed by the scores is important. Normal curves, or approximations to normal curves, are bell-shaped curves that are common in psychology. Measures of central tendency represent the center of the distribution, indicating a typical score in that distribution. The mean and median are two measures of central tendency that are based on different definitions of the "center" of a distribution. Measures of variability express the degree to which scores tend to vary from the central tendency. Variance and standard deviation are common measures of variability.

Sometimes we wish to compare scores. In order to do so, we need a language for sensibly describing relationships among scores. A score's percentile rank indicates the percentage of scores in a distribution that fall at or below the score of interest. Thus, if a person earned a score of 64 on a test and that score is at the 88th percentile, then 88 percent of the scores are at 64 or below. Standardized scores, such as z scores, provide another way of converting scores into a form that can be used for purposes of comparison.

Psychologists often ask how two variables are related. How is IQ related to success in college? How are scores on a test of artistic creativity related to later success as an artist? How is age related to performance on a memory test? As explained in Chapter 2, a correlation coefficient indicates the strength and direction of such relationships. This appendix illustrates the computation of a product-moment correlation coefficient for a small set of data.

The final section of the appendix does *not* supplement Chapter 2; rather, it supplements the material on psychophysical scaling in Chapter 7. This section is not dealt with in this guide.

LOOK over the table of contents for this chapter in your textbook before you continue with your study.

The Integrated Study Workout

CONSIDER these questions before you go on. They are designed to help you start thinking about this subject, not to test your knowledge.

If a group of people are tested, how can we describe the performance of the group as a whole?

If people are given two tests—one on ability to speak French and the other on ability to comprehend it—how can their standing as speakers be compared with their standing as comprehenders?

What does it mean to say someone is at the 45th percentile on a particular measure?

How can we determine the degree of relationship between two variables, such as IQ and GPA?

READ the Appendix lightly. Then go back and read thoroughly, completing the Workout as you proceed.

Statistics are an important tool for psychologists, helping them to make sense of the data they collect. Descriptive statistics are useful for learning about the shape, central tendency, and variability of a set of measurements.

1. What is a frequency distribution? Describe how it is constructed. (See Table A.1 on text page A-1 and Table A.2 on text page A-2.)

2. Why is a graphical representation of a frequency distribution helpful? (See Figure A.1 on text page A-2.)

The shape of a distribution can be described in a number of ways. (See the four panels shown in Figure A.2 on text page A-3.)

3. Describe the shape of a normal distribution, or normal curve, and produce a rough sketch of one.

4. Why are normal distributions important in psychology? In general, when might we expect a distribution to approximate a normal curve?

5. Define the term *mode* and then distinguish between bimodal and unimodal distributions. Into which of these categories does a normal curve fall? Sketch a bimodal distribution.

6. Describe positively and negatively skewed distributions. Sketch an example of each type of distribution.

A measure of central tendency summarizes a set of scores in terms of a single number. That single number represents the center of the distribution. However, the "center" can be defined in more than one way.

7. Define the following two measures of central tendency.

    a. median

    b. mean

8. Compute the median and mean for the following set of scores: 3 5 6 9 12.

    a. median _____

    b. mean _____

9. Where will the mean be relative to the median in each of the following kinds of distributions?

    a. normal distribution

    _____

    b. positively skewed distribution

    _____

    c. negatively skewed distribution

    _____

10. Which measure of central tendency—the mean or the median—is preferable? Explain.

Variability is another characteristic of a distribution of scores. As with central tendency, there is more than one measure of variability.

11. Explain the concept of variability. Sketch two distributions that have the same mean but different amounts of variability. (See Figure A.3 on text page A-4.)

12. What is the range of a set of scores and why is it inadequate as a measure of variability?

13. Two measures of variability that take into account all the scores in a distribution are _____ and _____ . The measure of variability that is expressed in the original units of measurement rather than in squared units is the _____ .

It is often informative to compare a given score with other scores. For example, we may want to know how a given score stands relative to the other scores in the same distribution. Or we might want to compare score A's standing within its distribution to score B's standing within its distribution. In order to make such comparisons, we must convert scores into a form that permits us to speak of relationships among scores.

14. Define a percentile rank. Look at Table A.1 on text page A-1 and indicate the percentile rank of the score 61.

15. A _____ is one that is expressed in terms of the number of standard deviations that the original score is from the mean of original scores.

16. Answer the following questions about z scores.
   a. How is a score converted to the type of standardized score called a z score?

   b. In a distribution with a mean of 50 and a standard deviation of 10, the z score of the score 65 is _____ .

   c. If a z score is positive, then we know that the original score is _____ (above/below/equal to) the mean.

   d. The percentage of scores that lies at or below a z score of +2 is _____ . The percentage of scores at or above a z score of +1 is _____ . (See Figure A.4 on text page A-7.)

Statistical techniques also permit us to describe the relationship between two variables—such as the relationship between age and income, between IQ and creativity, between hours of weekly television viewing and grade point average. A correlation coefficient summarizes in one number the strength of the relationship (how related the two variables are) and the direction of the relationship (whether high scores on one variable tend to go with low scores or high scores on the other variable).

17. Which aspect of the correlation coefficient indicates the strength of the relationship? Which indicates the direction of the relationship?

18. Look at the scatter plot below and indicate whether there appears to be a negative or a positive relationship between variables X and Y. Is the correlation perfect? Support your answer. (See Figure A.5 on text page A-8, along with the corresponding discussion.)

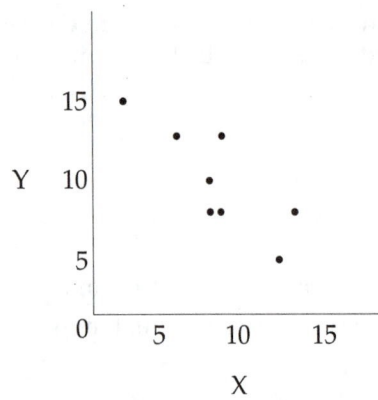

19. In "25 words or less," explain how a correlation coefficient is calculated. In other words, explain where this number comes from.

After you have studied the Appendix thoroughly, CHECK your understanding with the self-test that follows.

Self-Test

Multiple-Choice Questions

1. A normal curve is:

    a. unimodal and asymmetrical.
    b. unimodal and symmetrical.
    c. bimodal and asymmetrical.
    d. bimodal and symmetrical.

2. The scores on a particular test range from 30 to 100. Most scores center around 85, but a number are lower. The frequency of these low scores gradually declines as we approach the lowest score of 30. This distribution sounds as if it is:

    a. positively skewed.
    b. negatively skewed.
    c. normal.
    d. bimodal.

3. In which of the following cases are the mean and median of a distribution necessarily identical?

    a. bimodal distribution
    b. positively skewed distribution
    c. negatively skewed distribution
    d. normal distribution

4. If a distribution is skewed, is one measure of central tendency generally preferred to another?

    a. yes, the median
    b. yes, the mean
    c. yes, the mode
    d. no

5. Which of the following measures of variability take(s) into account all the scores in a distribution?

    a. only the range
    b. the range and the variance
    c. the variance and the standard deviation
    d. only the variance

6. Liz says she scored at the 57th percentile on a test of eye-hand coordination. This means that:

    a. Liz's measured score, out of 100, was 57.
    b. 57 percent of the people tested earned the same score Liz did.
    c. Liz has 57 percent as much coordination as the most coordinated person tested.
    d. 57 percent of the people tested had a measured score equal to or lower than Liz's.

7. If Carmela scores a 70 on a test with a mean of 60 and a standard deviation of 10, her z score is:

    a. $+1.00$.
    b. -1.00.
    c. $+10.00$.
    d. -10.00.

8. Which of the following statements is true?

    a. If a distribution of scores is normal, one can convert from a percentile rank to a z score, but not vice versa.
    b. If a distribution of scores is normal, one can convert from a z score to a percentile rank, but not vice versa.

c. If a distribution of scores is normal, one can convert from a percentile rank to a z score, and vice versa.

d. There is no way to convert between percentile ranks and z scores regardless of the shape of the distribution.

9. The best way to express the direction and degree of relationship between verbal SAT scores and interest in reading is a:

a. correlation coefficient.
b. percentile rank.
c. psychophysical scale.
d. measure of central tendency.

0. The correspondence between variable X and variable Y is illustrated below.

X:	1	2	3	4	5	6
Y:	4	5	8	10	13	19

the relationship between X and Y linear?

a. yes
b. no, because each value of Y differs from the corresponding value of X
c. no, because the increase in Y that corresponds to a unit of increase in X varies
d. It's not possible to say from the information given.

Answers

he Integrated Study Workout

3. a. 6, b. 7

9. a. identical to it, b. above it, c. below it

3. variance and standard deviation; standard deviation

14. 75th percentile ($\frac{15}{20} = 0.75$))

15. standardized score

16. b. +1.5 [(65 − 50)/10 = $\frac{15}{10}$], c. above, d. 97.72%; 84.13%

18. The scatter plot suggests a negative correlation, which is not perfect because the points do not lie on a straight line.

Self-Test

1. b. (p. A-2)

2. b. On the x axis, negative scores lie toward the left and positive scores toward the right. You can remember that a negatively skewed distribution is one whose tail "points toward" the negative end of the axis; a positively skewed distribution is one whose tail "points toward" the positive end. (p. A-3)

3. d. They could be identical in a bimodal distribution, but they are not necessarily so. (p. A-3)

4. a. (p. A-4)

5. c. (pp. A-4–A-5)

6. d. (p. A-5)

7. a. (70 − 60)/10 = 1 (p. A-6)

8. c. (p. A-7)

9. a. (p. A-8)

10. c. (p. A-8)